SECOND EDITION

PUSH IT
TO MOVE IT

LESSONS LEARNED FROM A CAREER
IN NUCLEAR PROJECT MANAGEMENT

PRAISE FOR
PUSH IT TO MOVE IT

"I've worked with Dave Amerine for several years and in the nuclear industry for many decades. No one is more qualified to serve as an example to those who begin a career in the power industry. The experiences of his illustrious career — both the high successes and the lows, when external events conspired to prevent success — can be worthwhile lessons of the necessary work ethic, of which paths to take and to avoid, and of the importance of knowing the details, without ever losing sight of the big picture. In our association, I was fortunate to directly profit from Dave's insights, and firmly believe others who read his book will be able to do so as well."

Dr. Robert Iotti
Former Senior Vice President, CH2M Hill Nuclear Group, and Member of the Board of Advanced Reactor Concepts LLC

"A vivid storyteller and remarkable leader, Dave Amerine shares a compelling life story — one that takes you on a journey linking his values and experiences to a life of service and admirable accomplishments. His commitment to excellence in his endeavors — combined with personal humility, genuine esteem for others, and a penchant to leverage his life and work experiences as learning opportunities — have enabled Dave to excel and overcome adversity. This must-read book shines a light on wisdom produced by knowledge and experience, and affirms the axiom, 'leadership matters!'"

Victor M. McCree
Former Executive Director for Operations, US Nuclear Regulatory Commission

"A very inspirational book on Dave's lifelong commitment to management results and leadership. Well done!"

John R. Longenecker
Nuclear Industry Leader, Managing Director of the Energy Facility Contractors Group (EFCOG), Former Deputy Asst. Secretary for Nuclear Energy at the U.S. Department of Energy, President of Longenecker and Associates, Inc.

"David Amerine is the picture of ethical and compassionate leadership. He's intelligent, keeps a cool head, listens to people, finds solutions, negotiates well, and always speaks from a well-informed position. David leads by capturing the essence of other people's character and strengths, by nurturing those strengths, and by exercising forward thinking with excellent leadership capabilities. He is a model of decency and good character, and has demonstrated successes with an abundance of energy. He's the kind of man whose collective qualities leave me hopeful about the leaders he has trained and the countless people he has inspired. He's a leader who the next generation would be wise to emulate."

Kathleen D. Gordon
High School Classmate and Life Long Friend

"I've worked with many project leaders over the years, but Dave Amerine is by far the most committed and qualified of all. No one can out-work him! He has the bigger picture always in view, while knowing the details that provide the day-to-day management of the critical paths to completion. He has drawn top talent to his teams and has developed outstanding future leaders. Dave always makes sure that the '3 Ps' of plant, paper and people are well integrated going into startup."

Ambrose Schwallie
Former President and Chief Executive Officer, Westinghouse Government and Washington Group International Government

"*Push It to Move It* is a remarkable compendium of insights, derived from a diverse and challenging series of assignments across the spectrum of nuclear enterprises. Dave conveys his learnings in a most authentic and heartfelt manner, blending the personal and the professional to yield a compelling read. By internalizing these insights, you will become a more effective leader, and a better person."

Rick Kacich

Former President of Yankee Atomic Electric Company

"In this book, Dave shares his hard-earned and proven secrets about how to successfully run complicated nuclear concerns in a highly regulated environment. Further, he shows how to integrate those efforts as a caring father, husband, friend and engaged American Christian. I consider *Push It to Move It* a must-read for upcoming nuclear executives."

Chuck Spencer

Former President of Y-12 National Security Complex and Hanford Environmental Cleanup Corporations

"Dave Amerine possesses that unique natural blend of leadership and humanity that inspires people to follow him and want to make him proud. His logic chart to life led him to choose the perfect wife for his lifetime adventures and to become the patriarch of a wonderful family. His ability to learn life lessons from every stop along the way and add those lessons — whether from mistakes or successes — to his playbook for teaching *others* has been impressive. This book captures only some of the best stories of an incredible career — and reading it gives you a good glimpse into the extraordinary experiences and wisdom of a good man. I urge those at the beginning of a career to read it to learn which paths to take and avoid. And it's an equally great read for those at the end of their careers, who will enjoy some kinship with Dave through his experiences and insights. There is a chuckle and a tear in every chapter. Dave, I am proud to have passed your way."

Billie Garde

Attorney, Partner at Clifford & Garde, LLP

"Dave Amerine epitomizes the highly effective and successful project manager. This book is unique because he shares how he carried early life lessons forward in his career. Dave shows how building a solid foundation of experience, hard work, drive and perseverance make a huge difference. A hallmark of Dave's success, and most interesting to future project managers, are the stories of how he helped 'troubled' complex nuclear projects by giving them new life and purpose. I was privileged to work with Dave, as a client and a direct report, and learned from him. He recruited talented staff and molded effective teams. He cared about people, listened to them, encouraged them to speak up and make an impact, and taught accountability. This book will profit all who are interested in technical and business careers!"

Charles Hansen
Former Deputy Manager, Savannah River Site, US Department of Energy, and Vice President, Parsons Corporation (Aiken, SC)

"*Push It to Move It* provides a wealth of lessons learned for managers and leaders in the nuclear industry who strive to establish and maintain a strong and healthy safety culture. Based on his 40+ years of experience, Dave Amerine describes the core values and behaviors that emphasize safety over competing goals, such as production, schedule, and cost. He illustrates the patterns of thinking, feeling, and behaving that enable sustainable and safe operations. It has been a pleasure to work with Dave throughout my career."

Shirley Olinger
President, ISMSolutions, Inc., and Former Department of Energy Manager, Office of River Protection (Hanford, WA)

"Dave Amerine embodies all the essential qualities of a great leader. He is a visionary who gravitates toward big and meaningful challenges, he has a broad command of the tactics and tools necessary to achieve his visions, and he can assemble and inspire highly talented teams to perform at peak levels of productivity and quality. He has also been a great personal mentor to me and countless other leaders in the nuclear industry. I consider it a rare privilege to have had the chance to work with and learn from Dave, and I am forever indebted to him for his leadership and guidance throughout my career. With his book, *Push It to Move It*, Dave has captured his immense knowledge and experience base in a well-crafted narrative that is a true gift for the future leaders in the nuclear industry."

Dr. Thomas D. Burns, Jr., PE
Senior Vice President, Parsons Government Services; Salt Waste Processing Facility Deputy Project Manager/Director of Engineering

"*Push It to Move It* is a must-read book for project managers. Over the years, Dave Amerine and I worked closely as client and contractor to ensure successful completion of highly complex technical projects. We both believed in focusing on the end, tackling problems head on, supporting the people in the trenches by walking the site and knowing their needs, working hard long hours and celebrating weekly accomplishments to the end. This book tells you how to do precisely that, and more."

Roy Schepens
Former Department of Energy Assistant Manager, Savannah River Site, and Former Department of Energy Manager, Office of River Protection (Hanford, WA)

"In *Push It to Move It*, Dave Amerine provides more lessons learned on the application of nuclear safety culture — in a clear and very effective way — than I have ever seen! I have taught nuclear safety culture for years and the examples and real-life experience in leadership he offers is equivalent to what John Wooden provided in his book on basketball leadership and life. Dave is also humorous and thorough in recounting a grand history of nuclear energy in the civilian and DOE sector over more than 40 years. I recommend this book for newcomers as well as experienced engineers and scientists who lived and worked through the turbulent times described in this excellent book!"

Ted Quinn

Instrument Society of America Fellow, American Nuclear Society Past President 1998-99, International Electrotechnical Society SC45A WGA9 Chairman, and President of Technology Resource

SECOND EDITION

PUSH IT
TO MOVE IT

LESSONS LEARNED FROM A CAREER
IN NUCLEAR PROJECT MANAGEMENT

DAVID AMERINE

SILVER TREE
PUBLISHING

DEDICATION

This book is dedicated to all those who have supported me and taught me life's lessons, but most especially to my wife, Cindy. As the last line of my rather turgid resume states, "none of the above would have been achieved without her support." And it's so very true.

When I edited the first full draft of this book for its initial publication in 1st edition format (in 2016), Cindy and I were dealing with her recent diagnosis of Amyotrophic Lateral Sclerosis, commonly known simply as ALS or as Lou Gehrig's disease. I was then, and still am now, in awe of her attitude and courage after two years of exams, analyses, tests, and more tests resulting in the determination that she had a variant of this awful disease.

Wife, partner, lover, mother, athlete, dancer, and funny lady are descriptors that only begin to paint the colorful portrait of my beautiful best friend ... who I ultimately lost far too soon. During her valiant fight and her final acceptance, I learned so much about her spirit and I came to add — to the myriad accolades she so deservingly amassed from us all — her most defining attribute of all: my hero.

Cindy passed away on August 11, 2018. This book will not adequately convey all this amazing woman has meant to me. But I have tried.

TABLE OF CONTENTS

FOREWORD

by Mike Morris

From the moment I met him, I knew Dave Amerine was a dynamic, no-nonsense leader. My career in the energy business and Dave's career in the nuclear industry intersected at the Millstone Nuclear Power Station in Waterford, Connecticut. Northeast Utilities was the owner/operator of the Millstone Station, where I was hired as President, Chief Executive Officer (CEO), and Chairman. At that time, Northeast Utilities, as a whole, was in some degree of extremis, due — in large part — to the Nuclear Regulatory Commission-enforced shutdown of the Millstone Nuclear Station. We brought in a new senior management team at Millstone, with Dave serving as the Vice President of Engineering and Services.

Millstone was unique in the fact that the operating license for that three-reactor plant station was revoked by the Nuclear Regulatory Commission (NRC) due to untoward treatment of employees who had brought up nuclear safety issues. The senior management team that was replaced at Millstone had been focused on preparation for deregulation and the competition in the marketplace. They were not as sensitive as they should have been to issues being brought up by employees, especially if those issues threatened to detract from that overarching goal. While there was a spectrum of employee concerns and management assessments of employee motivations for voicing those concerns, some leaders ultimately let those considerations cloud their judgment about how to address the concerns. In any industry, such clouded judgment can create an environment that discourages employees from raising issues in the future. Morale and safety will ultimately suffer.

The new management team at Millstone, however, was immediately focused on how to correct the milieu that had been created and how to manage in that new environment. We needed to convince the NRC that we had, indeed, figured that out and had created and could sustain a new approach to handling employee issues. The most important challenge was to gain the trust of the employees and nurture that trust on a continual basis. Dave was given the lead to address this challenge.

In this new and remarkable book that Dave has written, he discusses what was done, and how the lessons learned had applications across the nuclear industry. From the brave new world created at Millstone, Dave went on to apply those lessons learned at other venues, culminating in his selection as President of Nuclear Fuel Services, which — a decade later — had some of the same issues that existed at Millstone.

I agree with Dave that the approaches that applied to handling employee concerns in the nuclear industry have the potential for broader application to any industrialized endeavor. Dave also provides the approaches he used in rescuing troubled projects and I believe those concepts, tools, and methods can have a broader application than just nuclear projects as well. As for the more personal, autobiographical elements of this book, Dave does a great job explaining why he included glimpses, throughout the book, of his time growing up and his education as a background for his project management endeavors. Those recollections are not only informative but, in many cases, also entertaining. The book is a good read and a useful one, too.

The approaches that applied to handling employee concerns in the nuclear industry have the potential for broader application to any industrialized endeavor.

Based on our experiences together at Millstone, I wasn't surprised to see Dave achieve so much in his career, nor was I surprised that he ultimately wrote this book to share his insights — about business and life — with a broader audience. His willingness to offer the perspectives he gained as a leader and high-stakes project manager in the nuclear industry fulfills an imperative to help the public better understand this essential industry. And his vulnerability and good humor in sharing the lessons of a life well lived are a gift to us all.

Based on our experiences together at Millstone, I wasn't surprised to see Dave achieve so much in his career, nor was I surprised that he ultimately wrote this book to share his insights — about business and life — with a broader audience.

For rising leaders in the nuclear industry, this book should be required reading. For everyone else, this book will help you, too, lead and connect differently and better.

Mike Morris

Mike Morris led Consumers Power Company before being recruited to join Northeast Utilities as President, CEO, and Chairman. After receiving the Nuclear Regulatory Commission's approval to bring two of the Millstone units back on line, Northeast Utilities sold the plants to Dominion Energy. Morris went on to be President, CEO, and Chairman of American Electric Power (AEP) and its two-unit Donald C. Cook Nuclear Station. He served on the Board of the Institute of Nuclear Power Operations (INPO), ultimately as Chair, and at Nuclear Electric Insurance Limited (NEIL), where he also served as Chair for a number of years.

PROLOGUE

When my wife, Cindy, and I were in Florence, Italy, in our 20s, we went to the Museum Academia. Among the many works of art were Renaissance paintings. These paintings were known for the creative and deliberate use of perspective — the way they seemed to provide a window into space and time. In addition to giving a more realistic presentation of the subject matter, Renaissance painters were practically composers; they used their paintings to tell a story, as well as provide a picture.

One approach these renowned artists used is known as "foreshortening," which refers to the artistic effect of shortening lines in a drawing so as to create an illusion of depth. They also used a technique called "sfumato," the blurring or softening of sharp outlines by subtle and gradual blending of one tone into another through the use of thin glazes, to give the illusion of depth or three-dimensionality. "Chiaroscuro" refers to the modeling effect of using a strong contrast between light and dark, also to give the illusion of depth. The results were paintings of great detail and scope that gave the impression that what one saw on the canvas had just flowed from the artist as he saw the world, in his mind or in reality. The paintings were of a multifaceted grandeur, often illustrating multiple activities, leaving one wondering how the artist could capture all this on one canvas. Did they really create such masterpieces from raw talent and inspiration alone, or were these complex techniques proof that there is craft — even science — in the creation of art?

As we walked around the museum, Cindy and I came upon a painting that was only partly finished. What could be seen on the part that had not been painted were lines and arcs, and even letters and numbers. It was obvious that there was a lot of geometry, architecture, and even mathematical preparation that preceded the actual flow of painting. I was awe-struck to see such left-brained strategy behind what I had always believed was right-brained artistic talent.

Some years later, I was listening to a conversation on the radio between the great jazz/blues/soul musicians Ray Charles and Miles Davis. They were discussing how they developed a song. Not unlike my impression of the detailed and multifaceted Renaissance paintings, I had always thought that these great musicians just sat at their piano and let the mood of the moment create their masterpieces. I assumed great music was "inspired" and even improvised. What I learned from this conversation between two musical legends was that there was a tremendous amount of support work and an almost tedious fitting of beats, rhythms, melodies, and even an act of agonizing over individual notes that preceded the "improvisation." Once again, there was tremendous architecture and preparation required to produce the finished product.

In thinking about writing a book that might have some value beyond my own satisfaction, it became clear to me that it would require some construction. It would not just flow from my fingers onto the keyboard and into the computer as a masterpiece. In fact, I had no hope that it would ever be a masterpiece at all. But I do hope that it will provide some interest — some ideas to ponder on life and work — to others who pursue life paths similar to mine. I hope you will find the following chapters — whether you read them in their entirety and in chronological order, or whether you choose your own adventure, selecting individual sections with topics that appeal to you — to be of inspiration, or support, or clarity.

I believe everyone has a story of some interest. And perhaps everyone's interesting story ought to be shared with a wider audience. I am honored and humbled to share mine here.

Writing a book, at its very best, involves first examining your own experience so you can tell it fully and authentically. To author your story, you must first understand and appreciate fully where you have been, where you are headed, and what it all means. So, I endeavored to do precisely that when preparing this book for its readers.

It has been suggested to me that the best way to examine a life is in the context of domains and stages, such as:

- Growing Up
- Education
- Career
- Marriage
- Family
- Friends
- Leisure
- Retirement
- Spirituality

Additionally, within each of these aspects of our existence, as appropriate, one should focus on the following:

- Triumphs and Tragedies
- Words of Wisdom (usually born from experience)
- Gratitude

I have followed this advice to the extent I think it applies or is useful. In the beginning, examining my life benefits me. In the end, as such examination gives way to the publishing of a book (now in its 2nd edition), the beneficiary of the insights is hopefully you — the reader.

Some years ago, I read an article that suggested that everyone should write what the author of the article called an "Ethic Will." His contention was that smart people typically paid a lot of attention to preserving as much of their estate as possible (from the always-greedy clutches of the government), and passing those worldly goods along to their chosen relatives (usually their spouse, followed by their children). This task has become increasingly difficult as the Federal government has become more and more intrusive and voracious with respect to taxation. These instructions for passing along the estate are contained in a document called a will.

What is not contained in that legal document and passed along is the essence of the person who has become deceased. What did he or she think about things? What did he or she care deeply about? What were his or her guidelines for living, and how did those guidelines evolve (through trial and error, or education, or example of others, or ... you get the idea)? What thoughts, ideas, suggestions, or just interesting anecdotes do they want to pass on to those about whom they care that may (or may not, depending on the reader) be of some value or interest? I began to capture those thoughts and have drawn upon them in this life story, which may, hopefully, be a more interesting and entertaining presentation of the information contained in the initial Ethic Will endeavor.

I have merged that Ethic Will effort into this book. I am sharing with you my life story, which should contain the background that led to the philosophies and thoughts that ultimately guided my adult life and my decades of work. I have endeavored to apply my life's experiences and lessons into insights and suggestions for the benefit of others. I believe these thoughts may be of some use to those of you who work in what I call high-hazard/low-probability industries, such as the nuclear industry, where I spent my career.

In trying to capture things that might be of interest and use to others, I have been as honest and revealing as possible. I have avoided anything that might be embarrassing to those I leave behind, or that is best kept between me and my God. I think I have led a decent life and have had primarily a positive impact on those with whom I have interfaced and with those I love.

On the other hand, I am reminded of a saying that certainly applies to me: **"There are things I did in my youth of which I am no longer proud."** (And you will see that, throughout this document, I highlight those anecdotes and lessons learned in bold.)

So, I have made mistakes, both personal and professional. The professional mistakes provided learning opportunities. Fortunately, none were so severe or occurred with so much visibility as to set back my career or work opportunities. I think I learned from those situations and avoided making the same mistake twice. I also passed along those lessons learned to others, so that they could benefit from my experience regardless of what vocation they chose. I worked in the nuclear industry, which is just one of the high-impact/low-probability industries I made mention of above. There are many other industries, businesses, and vocations that fall into this category — from space exploration to oil refineries, and more. I hope the lessons I learned and the approaches I applied in my career will be of assistance to those who work in those types of fields, and beyond. It is said that a fool does not learn from his mistakes, a smart man does, and a truly wise man learns from the mistakes of others. I will attempt to give others the opportunity to be that wise.

It is said that a fool does not learn from his mistakes, a smart man does, and a truly wise man learns from the mistakes of others.

My personal mistakes were always the result of selfishness and thoughtlessness, which I think is true for most people. Fortunately, those mistakes did not cost my family or friends any significant sorrow, and for that I thank God.

The Techniques Behind the Brushstrokes: How this Book is Organized

As you embark upon reading the pages ahead, I think that the stories of my childhood, young adulthood, and career, as well as highlights (and lowlights) of marriage and fatherhood will set the stage for the philosophies and approaches I will express later. Those early years do, in my opinion, determine how we will approach the challenges in life that we all invariably face as adults, both personally and professionally. The author Malcolm Gladwell, in his book *Outliers: The Story of Success*, argues that what is often overlooked when trying to understand why some people are so successful is an exploration of where successful people come from and their particular circumstances that helped *lead* to their success.

I have seen studies that indicate that the more secure one's formative years are, the better able one is to handle the vicissitudes of life. This seems counterintuitive. You would think the tougher one has it as a child, the tougher and more resilient one would be as an adult. Sometimes I am sure that hardships as a child do indeed toughen us up, but according to the studies, not on average. I was fortunate to have a very secure and nurturing childhood, with parents and in a community, who made such privilege possible.

I have divided this book into five sections.

I.   The first is a remembrance of my life growing up and certain things that happened that seem important to me.

II.   The next section is about the career I pursued, and the life I lived with my wife and two daughters ... about the many homes we owned and decorated, the adventures we had together, and the challenges we faced.

III.   The third section of the book focuses on what I learned and what it all means, in the grand scheme of things.

IV.   The book's fourth section is dedicated to how those experiences and personal lessons of mine are combined to provide some suggestions or advice for you — insights and ideas that may be of value in managing complex activities, such as complicated projects in the world of business and challenging endeavors in avocations as well. This section hinges on my philosophy on leadership and life, which may be germane to project management of complex endeavors in some initial state of exigency. Here I have also included a tribute to my wife Cindy, who you will surely come to admire and adore if my stories do her justice.

V.   The fifth and final section of the book is a sort of reference guide — an optional-reading section that contains deeper dives into some of the topics explored in the book's main sections, with personal glimpses at speeches I've delivered and leadership tools that served me well.

I hope my journey to become a project manager in the nuclear industry will be of interest. I hope the lessons learned and the practices that led to successful recovery of complicated projects and facilities will be of use to engineers, managers, and executives through-out the industrial complex. I think some of those approaches to the human side of management have even wider application. This accounting is submitted for the benefit of those who find themselves in similar situations.

If this prologue piques your interest, please read further. For as long as I am alive, feel free to give me your comments, questions, or suggestions .... as this endeavor will be a work in progress until I no longer have the ability to amend it. (See the Keep in Touch section at the end of the book.) If you do read the book in its entirety, I thank you in advance for doing so. I suggest little gulps. With books and with life, it's always the best approach.

SECTION I

MY LIFE STORY

This book includes anecdotes from my childhood because they shed some light on the professional I ultimately became. These stories provide some background that lays the groundwork for my philosophy and general outlook, which impacted my work as an adult.
In a few cases, you might find the stories to be entertaining and humorous — not only in their own right, but also as a reminder of similar personal stories from your own life. I hope that the opportunity to remember your own stories may give you pause to consider how you came to the place where you find yourself now — that you will enjoy reflecting on those stories and the events they represent in your life. Taken together, these events help form how you see the world, including your work environment and family life, which are, in reality, usually inseparable. That perspective can help you apply the lessons of this book to the extent you feel motivated to consider them.

MY PARENTS

My parents were both born in 1918 and grew up less than 150 miles from each other. The year of their birth was the year the last of George Washington's step-great-grandchildren died, which tells you how young our country really is. My dad was the youngest of three children and the only boy. His father was an itinerate farmer, farming other peoples' property around Columbus, Ohio. My dad loved the animals on the farms — the cows, pigs, dogs, and cats. He went to several schools in rural Ohio, each of which educated multiple grades in one shared classroom. Although not an athlete, he participated in school activities and was a manager for the high school basketball team. Most of his spare time involved helping my grandfather with farm chores.

Eventually, my dad put himself through The Ohio State University, including the school of veterinary medicine because his love for animals never left him. While attending college, he worked several jobs to help meet his financial obligations. When he graduated, he didn't immediately embark on his career as a veterinarian, but instead enlisted in the Army. World War II had just begun. He was made an officer by virtue of his degree in veterinary medicine and, after attending several training camps in California, he was sent to the Pacific theater. Like a lot of young men who were thrown into the war, he found that it was an exciting and scary way to see the world.

My mother was the eldest of five children — three girls and two boys. Her parents were schoolteachers in rural Kentucky, near Bardstown. They bought a farm five miles outside of Bardstown and, at some point, turned their attention full-time to tending the farm and raising the kids. My grandfather was a tall, white-haired, regal-looking gentleman, respected throughout the county. He had his opinions and did not hesitate to express them. His oldest child — my mom — seemed to emulate him, and the societal limitations of being a girl in the 1920s did not seem to matter to her when it came to saying what she thought. By all accounts, my mother was headstrong and determined from the very start.

She graduated high school at the age of 16, and headed for nursing school in Louisville at Nazareth College for Girls. After receiving her degree, she enlisted in the United States Army Nurse Corps. She received training at various places and excelled in her profession, even under the trying circumstances of the war. Like my dad, she too found herself shipped to the Pacific theater in short order.

Both my parents grew up during the Great Depression and had some good fortune to be raised on farms during those trying times. They grew most of the food they needed, which helped a lot and sheltered them from some of the hardships endured by other families of this era. Even though their families raised most of their food, they still did without many other things, such as new clothes. WWII and the Depression were defining aspects of my mother and father's early lives, leaving lasting impressions on them both.

Years after the economy recovered, my dad could still tell you exactly how much money he had on him at any given time, and it was always around $500. He was a man with a back-up plan, ready for hardship if it were ever to return. Within reason, both of my parents desired to ensure that their children had everything they needed and wanted. I think this was partly because they could not have what they wanted while they were growing up. They also passed onto us, mostly by example, the values of hard work, goal-setting, and determination.

These two, who grew up in neighboring states, met in New Guinea and were married in Australia. I was conceived there. My mother never missed a chance to tell me I was her ticket home from the war. Any time someone would talk about having visited or about planning to visit Australia, my joke was to tell them, "I had been there." When they would ask what was it like, I would say, "I don't remember much. But it felt warm, wet, and safe." When the puzzled looks would come, I would explain I was just a fetus when I lived in Australia.

Dave's parents after their weding in Sydney, Australia, during WWII

My mother gave birth to me in a Catholic hospital in Louisville, Kentucky. I contracted infantile diarrhea and the doctors were worried I would not survive. I learned that my aunts and a friend donated blood for money, in an effort to pay the hospital bills. We were many decades before the invention of the GoFundMe campaign on social media and, suffice it to say that charity was to be avoided in those days, and welfare was unheard of. The priests baptized me in the hospital and gave me last rites. But my mother insisted we be discharged, and she brought me home to her parents' house in Bardstown "to make sure I lived." There, she nursed me back to health with a lot of home remedies and constant attention from her family support group.

I think my mother had moments of discontent with the Catholic Church before the time in the hospital, but that situation with the Catholic hospital's management of my birth and health seemed to be the last straw for her. Years later, when it came time for me to be

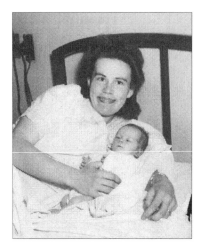

Margaret Amerine with newborn
David, October 1944

confirmed in the Episcopal church, the Catholic church in Louisville would not release the record of my baptism to my mother, so I was baptized in the Episcopal church at the age of 12 and confirmed soon thereafter. I am sure my mother sent notification of that Episcopalian baptism to those priests in Louisville with some salty suggestions on what they could do with their records of my earlier baptism.

It wasn't until after my birth that my dad came home from the war and met his in-laws. I am sure he had a lot of trepidation about that first meeting, but my Aunt Grace said everyone immediately liked my dad. He was able to get a placement through The Ohio State University as a meat inspector (back then, all meat inspectors had to have a veterinary degree) in Sandusky, Ohio, on the shores of Lake Erie. He went up to Ohio to make sure he had a job, and then fetched my mother and me. We moved into a little bungalow at the end of Columbus Avenue in an area known as Plum Brook because of its proximity to the Plum Brook Ordnance Works, which produced explosives during World War II and still exists today (2019) as a National Aeronautics and Space Agency (NASA) facility.

It is reported that I spoke my first logical sentence at the age of two, while we lived in that first house. I came in from playing in the back yard and, according to my mother, declared, "Doggy shit on brown shoe." My language and eloquence have not improved much over the years, some of which I attribute to my parents, who used profane language whenever it pleased them to do so. My mother's colorful sayings reflected both her Irish background ("Jesus, Mary, and Joseph," which seemed to fit almost any occasion) and her Kentucky upbringing and Army experience ("Your face looks like a Jaybird's ass in blueberry season." or "He/she doesn't know shit from Shinola.") I never did learn what Shinola is.

My mother's colorful sayings reflected both her Irish background ("Jesus, Mary, and Joseph," which seemed to fit almost any occasion) and her Kentucky upbringing and Army experience ("Your face looks like a Jaybird's ass in blueberry season." or "He/she doesn't know shit from Shinola.") I never did learn what Shinola is.

I remember coming home from the first day of my sophomore year in high school, and my mother, who was taking night classes to get her civilian nursing certificate, asked me who I had for teachers. When I told her that I had Mr. Sherer for English, she said, "Oh, I have him, too. He is a real prick." Later, my mother suggested I read Steinbeck's *Grapes of Wrath* for a book report. That novel was a bit racy for the time (it was, after all, only the '50s) and when I stood up to give my book report, Mr. Sherer told me to sit down as soon as I announced the name of the book. When my mother heard that, she went on the warpath. I received an A on the written report, but still was not allowed to give the report verbally. In retrospect, I think my mother planned the whole thing. I know the kids in my class could not wait to get their hands on the book.

We lived in that first house for a little more than two years, and then my dad bought a retiring veterinarian's business and adjoining house, still on Columbus Avenue but about five miles closer to town. (He was to repeat this transaction in reverse almost 40 years later. Today, that veterinary practice is the longest continuously running veterinarian clinic in the state of Ohio.) My three siblings — Judy, Phillip, and Debbie — were all born in Sandusky. Each child had their own room upstairs in the house until my mother agreed to adopt my sister, Pat, the child of one her Army buddies who was going through a nasty divorce, something that was still fairly rare in the 1950s. I remember Pat moving in and sharing the big front upstairs bedroom with Debbie.

My parents' bedroom was downstairs, as was a guest bedroom that also served as a sewing room for my mother. We had two living rooms, although at one time I am sure one was considered a "parlor" in which visitors would sit. Our dining room adjoined the kitchen and there was a full basement. Basements in those days were not finished but served as space for storage, utilities, and a wringer washing machine (clothes were hung outside to dry until the 1960s). The basement also had a coal room until the coal-burning furnace was replaced by an oil-burning furnace, which also happened in the 1960s. While I was still living at home, my parents remodeled the kitchen and added what they called a sunroom, which ran along the side of the house parallel to the kitchen and the first living room. It served as a TV room and a place to sit when those you did not want to sit with were using one of the other rooms.

My dad's hospital was separate from the house and was part of an L-shaped structure that included three garages, which had previously been stables for horses, and a storage/work area. There was a small back yard right behind the house that was virtually consumed by a swing set my dad erected and a huge open parking area for people who brought their pets in to see my father or to be boarded. This parking area was at the end of a long cement driveway that ran along the left edge of the property. The previously mentioned sunroom addition was on the other side of the house, leaving very little room between it and the line that divided our property from that of our neighbors, the Bradys, who had two boys around my age — Dickey (a year older) and Ronnie (in my class). More about the Bradys later.

Behind the hospital there was a big backyard. Roughly one half of it was dedicated, for many years, to my mom's rose gardens and the other half to my dad's vegetable garden. Dad always had a garden. I think those gardens brought him closer to his roots. The only thing I asked for on the day my dad died was the stone he had in his last garden, on which there is an inscription that says, "He who plants a garden, plants happiness."

Dad always had a garden. I think those gardens brought him closer to his roots.

Both areas were roughly 1,500 square feet in size, although my mom's area also had to share space with a barbecue pit and a picnic table. Our backyard abutted a railroad track and, beyond it, a field in which I played a lot when I was in grade school. On the other side of the field was a park, which included a baseball diamond, large swings, and a large open area. The baseball diamond was used by the older boys' baseball league. Little League and Babe Ruth League played at other parks, but I used to go over to watch Dick and Don DeHaven play. They were the sons of the high school football coach at the time and were in high school when I was in the third to sixth grades. They were good athletes and the neighborhood idolized them. I dreamed of the day when someone might idolize me.

I dreamed of the day when someone might idolize me.

My favorite books in those preschool days were *Good Enough Gismo* and *The Little Engine That Could*, both books about overcoming obstacles and striving to do one's best. They may have been harbingers of what kind of life I was to lead. I had to try hard with my meager talents, but I think I came close to being the best I could be in whatever I chose to do.

Dave with one of his favorite books as
a four-year-old, 1948

THE GRADE SCHOOL YEARS

When I was growing up, things seemed a little more carefree than they are now. In those days, parents could let their children roam free with very little care other than getting hit by a car due to carelessness, usually on the child's part. My mom made it clear to us kids that if we didn't look both ways when we crossed the street, and got hit by a car because we ran out into the street without looking, she would "beat you to within an inch of your life." I did not know what that meant exactly nor did I follow the logic of beating a child who just got hit by a car, but we all looked both ways and were never hit.

I think I was four or five when we moved to the neighborhood in which I was to finish growing up. Besides the Brady boys, who mostly stuck to themselves and did not seem interested in usual kid things — like hide-and-seek, playing cowboys and Indians, baseball and football, fishing, or just hanging out — the immediate neighborhood had about seven other children around my age.

The Samkos were our neighbors on the opposite side of the house from the Bradys. They had two kids — Pete, who was a year older than me, and Marla, who was four years younger than me, the same age as my older sisters. The Ordways lived two houses down and Gloria was in my class, Denny was two years older, and Tony was my brother, Phil's, age, which is to say five years younger than I was.

Then came the Grosscosts. Jim was Denny's age and Joe was a year older than me. Then there was a house full of three beautiful girls,

Carol, Kathy, and Emmy Weis. Carol was four years older than me, Kathy one year older, and Emmy was in my class. There were the Scheulers, who lived in the apartment at the end of the block; John was a year older and his sister, Ann, was Judy's age, four years younger than me. A few streets away was another neighborhood, in which lived all the boys with whom I would play sandlot sports while growing up. But my immediate neighborhood — where I had to get accepted as the new kid — was our block on Columbus Avenue.

The neighborhood kids had lived there all or most of their lives. I was new. When I ventured down the street on our block, I encountered the group, and they said I had to fight them. Several of the boys were bigger than I was, and it seemed a little unfair that I had to take them all on. Their idea of fairness was that it would be one at a time. At least there were no weapons involved. That initiation included the girls and, even then, I knew it was not appropriate to hit a girl, so I just let them shove me down. To this day, when I see her at reunions, I still remind Emmy of that initial introduction.

After that introduction, I was a member of the neighborhood group of kids in my age range. From my vantage point, it was a great time to be a kid. We could run all over the neighborhood and, as we got a little older, venture beyond the neighborhood boundaries without any fear — and, apparently, without any concern on the part of our parents. As I said, just a few blocks away were the boys with whom I spent the most time playing all variety of sports and other kid activities. They included my lifelong friend, Tom Rutger, and Bill Poeschel, Mike and Tom Yeager, Tom Petersen, and others. There were also a handful of black kids from a few blocks over, who also joined in on most of the activities, like Ed Bryant, Al Graves, Bob Hunter, and Ronnie Craig. We played games of all kinds in the field, in the park, in each other's homes, and just generally enjoyed life. We were a cluster of boys from different grades, different religions, different races, and different backgrounds, having fun and growing up together. The color

Dave and Tom Rutger, friends since kindergarten, all grown up

of a kid's skin just did not seem to matter, or at least it did not register on me at that age.

I'll always remember the time I came wheeling into the driveway on my tricycle and, just as I got off the bike, the center bar of the bike's frame broke in two, and my tricycle became two distinct irreparable parts. I cried. But my dad figured it was time for me to get a big-kid bicycle anyway (with training wheels, of course). I remember my dad helping me to master the bike without training wheels. He would guide the bike from the rear as I tried to get the balance, and we would go up and down our long driveway. Then one time I looked back, and he was several yards behind me, having let go without telling me. I immediately fell over, but the point had been made. I could do it by myself.

That bike was freedom itself. I went all over Sandusky on it. Over time, I cut the fenders, added playing cards to rub against the spokes to make motor sounds, put a basket on, and then quickly took it off when other boys made fun of me for having a girl's apparatus on my bike. I added a cereal box license plate, added handlebar streamers, and did everything every other kid did. The bike was the primary mode of transportation all the way through the summer leading into ninth grade. Then, suddenly, it was not "cool" anymore, and the bike found its way deeper and deeper into the garage, where all things no longer used were kept by my dad. That nothing was ever actually thrown away may have been a hangover from the Depression.

In those days, milk was delivered to the home and sat outside on the milk stand just outside the back door. The cream always rose to the top and was skimmed off by my mother for coffee and other uses. Sometimes the milk froze, but we were careful to always grab it first thing in the morning when it was delivered, so it did not get too hot and spoil. We bought our groceries at small neighborhood stores, usually with the family who owned the store living above it. There were at least three within a block of our house on Columbus Avenue. They always seemed to have whatever was needed and were the source of an occasional candy bar. I still remember my mother taking me to the first supermarket in Sandusky. I did not think much about it at the time, but now in my memory that seems to have marked the beginning of the end of the small-town atmosphere of the '40s and '50s.

Competition and Camaraderie: Childhood Sports

From about the fourth grade on, it seemed sports dominated the lives of most Sandusky boys. We played whatever game the season brought and there was very little adult supervision. The sandlot games were the best, equipped by kids, organized by kids, ruled by kids, played by kids. As we got older, kids would come to various places in town where they knew there would be a good game. For my neighborhood, whose boundaries started to expand as I got older, that seemed to center on Campbell Grade School. Occasionally, disputes were settled by fights, but not very often. I can't help but observe that arguments are more prevalent when adults, uniforms, and accurate scores are involved.

We played whatever game the season brought and there was very little adult supervision. The sandlot games were the best, equipped by kids, organized by kids, ruled by kids, played by kids.

Campbell School is where I went to grade school. It was a three-story limestone building, as were all the grade schools and other public buildings in Sandusky at that time, because limestone was so prevalent in the area. Campbell was three blocks from my house. I walked there almost every day for seven years, including kindergarten. If the weather was really inclement, my mother would drive us the three blocks, but it needed to be a near hurricane before that happened. In those days, school never closed down for weather and you had better be at death's door if you stayed home sick or were even late, for that matter. I still remember some of the teachers, like Mr. Niehm, who years later called me to inform me I had been inducted into the Sandusky Athletic Hall of Fame. Although he told me to call him Ray, some 50 years later, I could not address him as other than Mr. Niehm.

Then there was Mrs. Grindle who, like her name, struck fear in the heart of her students because she was so no-nonsense and demanding. I remember her scrubbing one young boy's hands raw because he came to class with dirt under his fingernails. She was tough and exacting and yet she may have been the best teacher I had at Campbell. Her expectations were high and her students wanted to excel because when she gave a rare compliment, it was like the sky opened up and light came down on your head. You knew you earned it!

I do remember two times my mother brought me to school. One time was when it was "raining cats and dogs," as she used to say. It was a cold, dark late fall day, and I think I was in the third grade. For whatever reason, she dropped me off on the street that ran parallel to the schoolyard, which I then had to cross. It was wider than a football field. But what I remember was looking through that dark rain up at the old school building with all its lights on in the windows. To this day, I cannot remember whether, as a third grader, that image evoked feelings of a safe harbor or something more ominous.

The other time she brought me to school was in kindergarten, when she had some matter to discuss with the principal. I thought I was being brought to school to attend class, not to sit in the principal's office, so when left alone for a moment, I went running into the ongoing kindergarten class. As I ran across the front of the room, I looked at the class, saying "I'll be right back as soon as I hang up my coat." Once I got in the cloakroom, it dawned on me that I did not know any of those kids in that class, and they were not my friends from my kindergarten class but complete strangers.

Just as I was thinking, "*Who were those strange people?*" the teacher came into the cloakroom to see who this new little boy was that had just sprinted across the front of her classroom. She asked me if I would like to come into the class or what would I like to do. Being totally confused, I said I was going to stay right where I was.

No amount of talking could get me to budge, so she left to go see the principal. I'm pretty sure that, like me, she didn't know what to do either.

Fortunately, there was another entrance to the cloakroom and, pretty soon, my mother came through that door and said (loud enough for all those kids in the classroom to hear, I am sure), "David, get your coat and get your little butt over here right now so we can go home."

Apparently, she had finished her business with the principal which, at the time, I was sure was to put me in a class for idiots. At least she didn't say she was going to beat me within an inch of my life!

Speaking of classes for idiots, I do remember public school being segregated by "tracks" of sorts. The kids were divided up into basically three groups. They consisted of those who appeared to be either very smart or at least worked very hard at their studies, those who were of seemingly average intelligence or just did not want to work as hard, and those who had difficulty with the material or just would not work at the material at all, for whatever reason. Similarly, grades were posted in a public manner, and some students took pride in receiving a good grade while others didn't seem to care what they received. Again, students were judged by and acknowledged for their ability to assimilate the material as based on their homework and test scores, which in turn was as much a function of effort as talent.

The teacher seemed to handle the situation just fine, and the kids (or more importantly, the parents) seemed to accept the groups into which the students were settled. Over time, some kids seemed to move from one group to another with no great fanfare, and some kids were even held back to repeat a grade. There was none of this "everyone is the same" crap that exists today (with everyone pushed toward college). There was equality of opportunity, but no guarantee of outcome. The outcome was up to the students and whatever direction their parents provided. I think today's approach results in the gifted students having the same attrition rate as the extremely challenged students.

I believe that our educational system, nationally, started its decline with President Carter's creation of the Department of Education, along with this idea that everyone should go to college. Federal interference at the local and state levels has added administrative burden but very little value. Common Core is a disaster. The shop wing at my old high school doesn't even function during the day for high school students anymore. There were kids who would disappear down that wing when I was in school and got jobs as carpenters, welders, pipefitters, mechanics, nurses' aides, secretaries, etc. And four or five years later, they were making a hell of a lot more money than classmates graduating with degrees in sociology. Those jobs are going begging for people today. Starting with the premise that everyone is the same ignores reality and eliminates or restricts the tailoring that can keep all students — regardless of their interests and academic gifts — engaged.

The shop wing at my old high school doesn't even function during the day for high school students anymore. There were kids who would disappear down that wing when I was in school and got jobs as carpenters, welders, pipefitters, mechanics, nurses, secretaries, etc. And four or five years later, they were making a hell of a lot more money than classmates graduating with degrees in sociology.

I'm guessing that most parents at that time were like mine. If any of us Amerine kids got in trouble at school, it was understood we were also in trouble at home. And our parents had better hear about it from us instead of from the school. The teachers were always right, period. We were to show them respect at all times.

The rules of engagement for sports were much the same as in the classroom. Whether it was adult-supervised sports (which seemed to begin in the fourth grade with both grade school competition and summer baseball) or the sandlot games run by the kids themselves, you did your best and the chips fell where they may. Some kids lost interest in sports, presumably because they were not very good and got tired of trying, or maybe because they just were not interested in the first place and had other interests. Back then, there weren't many pushy parents trying to achieve vicariously through their children. No over-exuberant football dads who wanted their son to play first string, and no obsessive tennis-coach moms who came to every practice. Adults had their own lives to live and the focus seemed to be on providing for their families. The adults who were involved seemed either interested in coaching kids or were teachers (who may or may not have been reimbursed for their coaching time).

When I drive around towns now and happen to think about it, I see very little sandlot sports going on. It seems that everything is ultra-organized and adult supervised, or it doesn't exist at all. I also think there is an unhealthy emphasis on specializing in one sport way too soon in a young person's life. Not only is the kid missing out on variety and maybe not learning that there is an entirely different activity they might like or be good at, but studies have shown that it is not physically healthy to focus on one set of muscles or one skill set at too early an age.

When I drive around towns now and happen to think about it, I see very little sandlot sports going on. It seems that everything is ultra-organized and adult supervised, or it doesn't exist at all.

I was not a very gifted athlete (my brother got all the athletic talent), but I tried hard and was pretty strong for my size, which was above average in grade school and junior high. In high school, it seemed I stopped growing. My mother told me I would be taller than six feet every time I asked. I think she based that prediction on the fact that her father and brothers were all six feet tall or taller, and the Hagans in Kentucky could brag that they had two All-American basketball players in the family who were 6'5, Cliff Hagan and Charlie Tyra. It was also a way to get me to quit asking the same question all the time. Well, I barely made it to 5'9, while my brother was pretty much exactly six feet. In our later years, he also inherited my maternal grandfather's white shock of hair, while I got my dad's family height and hairline: short and bald. Genetics are a crapshoot.

When I started playing baseball, I was lousy. I just could not hit the ball. My first two years in Little League, I struck out every time except once and that was an accident — pure luck swinging with my eyes closed. My dad heard me whining about it and decided he would take me over to Campbell School one afternoon and show me how to play baseball. That was kind of embarrassing, especially because he brought along my sisters and brother. But at least he tried even though, as I said, he was no athlete himself. Then a funny thing happened. Between the fifth and the sixth grade, I seemed to get my hand-eye coordination. I went from being the last guy chosen in sandlot to leading Little League and then Babe Ruth League in almost every hitting category. **Sometimes it pays to just not give up too soon.**

Church Days and Neighborhood Ladies

Nearly every Sunday, everyone went to church. My parents made sure we went each Sunday, but they themselves did not attend. My sister, Judy, told me that my dad chose Grace Episcopal Church after Reverend Carey brought his dog in one day when my dad's practice on Columbus Ave was just starting out. Dad liked the Reverend, who was indeed a nice man with an appropriate authoritarian way about him, and Dad decided we Amerine kids should attend Reverend Carey's church. As Judy says, we are lucky Mr. Carey was not from the Hare Krishna sect, or we might all be in airports asking for contributions.

My dad tried once to attend church with us and made each of us kids sit with him. I did not like sitting with my siblings, and I was embarrassed by my dad's singing. I think he sensed that and never went again. Years later, when I think back to that time, I still feel bad about it. Mom never went. I think she was still pissed at the Catholic priests and was daring them to send her to hell. However, she made me sing in the choir and go to confirmation classes. I did not like either, but felt that I needed to please God (as well as my mother). I became an acolyte (which, in the Episcopal church, is someone who performs ceremonial duties) and I eventually was selected to be the head acolyte. I liked being an integral part of the church service. The acolytes also went on some great trips, like to the National Cathedral. The bottom line is that church was an important part of my growing up and I was somewhat active all through high school as an acolyte. I always felt that God was there, even though I was not sure what that meant to me personally. I did say my prayers, although probably not too well.

There are other things I remember from the grade school days, some funny, some poignant. I remember that there was a kindly old lady who lived a few houses from us. One day, when three or four of us were playing around near her house, I somehow ended up accidentally throwing a rock through one of her basement windows. I was six or seven at the time. I knew that she saw me do it, but I assume she never called my parents because I never got in trouble, although I worried about it a lot. First, I was worried that I would get in trouble, and then I was worried that I did something very bad to a person who had done nothing but been kind to me. I got up the courage, knocked on her door, and apologized. She said that little boys just needed to be more careful.

Time passed and then, one day, there were a lot of cars at her house. I asked an adult going into the house what the occasion was. He told me that the lady had died, and this was a memorial for her. I went up to the door and asked the man who answered it if he would tell the woman I wished her a happy dying. My parents did hear about that, and told me that was a nice thing to do.

Forbidden Fruit

You may recall that I mentioned that Denny Ordway was taller than the rest of us. Our next-door neighbors, the Bradys, had a small orchard in the part of their yard that was parallel to my dad's garden. One day, some of us had jumped the fence to help ourselves to some of the apples and pears. Mr. Brady saw us and came out of his house, screaming, as we all jumped back over the fence. He yelled that if he caught any of us in his yard again touching his fruit, he would call the police and have us all arrested for stealing. As it happened, some of the tree limbs hung over the fence into my parents' space. Well, Denny could just about reach the apple with his mouth, so he stood on his tiptoes and ate it while it hung on the tree. Apparently, my mother had either heard the commotion or more likely had been called by Mr. Brady about her son and his hoodlum friends, and she came into the backyard just as Denny was finishing the apple. When she saw that core hanging there, she burst out laughing so hard I thought she would bust a vein.

She did not think Denny was so funny, however, on another occasion when he slammed the Grosscosts' backyard gate just as I was coming through it, and it hit me square in the mouth. It chipped my front tooth and that tooth remains chipped to this day. I used to tell people it got chipped when I was making a tackle in football, but the truth is less heroic or interesting. The truth is that neither Denny nor I was paying attention to what we were doing. However, my mother was angry. She had paid a lot of money to the dentist to make sure her kids had healthy teeth (none of us had braces but we did have a number of fillings). I think she hated to see me "scarred for life." She made me wear a mouth guard on my football helmet in grade school football. The mouth guard, though, had a very short life span before I took it off out of embarrassment. None of the other kids used one back then, and I didn't want to either.

I did eventually get Denny back with a trick Joe Grosscost and I played on Denny and Joe's older brother, Jim, and a couple of other older boys. We were hanging around an old barn at the end of the alley that ran through our neighborhood, and someone said that there had been a murder years ago in the attic of the barn. Well, the older boys said that Joe and I should go up there and check it out. We did not want to do it, but they made us. While we were up there, we found a bee hive, so we went to the trap door, got ready to go down the steps, and just as we closed the door we moved a rake hard against the hive and slammed the trap door shut as we hurried down the steps. The older boys asked us what was up there when we came out of the barn, and we said some really neat old bikes and farm tools. They said, "Step aside. We will go see if there is anything worth salvaging." As they went in the barn, Joe and I took off running to find a good place to hide for the rest of the day. We could hear them screaming from a block away. Later, Joe told me that he stayed really close to his dad that night while his mom treated his brother for multiple bee stings.

As I reflect on these precious memories from childhood, one moment burned in my memory is my first pair of ice skates. I got them for Christmas. My mother took me down to Battery Park, where the marina had a large open area that froze over, and all of Sandusky seemed to go there to skate. The first time she took me, she just dropped me off and said she would be back in a couple of hours. Even though it was bitterly cold, the ice had melted a little the day before and there was a film of water on top of the ice. I fell a lot and was soaking wet when she returned. Worse than that, there were some older girls there, who saw my futile initial efforts. Worst of all, they offered to help me. Embarrassing!

I did eventually learn to skate and could do all the tricks the other boys could do, like skating backward. We also played hockey, which was brutal. The puck hardly seemed necessary, as we beat the hell out of each other, which as it turned out was a good precursor for playing lacrosse at the Naval Academy. Every year, Lake Erie would claim some people during the winter season, ranging from ice fishermen who pushed their luck as the Lake started to thaw to kids doing something stupid. I remember one day when a bunch of us were playing hockey, a mother who had heard three boys had drowned came to the edge of the ice in a panic asking if we had seen her boy. It turned out that her son, who was a year behind me in school, was indeed one of the three. I will never forget the fear in her voice. It is every parent's worst nightmare to be predeceased by one of their children.

We also played hockey, which was brutal. The puck hardly seemed necessary, as we beat the hell out of each other.

The Truth About Cows and Dogs

Like most primary care veterinarians, my dad treated small animals at his hospital. He also treated large farm animals. For quite some time, he was the only veterinarian in Erie County. That meant he had to go visit farms when they had a sick pig or cow or when their animals needed vaccinations. I remember being present on many occasions when my dad assisted in the birth of a calf. Sometimes both he and the farmer (and even I!) had to help pull the calf out if it was somehow caught or in the wrong position. A few times, this had to be done with a great sense of urgency or the calf might drown in its own fetal fluids. The cow never did seem to appreciate the help of these humans, judging from the noise she would make.

My dad's father was a farmer, and my dad was a farmer in his heart. He loved his farm calls. He loved putting on his overalls and boots to go on a farm call, and I loved to go on farm calls with him. I could always tell when we were getting close to the designated farm because he would put a wad of chewing tobacco in his mouth, which I never saw him chew any other time. An obligatory part of the farm call was leaning on the fence with the farmers and chewing, spitting, and philosophizing. Dad just loved that. He loved those farmers because he admired and respected the life they had chosen, and he loved that he could help their animals.

My dad's father was a farmer, and my dad was a farmer in his heart.

I helped my dad do a lot of things that were unique to being a vet's son. I was there when he delivered kittens and puppies, and it was my job to gently rub them and clean them. And, as I mentioned, sometimes I was there when he delivered a calf, and sometimes that was a real struggle. One time, the farmers had to wrap a chain around the calf's hooves to help pull it the rest of the way out. I have wrestled down calves and piglets for vaccination, and even held the pigs for castration.

I'll never forget having gone with my dad to a farm after the sun had gone down. I got bored in the barn and went out to see what was in the pens near the barn. There were some cows in one pen, and I hopped over the fence to see if I could actually pet one of them, seeing as they didn't have much room in the pen and I thought it would be easy to approach them. Usually cows are pretty skittish and will back away, but when I went up to one and pushed on its nose, it pushed back. Some of the other "cows" came over to check me out. About that time, my dad came out of the barn to see where I was and, when he saw me, he yelled, "David, get the hell out of there!" I was in a pen full of bulls. I calmly climbed out of the pen, not appreciating the sense of urgency, because he didn't tell me that until I got up to the barn. I could have really gotten hurt.

Starting sometime in grade school, fifth or sixth grade, my dad would get me up at 5:30 a.m. on Saturdays and Sundays, to clean dog cages. His hired help, Fred, was off on the weekends, so cleaning cages was my job when Fred was away. I didn't like getting up early, but I liked being with my dad. He worked hard and fast, and it was difficult to keep up with him. It was messy work, and occasionally I had to deal with a dog or cat who didn't want to come out of its cage. Dad taught me how to use a catch pole (a loop on a rope that was threaded through a steel pipe) around the animal's neck and pull it tight and then pull them out of the cage. The pipe, about a yard long, kept the dog at bay until you could get it out to the run, loosen the rope, and lift it off the animal's head. The cats had to be moved to a different cage because, unlike the dogs, they could climb out of the kennel runs and make their getaway, if they were so inclined. One really sad thing that always bothered me was that there was a Doberman named Boy, whose owner kept him there 24/7, all year round. That did not make sense to me nor did it seem at all fair to condemn the dog to that existence. He was still there when I went off to the Naval Academy as a young man.

Adult Lessons at a Tender Age

There were a couple of other things that happened during my grade school years that shaped my view of things as an adult. One enduring lesson my dad gave to me is illustrated by this singular story. It was a hot summer day when I was 12 or 13, and a group of my friends and I had just finished playing baseball. We were walking by my house when I remembered that my dad kept a stash of Popsicles in the freezer in the animal hospital. I asked my friends if they would like one and, of course, they said yes. However, two of the guys, who were black, said they did not want any and sat on the curb, waiting for us to return. Focused on the Popsicles, I didn't think anything of it as the rest of us proceeded back to the hospital. It didn't register with me that all the white boys came in for a Popsicle, but the two black boys hung back. But my dad had seen everything from his hospital window, and he asked me why those other two boys did not come back. I said that they were not interested. My dad said, "You go tell those boys that your father said for them to come back here and get their Popsicles." It was years before that lesson registered on me: at that tender age, those two fellows worried that they might not be accepted by the adults in the house due to the color of their skin. They never forgot that kindness and always stopped by to see my dad even when they returned to town from college or the service.

For several years in a row, my mother invited a few kids from the city orphanage to spend Thanksgiving Day with us. Although I felt a bit uncomfortable the first time she did it, because I did not know these kids, I think the Amerine kids did the best we could to make these children, who were a few years younger than me at the time, feel welcome. My mother did other things with little to no fanfare that I noted at the time were acts of charity. Even though we did not talk about it, it made an impression on me that those who are able have a duty to help others.

My mother did other things with little to no fanfare that I noted at the time were acts of charity. Even though we did not talk about it, it made an impression on me that those who are able have a duty to help others.

I remember the last spanking my dad gave me, which I think happened when I was in the fifth or sixth grade. I must have done something very bad because my dad rarely spanked any of us. Being a veterinarian involved a lot of physical exertion besides medical analysis, so my dad was pretty strong and in good shape. We went into his bedroom and he got out his belt. Then he said, "This is going to hurt me a lot more than it will hurt you." I remember thinking at the time, "*Then why do it?*" but I was smart enough not to say that. However, I could tell that, as strong as he was, his heart was not in it because he could have made it hurt a lot worse. I remember thinking afterward that I did not want to put him in that position again, because I knew he had gone easy on me and he really did not relish corporal punishment.

When I was in the fifth grade, two things happened with my mother. One was a bunch of us boys got into a snowball fight, which meant a lot of rolling around in the snow wrestling as well as throwing snow at each other. That night, one of the boys, whose name I cannot remember, died of spinal meningitis. All the mothers of the boys who had been involved in that snowball fight were called by someone. My mother rushed me to a doctor, where I got a series of shots. She watched me like a hawk for the next several days and I could tell she was really worried. The good news was I got to stay home from school until it was determined I did not have the dreaded disease. No other boys died besides the first one, but I never saw the same fear in my mother's face before or since.

Sometime after that but still in the fifth grade, I got in a fight at another boy's house and hit him in the mouth. He went downstairs and told his mother, who screamed at me and told me to leave her house. When I got home, my mother was waiting. She asked me if I had hit Mark and I said yes. Then she said, "Did he deserve it?" I said I thought so. Then she said, "Well, there are other ways to settle disputes and you might consider that. Now, tomorrow in school, you apologize to Mark."

The next day, I told Mark I was sorry and he said, "For what?" I wasn't sure, so I told him my mother told me to find other ways to settle disputes. He said, "What dispute?" I think it goes to show parents can make a mountain out of a molehill. But somehow that event said to me that I was too hot-headed and needed to channel my aggression to the playing fields if I was to stay out of trouble.

Good Laughs, Good Lessons

One other thing I remember about the fifth grade was racing home to hear my favorite radio show on Saturday night, *The Shadow*. I slid into the living room and sidled up to the radio ready to hear, "The Shadow knows!" when I noticed everyone was looking at the far wall. I turned around and there was a television set. It was in a big console and the screen was about a foot square with a fuzzy black-and-white picture, but it spelled doom for the Shadow just as much as any of his fictional enemies. We had a TV!

There is something I should mention about these years. I liked school, but unfortunately only from a competitive standpoint. I wanted to get better grades than everyone else and worked hard to make that happen. If I learned something along the way, that was incidental. I did like math and figuring things out, but it came pretty easily. My mom would work with me whenever I ran into a difficulty, like drawing my sevens backward when I was in the first grade. However, by the time I got to junior high, she began to not be able to help me with my math.

My dad was always working, so he was not much help with the studies. On the other hand, he gave all of us kids a dollar for each A we earned, so I know he wanted us to do well in school. I say "unfortunately" about my attitude toward academic success because it seemed doing well grade-wise was always more important to me than true understanding. Many times, the two go hand in hand but not always. It is better for students to be driven by the thirst for knowledge. While I did well in school, I think I could have done better — or at least gotten more out of it — had the driver been learning rather than earning.

While I did well in school, I think I could have done better — or at least gotten more out of it — had the driver been learning rather than earning.

One interesting thing that happened in school involved a math test, a subject I liked and for which I seemed to have an aptitude. We were instructed to take the test papers we had just completed and pass them to the back of the classroom, to be picked up by the teacher. The next day, I was floored when the grade on the test I received was a D. I was so confident when I handed in my test that I just could not believe it. When I got home, my mother said she had received a call from the principal about the test. She asked me if I had knowingly switched my test with Ronnie Brady, my next-door neighbor. I was shocked and she could tell that I had no knowledge of such a thing. (My mother could always tell when one of us kids was lying and she did not abide lying at all.) I really do not know what occurred after that except that I got my real test back with an A on it, but I am pretty sure Ronnie did not sit down comfortably for some time. It is interesting to note that Ronnie became a successful insurance salesman as an adult and liked to let everyone know how much money he had when he would come back for reunions. I am surprised he did not become a politician.

I do remember that it was during my grade school years that my dad introduced me to chores. Besides cleaning dog cages on the weekend, it was my job to cut the grass, rake the leaves, sweep the driveway, shovel the snow, and clean the basement. For doing these things, I was paid an allowance. I did my chores religiously without my parents hassling me to do them. I do not know why, but I took pride in doing them, and as near as I could tell, I did them to my dad's satisfaction.

The family joke was that when I left to go to the Naval Academy, my brother took over the chores, and my dad had to track him down to get him to do them. Frequently Phil would enlist the help of friends, and my dad said the yard seemed to be getting smaller and smaller from my brother's mowing technique of not going close to the edges. A parental guidance that came out of doing chores was my father's admonishment that the job was not done until the tools were cleaned and properly stored. I carried that philosophy into the Navy and my personal life as well. Additionally, if any of us kids left a door open when we should have shut it, Dad would always ask, "Were you born in a barn? Go back and shut the door." I have no idea what the relationship was between failing to shut the door and being born in a barn, but then I never understood why my mother would say, "There is just enough time to shave, shit, and shower!" when she was in a hurry, but I liked the alliteration.

The job was not done until the tools were cleaned and properly stored.

Something that always bothered me, though, was the wind. When I swept the driveway or raked the yard, the wind always conspired to blow the leaves back to the place from which I had just moved them. Even when I tried to cooperate with the wind to the extent the yard or drive would permit, it still conspired against me. One day I got so mad, I threw my broom and it went through a garage window. I thought I would be in real trouble, but I saw my dad at the hospital door nearly doubling over with laughter. He had been watching the whole thing. That episode was another example that I was perhaps a bit of a hothead.

Reflecting on these years, it occurs to me that, as a child, I did not mind being by myself. In fact, sometimes I liked spending time with my thoughts. I liked looking at the sky, lying flat on my back in the backyard, and watching the clouds. I liked thinking about things and even just making things up in my mind. As much as I liked playing games and sports with the other boys, I did not feel like I needed anyone else to define me. That seems a little heavy for someone in grade school, but that is the way I remember it. I also felt I had a sense of humor. I liked to laugh and to make jokes. I especially liked it when I could make my parents laugh. I think even then I knew a sense of humor was important to keep things in perspective, and it was good to be able to laugh at yourself. Also, I liked to think of myself as tough and not afraid of anyone, but not ever mean.

I think the worst thing I did that was mean-spirited was to join in with the other boys in dropping a garden snake off the top of a vertical gas tank. These tanks, which contained gas for the mechanic's car garage, were about 40 feet high and 10 feet in diameter and had a ladder up the side that we would climb up and then drop the snake when we got to the top. We killed that snake for no good reason other than it was a snake, and I have always felt bad about that. The real takeaway from this train of thought? Even in grade school, I didn't think of myself as a joiner but as something different, something like a leader. And as a leader, I felt strong about some things that I couldn't clearly identify at that age, but it had to do with being fair and respectful to others ... even a garden snake.

When I was in the sixth grade, there was a family who lived across the street from the school. There were at least three boys in the family, one younger than me by a year and one older than me by a year. Their brother, however, was high school age and rode a motorcycle. He kept the bike in a small garage behind the house that I do not think was big enough even for a single car. Also in that garage was a set of weights with a big bar and two small bars for dumbbells. He also had a bench. I was attracted to the garage by a gathering of boys I noticed one day, and they were lifting weights. The older brother was showing off how much weight he could lift over his head. I also noticed that the garage had several pinups of scantily dressed girls. I cannot remember if I made the connection that making my muscles bigger was good for getting girls to notice me or good for playing football or both. In any case, that started me on a lifetime of lifting weights.

Even in grade school, I didn't think of myself as a joiner but as something different, something like a leader. And as a leader, I felt strong about some things that I couldn't clearly identify at that age, but it had to do with being fair and respectful to others ... even a garden snake.

In the 1950s, there were no gyms or fitness clubs like we have today. In organized sports, it was thought that lifting weights would make a person overly muscle bound and, therefore, hurt his athletic prowess (perish the thought that a girl would even be interested in athletics, let alone lifting weights). But I persisted on my own from then on, lifting in the garage with a set of weights I subsequently convinced my dad to buy for me for a birthday in the seventh grade. I got exercises from the pamphlet that came with the weights and later from muscle magazines. I dragged that set of weights around with me for years, even after I got married. They were finally replaced by a more sophisticated set and some weight machines as well, so I could work out before I left for work. That was years later, and by then the bodybuilding mindset of both the general public and the athletic community had come a long way from those first days in that small garage.

JUNIOR HIGH

In Sandusky, there were nine grade schools that fed one junior high school, which housed the seventh and eighth grades. The school was named after the street it was on, as were most of the grade schools, and most of those names (streets and schools) were named after Presidents. But it was just known as Junior High back then, although it was formally Jackson Junior High. It was also the center of many city activities because it was relatively new and had the biggest auditorium. All the high school basketball games were held there at that time, because the junior high gym was bigger than the high school gym. And we hosted all the high school swim meets too, because the local high school didn't have a pool.

At Campbell School, I had worked my way up to sixth grade, and I was the big cheese. My buddy, Tom Rutger, was clearly a better athlete, but I was a better student. I had friends I had known for six or seven years. Many of my classmates looked up to me. Teachers liked me and remembered me from when they had me in class and would say hi and ask me how it was going. Now I had to start all over with a new group of students, most of whom I did not know, and a new group of teachers, sometimes four or five in the same day, who definitely did not know me.

I remember the first day at junior high. It was intimidating. All the strange new faces, the stories I had heard about bigger, tougher kids, not to mention actually changing classes and teachers to change subjects. Oh yes, there was the matter of learning the new building and schedule as well as mastering the locker and lock situation. And now there was a greater awareness of girls. Somehow that situation had changed over the summer. I was noticing new things, like breasts pushing out sweaters and tight skirts (back then they came down to midcalf, but you could still tell if a girl had a nice butt). For the first time, I was noticing girls were using a little makeup. Had they been doing that before in grade school? I don't think so, but then who had time for girls back in grade school? Tom Rutger used to encourage me to go to Gloria Ordway's house to learn how to make out, but I was always afraid we would get in trouble.

Fortunately, as the huge crowd gathered outside the school on that first day, there were some eighth graders who had formerly attended Campbell School who recognized me and started introducing me around. They told me who the football players were and who the tough guys were. They also told me stories about some of the teachers. Some were reputed to be tougher than others, depending on the subject. My sense of it is that the approach to teaching was different in the '50s and early '60s than it is today.

In looking back, I feel like I was blessed to have gone through the Sandusky public school system when I did. I felt like I consistently had good teachers who were interested in the subject they taught and invested in their students. There was never a strike, and if there was a teachers' union, it was not pervasive like it is today. Surely it was true then as it is now — teachers' pay was low relative to many other vocations. But in large part, I think the teachers chose that job, not because they could not do anything else, but because it was what they wanted to do. It was a labor of love.

One person to whom I was introduced in junior high was Dean Earl. Dean was nearly 6'4 in the eighth grade and he was black. I came home from school that first day and told my parents, "There is a giant in the eighth grade! No, really!" I was in awe. As it turned out, Dean was everyone's hope to eventually lead Sandusky to championships in football, basketball, and track. That did not quite happen. Dean's interest was in music and the piano, where he was self-taught. His father actually put a record player in their piano and Dean would play along with Fats Domino as a way to learn the music. Dean became a friend of mine and we had many "important" conversations. He was a frequent visitor to my home, as I was to his. His parents were very nice to me, as were mine to Dean. My mother actually filled a request of Dean's to learn to play golf. They made quite a sight out on Mills golf course, this black "man" playing with a white "woman." My mother, who was women's lib before that term existed, couldn't have cared less about the image. In fact, knowing her personality, she may have reveled in any controversy. I wish I had been a better friend to Dean after high school, but we eventually went our separate ways.

I had a classmate named Gary King whose father was the seventh-grade math teacher. Mr. King helped nurture that spark I had for math that started in grade school, and I continued to do well as the subject matter became more sophisticated. I only remember two other teachers from junior high school, Mr. Pogoli and Ms. Homegardener.

Mr. Pogoli was the physical education teacher, a course that was mandatory back then. He was also the football coach. Ms. Homegardener taught library, which included Ohio state history. She was a colorful character who was reported to have a drinking problem and loose morals. However, she was "old" by the time we had her for a teacher, maybe in her late 40s.

Back to girls. Change that to back to sports. Mr. Pogoli saw something in me. Normally, the seventh graders had their own football team and game schedule separate from the eighth graders. However, he moved me to the eighth-grade team, and I started as a middle guard on defense. I had no idea what I was doing, but somehow was able to get into the backfield of our opponents and make tackles for a loss. I was the only seventh grader who lettered on the eighth-grade team. Now back to girls. Maybe my football exploits are what got Bonnie Martin's attention. I mean I was hanging out with eighth graders and she was an eighth grader. Actually, due I think to some illness, she was held back one grade somewhere along the line in grade school, so she truly was "an older woman." I would meet her at her locker and walk her to her class and then hurry not to be late to my seventh-grade class. Anytime I did not have a sports practice, I would walk her home. We would kiss every opportunity we got. I was in heaven. However, when the school year was over, she was headed for high school and I was still in junior high. It did not take long for this good-looking girl to come to the attention of older boys in high school and I was soon history. But it was a great introduction to the mysteries of the opposite sex.

New Sports, New Freedoms

Besides football, I went out for the swimming team. I swam back-stroke and was the number-one swimmer for that stroke. I did this again in eighth grade and actually set the junior high record, which stood for a number of years. However, what I really liked doing was going to the junior high gym on Saturdays for pickup games of basketball. I was not a very good shooter, but I was a good passer, which made me attractive to the guys who were good shooters. I also played defense pretty well. Each year in the spring in junior high, I went out for track. I ran the half-mile because I had found I liked running distances even then. We only had one meet, which was with ourselves, but I won those races.

The junior high years seemed to mark a time when I thought I was no longer a little boy and could do what I wanted to do. Because of sports and my concern for my health as an athlete, I never tried smoking. I did not drink in junior high or in high school, for that matter, where it was a little more prevalent but mostly relegated to beer when it did happen. It was still pretty rare compared to today's problems. Drugs were virtually unheard of back then in small towns like Sandusky, but I think I would have been smart enough to stay away from them also.

My parents gave me a lot of freedom. My curfew on Friday and Saturday nights was midnight and they never were too insistent on knowing exactly where I was going. I was good about observing the timeline and was usually home a little early. However, one time when I was in the eighth grade, a bunch of us were over at one of the girl's houses when some guys with whom I usually didn't hang around showed up with a car. Now these were eighth graders, and they definitely should not have had a car. For some reason, I thought it would be cool to go for a ride and I jumped in the back seat. We rode around for about ten minutes, and then I told them to take me back to the party. When I got home that night, I checked in with my parents, who were in bed, as I always did when I got home. My mother asked me if I knew anything about some boys who had been caught stealing cars and taking them for a "joy ride." I said no, which was lying even though I really did not put things together until right then. They said okay and told me go to bed because it was late and I had to get up early to help clean dog cages.

Well, of course, the boys who got caught squealed on everyone who had been in the cars regardless of how long. My name came up, and the police came to my house. That night, after my parents took me to the police station to be booked, my mother said she never wanted to speak to me again because I hadn't just been stupid, but worse, I lied to her. I was up in my room beating myself up for those two things when my dad came in the room and said, "Dave, I just wanted to tell you I love you." Then he turned around and left before I could say anything. That was the first time he had ever said that. Of course, now

I felt even worse, but I also felt good and promised I would never let my parents down again. When we went to court, the judge basically really chewed all of us boys out in front of our parents. When we were walking back to the car, my mother said, "David, never put yourself in a position where you deserve that kind of dressing down and have to take it." More than anything, she was angry that her son had been so stupid.

Adolescent Summers and Early Sports Injuries

I had two great summers of baseball during the junior high years. We still had great sandlot games at Campbell School. However, I moved from Little League to Babe Ruth League. The organizer of the Babe Ruth League, Mr. Palmer, had a son, Jim, who was a year older than me and a pretty good baseball player. His dad loaded up the team with good players and that included me. The team was sponsored by Smith Hardware and it trounced every other team in its first year. The next year, Jim moved up to the Knothole League and so did his dad. There were three or four other really great players, like Dick Acerto, who also moved on and left the league. (Incidentally, Dick also played football, and in his high school senior year was voted Lineman of the Year in the state of Ohio.) The Babe Ruth League organizers, who were also coaches of those teams we had beaten so badly, decided they would get even and replaced the departed players on our team with a bunch of little guys from Little League.

However, they did not do their homework very well because, even though they were relatively small in stature, it turned out those kids could really field the ball and could be counted on to bang out singles when needed. So, with the residual from that first season, which included players like Dave Milne, Jerry Jenkins, and myself, we beat everybody again.

The city of Sandusky was like a lot of Ohio towns, which all took their high school sports very seriously. I started to play football in the fifth grade for Campbell School, which was as young as was allowed back then. I also played basketball and softball for Campbell, but was never really very good at basketball and did not catch on to softball/baseball until the sixth grade. But football was king in Sandusky, and I considered myself tough enough to be good at it. Even though eventually kids caught up to me in size and my athletic limitations became more apparent as the competition became tougher, I was one of the best in grade school by the time I got to the sixth grade.

What was really cool in the sixth grade was "football Friday nights!" My parents let me walk to the stadium by myself or with some friends to pay our 50 cents to find a seat to watch the really big kids play before a packed crowd under the lights. Those crisp fall nights, the smell of popcorn, and the cheer of the crowd were just the best feeling ever. I could not imagine being good enough to play for the varsity team, but it was all I dreamed about. And, of course, my dreams had me as the star.

There was one thing that happened during the summer between my eighth-grade year and high school that was to set the stage for the rest of my athletic career and, ultimately, had a real influence on my life. The baseball coach was thinking about having me pitch. As I mentioned, in those years I was both of good size and fairly strong for my age. The coach would have me over to his house to practice pitching with his son, who was the team catcher, for several hours at a time. One time, I must have thrown really hard for at least two hours.

When I left their house, I went over to Campbell School to play in a pickup game, but the only person there was a 19-year-old who played in a lot of our sandlot games. Between us, we had our gloves and a ball but no bat. So, we played throw over, where each of us would throw the ball as high and as far as we could and the other guy would have to throw from wherever he fielded it. We must have done that for about an hour. Somehow, from all that throwing, I strained the ligaments in my lower back.

During the following two weeks, two things happened. Smith Hardware started to play in the Babe Ruth League World Series and high school football practice started. Even though I was about to start my freshman year, because of the success I had in junior high school football, I decided to go out for the varsity. (Freshman football would not start until school started, while varsity always started practice in the middle of August.) My back was getting worse and worse. I didn't get a single hit in the World Series because I could barely swing the bat. Football was becoming increasingly difficult and painful. Finally, just as school was starting, my mother took me to see Dr. Skirball, who diagnosed that I had strained the ligaments between my spine and my pelvis, and who said I should not play football that season. He went even further to say that he felt that I was injury prone and should focus on non-contact sports. I told my mom on the way home that I thought he should change his name to Dr. Screwball. Although she thought that was funny, she did say I could not play football my freshman year, period. So, I went from being on the varsity team to being the freshman football team manager. I was devastated. However, as it turned out, Dr. Skirball's analysis was prophetic.

Before wrapping up my reminiscing about my junior high school days, I need to tell you about my musical talent, of which there is none. My brother learned to play the piano, but I refused, thinking it was sissy. I could not appreciate that it would be fulfilling later in life, not to mention a girl magnet in high school, college, and beyond. However, my mother thought it would be a great idea for me to get a merit badge in Boy Scouts for playing the bugle. So she signed me up for lessons, which I hated. Fortunately, the teacher, a man, was interested in sports, so we spent more time talking about football than blowing on the horn. By the eighth grade, I quit Boy Scouts, but later in life wished I had some musical talent.

HIGH SCHOOL HIGHLIGHTS

High school was even more exciting and intimidating than junior high. At least in junior high, the older kids were only one year older. Now the seniors and juniors were a lot older, or at least that is how it seemed, and there were more of them. Some of the seniors were athletes I had watched play football and basketball during the past two years, and I was in awe of them.

My classmates and I were the second class to come into the new high school as freshmen. The old high school, which was a three-story limestone building near downtown, was to be made into the junior high for seventh graders, and Jackson Junior High — the junior high I went to for two years — would be for eighth graders only. The new high school was at the corner of Hayes Avenue and Perkins Avenue. It was a modern two-story brick building with a great gymnasium and auditorium. It was also across the street from the high school stadium, Strobel Field, which was built back during the Works Progress Administration (WPA), which was part of President Franklin D. Roosevelt's New Deal federal government-financed projects to provide jobs during the Great Depression. It is still today one of the nicest high school football stadiums I have ever seen.

Perkins Avenue marked the boundary of the town of Sandusky. On the other side, was Perkins Township, which had its own high school that we Sandusky kids considered Podunk High at the time. I have never understood that line of demarcation, and it helped lead to the financial downturn of Sandusky when residents and businesses started to move beyond the boundary line into Perkins Township, taking the tax base with them. But that was several decades in the future; during my high school years Sandusky was booming, along with the automobile industry it supported. I suspect the city leaders thought that the good times would continue forever and, at least in hindsight, no effort seemed to have been made to plan for the future.

However, at the time, Ohio had one of the best public-school systems in the country, and Sandusky was one of the best in Ohio. I was blessed to go to high school when the facilities were top notch, the teachers were dedicated and excellent, and strict discipline was the standard. The 1960s — which really meant the late 1960s with the Vietnam War protest, free love, and so on — was around a large corner when I entered high school in 1958. If anything, the sitcom *Happy Days* pretty well captured my high school experience.

The sitcom *Happy Days* pretty well captured my high school experience.

With respect to academics, as was the case in grade school and junior high school, it seems like my focus was more on grades than knowledge. My goal was straight A's each report card. I accomplished that goal more times than not and graduated high in my class — I think number three out of almost 400 students. However, there was an exception to this theme of grades over knowledge, and that was mathematics. It's the once place I really wanted to learn.

My approach to math I credit to two things. One is that math, in all its forms, seemed to come fairly easy to me. The other reason was Mr. Winkler, my sophomore math teacher who was teaching algebra. Mr. Winkler was an older teacher who was very approachable. He told us that, when he was a young man, he wanted to know how the radio worked, so he enrolled in college. He told us that the basic science of the radio, and everything for that matter, required an understanding of and ability to use math to solve equations that represented the world. Mr. Winkler said that everything in the universe could be described in mathematical terms, and that description in turn could lead to our understanding of it. That thought really resonated with me and seemed to light a fire within me to pursue math and science, although I could not tell you, at that time, to what end. Mr. Winkler was also the voice of Sandusky football — he announced all the games. He kept track of the football players even after they left their sophomore year and his algebra classroom.

As explained earlier, I did not play football as a freshman because of an injury. The freshmen had their own team and their own schedule, as did the reserves (those were kids in higher classes, usually sophomores, who could not qualify for varsity). I thought I could have made varsity, which would have been a very rare occurrence in Sandusky at that time. As it was, I could not wait for the season to be over so life could move out of suspended animation for me. Because I had swum in junior high, I decided to try out for the high school swim team. Even though my heart really was not into it, I did really well. The freshmen had their own meets, as did the reserves, but all were allowed to compete for a spot on varsity, and we all trained together.

I was soon moving up the ladder for the backstroke and swam in some reserve meets and won. I even beat the number-two man on varsity, so the coach was going to stick me into the varsity meets. I was all set to win a letter as a freshman, a rare event indeed. Then some guy came back from reform school, and he beat me out. Had that not happened, I might have actually kept swimming, which would have probably been a good thing given Dr. Skirball's analysis that my body was brittle and should not compete in contact sports. Of course, I still thought he was crazy.

After swimming, I went out for track, where again freshmen trained with the varsity and were allowed to compete on varsity if they were good enough. I was trying to win a place in the distances. Even though my body type did not fit the normal distance runner's physique, I liked to run distance and seemed to have the right mindset for it. In the junior high summers, I used to run out to the Soldiers and Sailors Home (later to be named the Ohio Veterans Home) and back in the morning as soon as I got up. The distance was a little under two miles, and I liked pushing my body as well as letting my mind drift as I ran. That may have been one thing my brother and I had in common. He became one of the premier runners in Sandusky High history — everything from the quarter mile to the mile and cross-country (two miles), where he held several records. However, later, I started to run marathons, which he never did, *so there*! I did get to run in most of the varsity meets in the mile, but I was, at best, third man on the Sandusky lineup and never finished high enough to earn points required for a letter.

There was a kid in the class ahead of me who is perhaps best described as "tough." His name was Tony, and every day he would come by my locker and kick it, leaving scuffmarks. At first, I thought it was a joke, but then a janitor cleaned off the marks, and Tony started in again. I was sure I was going to have to fight him, and he had a reputation for being a really dirty fighter. One day, when I was determined that I needed to make a stand and was sure it would lead to some pain for me, a friend of mine named Skippy Brown came by when Tony was just starting to kick the locker and as I was headed for it. Skippy was a big black kid, and I think he could sense what was going on. He got in between Tony and me and simply told Tony not to kick the locker any more. Tony was not stupid, and while he and I were the same size, Skippy would make mincemeat out of him without breaking a sweat.

Skippy and I remained friends throughout the freshman year and played basketball on Saturdays at the high school. Skippy just liked me, and I think he also sensed that, unlike some other white kids at that time, I did not have prejudice against black kids. In fact, this was not true for a lot of my white friends, and I would frequently argue with them about how black kids were the same as white kids and were entitled to everything to which we were entitled. That was just my sense of things, which I am sure I got from my parents. I enjoyed my friendship with Skippy until he and his family moved to Chicago between our freshman and sophomore year. He wrote to me from Chicago, and I answered the first letter but not the second or third. I am not sure why; I really am not. But all these years later, I still feel bad about it. It was like I deserted a friend, and I could not help but think it was partly because he was black and poor.

In high school, I was learning a lot about friendships and relationships. As far as girls are concerned, I went with one girl, Betty something or other, for a while but not really seriously. I would see Bonnie (the girl I went steady with in junior high when I was in seventh grade and she was in eighth) every so often and that would remind me of how it felt to get dumped. She would acknowledge my existence if she was not with one of the senior boys she dated, but that was about it. I was just a "kid" she used to know. When boys were hanging out, all they talked about were girls and what they had accomplished and what they were going to do. It was almost all fabrication. I still had only barely kissed a girl, but something was stirring.

I finished my freshman year with almost all A's and a pretty good athletic performance despite not being able to play football. However, I noticed that there were a lot more people, especially girls, at the basketball games than there were at the swim meets. I liked basketball a lot, even though my skill set was limited and I was not very tall. I think I was about 5′7 at the end of my freshman year. My mom kept answering that same question about how tall I would eventually become with the "over six feet" answer, so I decided I would try out for basketball my sophomore year. I went out to the basketball courts behind the high school and practiced every day, in the morning by myself and in the evening with the older black kids who lived in the nearby housing projects. I was always the last one chosen, but the regulars soon came to know that I could be relied on to pass the ball to them, and I had good passing skills. Their buddies had neither the same skill set nor, more importantly, the inclination to pass the ball, so I did get to play.

One morning that summer between the freshman and sophomore years, the varsity swim coach came to the high school and saw me out there. He came over and told me that I could get in the pool whenever he came to the school, and he would set up some regular times. I told him I would think about it and went back to shooting the ball. I think he could see the handwriting on the wall, and he never stopped by again. I felt sort of bad about that.

That summer was also my last to play organized baseball. It didn't seem the same in the Knothole League, and the really good kids were dropping out due to everything from jobs to girls to getting ready for the football season. I had visions of making the varsity football team and the reserve basketball team, and somehow baseball just seemed to be an impediment to that. Again, in retrospect and considering Dr. Skirball's opinion, I would have been better off to have chosen baseball over the other sports. We still had some good sandlot games, but they were fewer and far between. I continued to do my chores for my dad so I could make a little money for milkshakes and going over to Cedar Point, the huge amusement park that was part of Sandusky's makeup.

Sophomore Year: Big Moments, Big Heartbreaks

In my sophomore year, the decision was made to have a sophomore football team in the Buckeye Conference League in which Sandusky competed along with high schools from Fremont, Lorain (two schools), Elyria, Marion, Findlay, and Mansfield (two schools). These were all AAA-size schools, the largest in Ohio at the time, and the league was considered one of the toughest, if not *the* toughest, in all of Ohio. I dressed for varsity a few times with the intent of playing corner linebacker if the senior Norm Curtis got hurt, which, unfortunately for me and fortunately for him, did not happen.

However, on the sophomore team, I played fullback as well as corner linebacker on defense. We had a great team and went undefeated. I had several games where I gained more than 100 yards even though Otis Grissom was the premier back on the team.

As soon as football season was over, basketball started. It was about this time that really gifted athletes started to drop out of sports or found something else to do. Two really good basketball players fell into that category: Nelson Camp and my buddy from grade school, Tom Rutger. That left a hole at guard for me to fill, and so my dreams that I had while practicing all summer came true, and I started at guard for the reserve basketball team. In the first game, an away game, I hit a jump shot from several feet outside the top of the key the first time I touched the ball. The varsity guys watching the game went crazy. Little did I know that was to be one of my highlights for a rather dismal season after that initial basket. I do not think there was a game where I scored more than six points, and usually it was zero or two. However, I played good defense and could set things up pretty well, so I kept starting. But we won fewer games than we lost, and that did not fail to register with Bob Beachy, the varsity coach. I did get to dress varsity twice, but didn't even come close to getting in the game.

That sophomore year, I went out for track again, running the distant races, the mile and the half-mile. One of my buddies, Tom Petersen, a senior, was the best runner, and Teke Jackson was a close second. I hung in there as the third man, but did not score enough points for a letter. It was fun traveling to the track meets, and I really liked seeing athletes perform in different events, which stayed with me long after I gave up track myself. The bottom line was that I wasn't particularly fast at any distance but appreciated athletes who could run and jump well.

Finally an Upperclassman

The next year, Earl Bruce came to Sandusky to be the head football coach, bringing some great coaches with him, people who would affect my life in different ways for years to come, like Ernie Horning and Bob Reiber. Earl had *superb* coaching abilities and really started Sandusky High's Sensational Sixties, as the period from 1960 to 1970 came to be known. During that decade, Sandusky was a powerhouse in Ohio high school football. I played corner linebacker on defense my junior year and did a pretty good job, even intercepting two passes. I added halfback on offense my senior year. I was also voted team co-captain my senior year. Even though the offense centered around Stewart "Junebug" Williams, a high school All-American both his junior and senior years, I was averaging six yards per carry at the end of the third game. With teams focused on Bug, on those occasions when

Dave, Sandusky, Ohio, football, 1961

I did get the ball, I racked up a lot of yards before anyone noticed Stew didn't have the ball. However, in the third game, I had scored a touchdown from 10 yards out and was just about walking in the end zone when a dirty ball player from Elyria (with a reputation for late hits) tackled me — putting his helmet into the side of my knee long after the play was over — and tore the ligaments in my left knee. At halftime, I was taped up and I played a little more in the second half, but it was soon apparent that I was hobbled. After the game, the leg was put in a cast, and I never really played football again. That event led Coach Bruce to make his backfield runners run (not walk!) all the way through the end zone when they scored a touchdown. Again, Dr. Skirball's analysis of my body's propensity for injury seems to have been prophetic.

And that was it. All my athletic dreams and all my exercising had been focused on my senior year in football. In a moment, it was over. And that was it. All my athletic dreams and all my exercising had been focused on my senior year in football. In a moment, it was over.

And that was it. All my athletic dreams and all my exercising had been focused on my senior year in football. In a moment, it was over. In those days, they put the injured knee in a hanging cast that kept the whole leg immobile and you walked around on crutches. The quadriceps muscle immediately began to atrophy, so it had to be built back up along with other leg muscles once the cast was removed. At first, I thought I could make it back for the last few games of the season, but it was not to be. I dressed out for the final game and even went out for the coin toss, but Coach Bruce wisely kept me out of the game. It turns out Coach Bruce, who held the Maryland 100 – and 200-yard dash records, had his own promising career at Ohio State as a halfback brought to an untimely end by a severe injury to one of his legs. So he could empathize with my situation more than I knew at the time.

It was tough going to practices and the games and keeping a brave face on. I tried to be encouraging to my teammates, but inside it hurt to see them keep winning without me. Coach Bruce found a way to bring the talent to bear. Given my actual talent level, that injury, plus an article I describe below, probably changed the course of my life, ultimately for the better. But the situation was difficult for a 17-year-old kid who was experiencing the end of all his previous aspirations. I have come to believe all things happen for a reason, and I can now appreciate the course on which that injury sent my life. But at the time, it was a lot to cope with, and all things considered, I held up okay.

I have come to believe all things happen for a reason, and I can now appreciate the course on which that injury sent my life.

It is interesting to note that almost all the coaches on that football team went on to have notable careers. Coach Bruce had state and national high school championships at Sandusky and Massillon and ended his career coaching the Ohio State Buckeyes to nine winning seasons. Coach Ernie Horning and Coach Dick Crumm went on to coach at Miami of Ohio, and Coach Crumm had the head coaching jobs at Kent State and University of North Carolina, in addition to Miami of Ohio. Coach Horning was the backfield coach at Georgetown College in Kentucky when it won the national title in its classification. Coach Bob Seaman went on to have several state-championship teams at Sandusky and Massillon and had the head-coaching job at Wichita State University. Others had similar successes at the high school and college levels.

But football wasn't the only sport that occupied my time and energy as a high school upperclassman. My junior year, I went out for basketball after the football season was over. And after a few practices with what was one of the best basketball teams ever fielded by Sandusky (and the first time ever that the team showed ethnic diversity, with five black kids on the court at the same time), Coach Bob Beachy pulled me aside. He said, "Dave, as a basketball player, I think you could be a good wrestler." Not too subtle, but accurate, as it turns out. So I went out for wrestling, and that sport became a centerpiece of my athletics for the rest of my life. Coach Horning, the very good backfield coach for the football program, was also the wrestling coach, and frankly

Dave, Sandusky, Ohio, high school wrestling, 1961

he didn't know much about wrestling at all. To his credit, he would spend time over at Huron High School, getting schooled in moves by Chris Ford, a very successful wrestler and coach in Ohio. Coach Horning would then bring what he learned back to our practices.

Coach Horning made sure we were in good shape physically. I don't think anyone ever lost a match due to poor stamina. Coach Horning also insisted that we wear sport coats and ties on the days of the matches. I think that added some class and made us feel like a team. The blazers were provided by the school if a kid could not afford one, and that was done discreetly. Almost half a century later, I discovered that all the wrestlers for Coach Horning were, like me, still using a half-Windsor, which he had taught us, to tie their ties. Coach Horning's influence went beyond sports and included grooming and behavior, on and off the field or mat.

My junior year, I made the starting lineup at 165 pounds and won more matches than I lost, but my inexperience (and Coach Horning's) would cost me if I was evenly pitted athletically. Fortunately, I was usually stronger than most of my opponents, and the way we wrestled back then, that was important. Later, I would discover that quickness, balance, experience, and frame of mind were more important than brute strength.

I would discover that quickness, balance, experience, and frame of mind were more important than brute strength.

My senior year, I decided to cut down to 154 pounds, which, like my ears that eventually turned cauliflower from repeated blunt injury, I wore like a badge. Sometimes the weight cutting seemed to take precedent over the actual wrestling. It was a sort of obsession. And if done incorrectly, it can actually be dangerous. My mother sent me an article many years later that discussed three college wrestlers from different schools who had died from getting their electrolytes severely out of balance while cutting weight. She wrote on the article with a red Marks-a-Lot, "YOU WERE JUST LUCKY!" She might be right.

Anyhow, I spent the first half of the season undefeated, as did my buddy, Wayne King. Wayne and I were co-captains of the wrestling team. Later, we would be co-godfathers for Coach Bob Reiber's first son, who was also named after us, David Wayne. (That was a real honor!) I lost three matches in the middle of the season, I think due to my limited skill set and that "frame-of-mind" thing. In the Buckeye Conference tournament, I faced a black kid who had really big biceps. Thinking strength was the key, I let it get the best of me mentally, and I lost to him when I should have beaten him. Although I went on to recover and finished the season with only those three losses, I don't think I ever really gained that sense of confidence to always believe you can win. I did win the district tournament to qualify for the state championships. There I pinned my first opponent, but the next guy had a greater skill set. He narrowly beat me and went on to finish third in the tournament. However, because he lost his next match, I did not get to wrestle any more in the double elimination used in the state tournament.

One good thing that resulted from the high-school switch to wrestling was that I would practice on my brother whenever I could. That got him interested in the sport (maybe out of self-defense!) and, in junior high school, he practiced with the high school varsity wrestling team instead of doing something with his classmates. As a result, and due to his athletic skills, he lettered all four years in high school, which was a rarity. He was team captain and most valuable player (MVP) both his junior and senior years, an even rarer achievement. He had a great wrestling record in both high school and in college. He also went on to achieve success as a coach.

Ever the multi-sport athlete, wrestling wasn't my only focus during the final two years of high school. As far as track goes, I switched from distance to the high hurdles my junior year. Although I qualified as the number-three man, I again did not score enough to earn a letter. I'm not sure if I would have gone out my senior year even if I hadn't ended up wanting to spend time with my girlfriend. But because I was in love and because of my lack of success in the events, I gave up track my senior year, another sport at which my brother excelled — proving he got the athletic ability from our parents, or I should say from our mother.

Love, Work, and the Cuban Missile Crisis

I guess that brings me to my girlfriend, Connie. Like me, she was in the college prep classes, so we knew each other starting back in junior high. As I mentioned, I was smitten by an older woman in junior high, so at that time Connie was no more than a classmate friend who happened to be a good-looking girl. In high school as a freshman, I was hoping something would rekindle with Bonnie Martin. When that didn't materialize, I began to look around. Although I was making a name for myself in academics and athletics, enough so that I was elected class president (all four years), I did not have much confidence with the opposite sex. My buddy, Tom Rutger, and the quarterback, Jim Glick, seemed to have much more success getting girls and getting to second base and beyond, or so they said.

Connie and I started walking together between classes and talking at lunch. By our junior year, we were an item, and we fell deeply in puppy love. Without ever really announcing it to anyone or even declaring it to each other, as our class got their driver's licenses and moved into dating, we were exclusively a couple. Even though the hormones raged and we did some heavy petting on her parents' couch, second base was an infrequent conquest and neither of us "good kids" thought about going beyond that. Well, I thought about it but dared not to venture there for fear of offending both her and God. If she thought about it, she did not encourage me, although in retro-spect, she didn't really *discourage* me either. What were we to do?

We sat next to each other in church, and all those Episcopalian pledges seemed to indicate that God did not approve of even second base before marriage. Although we dated when I came home from the Naval Academy, time and distance took its toll.

And whose adolescence would be complete without their parents contributing to a memorable moment in dating history? You see, my dad had a wry sense of humor, and my girlfriend, Connie, liked animals. When she told me this early in our dating, I asked my dad if she could come on a farm call with us. He said sure, so we set a date for a Saturday morning. I had no idea what we were going to do, but my dad sure did. It turned out we were going to castrate 30 piglets.

My dad assigned me the job of catching them and holding them upright while he slit their skin where the testicles were, pulled the testicles out, and cut them off. It was Connie's job to pour the anti-septic in the slits. By the end of the morning, we were covered in pig shit, and I had gotten over my initial embarrassment, which my dad thought was so funny.

Despite how busy I was with sports and academics, I did find time to try my hand at the world of work. I worked between my junior and senior years for the Sandusky Water Department, a job a friend of my dad's secured for me. I remember that, on the first day, the boss informed me that he didn't care who I knew, I better do whatever he said. I worked hard and did all the dirty jobs of crawling in holes to fix equipment or getting meter readings, and soon I had the respect of all the workers — including the boss. One day, they even let me take the big dump truck home for lunch. The only problem was that I could not get the damn thing *into* third gear. So I limped home, winding it out in first gear and second gear and then stopping and starting over. At lunch, my dad showed me the trick of moving the floor shift as far to the right as possible and then up toward the dash to get into third gear. After that, fourth gear was easy.

That same summer, I also went to Boys State for a week of introduction into civics. Being chosen to attend Boys State was an honor, and I met some interesting fellows there, including Charlie Brown from Massillon, who later starred in football at Syracuse. I met him again when we scrimmaged and beat Massillon in the preseason. It was one of the best football games in which I ever played.

I continued to do well at schoolwork in my final year of high school, but again my focus was more on grades than on fulfilling a real passion for learning. I am not sure that is *all* bad, as my grades helped me get accepted to every college to which I eventually applied. My study habits have served me well for a lifetime. However, after reading about people like Thomas Jefferson and reading books written by Stephen Hawking, I wish my purpose in my studies had been a little nobler. On the other hand, the Sandusky High teachers I had were almost without exception, even after all these years, some of the best I ever had. I had to learn something to get the grades; there were no gifts and no favorites. Competition was the norm.

The school paper carried a list each month of those students in each grade who received all A's. Kids received C's, D's, and even F's if they deserved them. There was a curriculum for kids with different potential and for different apparent career choices. For some, it was college prep courses, which were tough and geared toward preparing students for college studies. There was a vocational curriculum, which was geared toward those who would be getting jobs, such as mechanics, carpenters, and secretaries, after graduation. As a result, I think we were all better prepared for life when we left high school. Did some people get unfairly or inappropriately pigeon-holed? I would have to guess the answer is yes. However, even as a student, I was aware that there were counselors on the lookout for students who should be encouraged in a different direction than they might currently be pursuing.

When I look back at high school, I recall that the dress code for both teachers and students helped set a more formal and respectful atmosphere than what I detect in our high schools and colleges today. Everyone dressed nicely, even though there was the same social strata there is today in the community (i.e., there were kids of company presidents and kids of manual laborers). The Sandusky High principal, Mr. Walker, seemed to rule the school with an iron hand; and students, teachers, and parents respected his authority. I don't remember one fight between students in the school or on the school grounds (though that moment with the locker-kicker came close for me!), although they occurred elsewhere. I honestly don't remember one student being disrespectful to his or her teachers. All in all, there just seemed to be a sense of pride in community, school, work, and family that I find has become diminished somehow in recent years.

Of a number of very good teachers during my Sandusky High School years, Mr. Danke, Mr. Spears, and Mr. Schneider stand out. Mr. Danke made my senior year in math both fun and interesting. His teaching methods helped me understand how to approach a problem of any kind in an organized fashion. Mr. Spears and Mr. Schneider taught science classes — physics and chemistry, respectively. Again, their friendly, open approach to teaching made me want to learn as well as get high marks.

In October of 1962, the Cuban Missile Crisis occurred. Although my awareness of public and international events was limited as a teenager, it seems like there was a buildup to the actual brink of war that occurred in the fall of that year. I remember that the previous summer, I was sitting on the front steps with my mom when Army trucks and other vehicles were rolling down Columbus Avenue in what seemed like an endless procession. My mother was a strong woman who rarely showed any weaknesses or fear. However, on that warm summer day in 1961, there was real fear in her voice when she said she hoped we were not headed for another war. I don't know if she was referring to World War II or the Korean War, because both were in our past at that time, but I think she was referring to the war of which she was part, World War II. Her apprehension at that moment obviously made an impression on me, a teenager without a real care in the world.

In the end, my senior year left me with many memories and many lessons. It was a year punctuated by the football injury, a modicum of success in wrestling, and the receipt of the outstanding graduating boy award known as the Malinovsky Award. When the senior girls did a composite of the perfect senior boy, I contributed "best body." I guess all that time lifting weights didn't go unnoticed, after all. Looking back, it was an ideal, even innocent, time to grow up in a wonderful town. In a certain sense, we were shielded from all the choices and temptations our children and certainly our grandchildren have faced or will face. For the most part, there was a certain respect and order that I fear is missing today. I know I need to be careful about generalizations, especially directed at the following generations. It was Aristotle who predicted the demise of the world based on his observations of the unruly youth of *his* time. It seems every generation considers it had things harder and did things better than those who follow. My lament is more directed at how our country seems to have changed, and the fault lies with my generation more than anyone else. We have moved away from those principles that have guided our country to its preeminence among all nations that have ever existed. Let me conclude this section of my story by saying I consider myself to be very blessed to have grown up with parents like mine, in a town like mine, at a time when I did.

Looking back, it was an ideal, even innocent, time to grow up in a wonderful town.

Before I turn the page on my high school years and regale you with tales from college, I must mention Bob Reiber again, and more fully. He was a football coach, who came to Sandusky, Ohio, with Earl Bruce, but stayed after marrying a Sandusky woman, Sandy. As I mentioned, he and Sandy asked Wayne King and me to be their first son's godfather and named him after us, David Wayne Reiber. Bob and Sandy later came to visit me at the Naval Academy, and we stayed in touch over the years. He nominated me for the Athletic Hall of Fame and the Erie County Achievers Award. Bob was a teacher, a coach, and a counselor at Sandusky High, and ultimately a true friend and mentor to me. His students and the community were fortunate he chose to stay in Sandusky.

COLLEGE

During my senior year in high school, I started thinking about college realistically for the first time. I had always dreamed I would go to The Ohio State University and play football for them. As reality crept in, I thought I would probably go to a Mid-American Conference (MAC) school, like Miami University, and play football at that level. However, when it came down to it, I thought I might have a chance to wrestle somewhere, instead of playing collegiate football. Academically, I vaguely thought about studying math, most likely with the intent to teach. The fact was that I didn't have a clue about what I wanted to do with my life, and I hoped college would provide the answers when I got there.

With one exception, I had not been contacted by any college to come play anything. Case Institute did contact me about coming there to play football and/or wrestle. I never gave it much thought. Finally, I applied to Northwestern University because I heard it was a good school, and for some reason, I thought I might have a chance to wrestle there. I also applied to Oklahoma and Syracuse, as well as Ohio State, Ohio University, and Miami of Ohio. I was accepted at all of them and was strongly leaning toward Northwestern.

My parents had a very relaxed attitude toward the whole thing. Several thoughts kept occurring to me. One was that my dad had mentioned one day — back when I was in grade school and we were watching an Army-Navy Game on our small black-and-white TV with its fuzzy picture — that it would sure be an honor for me to go to one of those two schools. He never said another word about it, but that remark stuck in my mind. Another thought that stuck with me until my late teens, when I started thinking about what was next after high school, was when we were driving down the Ohio Turnpike or Pennsylvania Turnpike and went under a large bridge built on a huge arc of steel. Dad said that some engineer somewhere had to design that bridge, and he had used math to do it.

It was also not lost on me that my dad and mom would have to put four other kids through college, and I thought that might pose a burden on their income. The fact was that my dad made a good living and was smart with his money. My mom's income from nursing helped their overall financial status, and even though college tuition would be a drain, in all likelihood, they could afford it. But I thought what I thought at the age of 17 and considered myself quite noble for having such thoughts.

With all these considerations in my head, I applied for an Air Force Academy appointment. Never mind that I quit Boy Scouts because I didn't like wearing a uniform! The Air Force Academy was relatively new, and an appointment would address my concerns. The academy produced engineers, would relieve my parents of the burden of one kid's college education, and seem to fulfill the honor my dad expressed many years earlier.

That year, the local paper started writing articles about high school seniors from around its area of distribution. They did an article on me, which mentioned that I was captain of the Sandusky High football and wrestling teams, nearly a straight-A student, was president of my class, went to Boys State, was involved in several other activities, received the outstanding senior boy award, and was under consideration for an appointment to the Air Force Academy.

The backfield coach for Navy football was visiting the family of a kid from nearby Fremont, Ohio, who he had recruited to play football for

the Navy. The mother was a friend of
my mother's and, for some reason,
had cut that article out of the paper,
and the coach saw it. He gave me
a call to ask if I would be interested
in going to the Naval Academy if the
Air Force appointment didn't come
through. I said "sure." That was
about the extent of our conversation. I didn't think much of it.
I think the coach probably called
Coach Bruce, who probably lied
about how fast I was, and, the next
thing I knew, I had an appointment

Dave in dress whites at the
Naval Academy, 1963

to the Naval Academy from Congressman Waggoner in Bienville
Parish, Louisiana. And once that happened and the word got out,
there was all kinds of subtle pressure to accept it. Northwestern was
soon history, and I would be entering the Academy two weeks after
I graduated from Sandusky High.

Sometimes when I look back on it, it all seems surreal and I cannot
help but think that it was part of God's plan for me . I had no
interest in making the Navy a career, although I had no idea what
I wanted to do for a career. I thought I would be a math teacher and
a coach, but that was all I had been exposed to other than being
a veterinarian's son. I knew I didn't want to be a veterinarian. I had
cleaned enough dog cages. Sometimes I felt like I took an appointment away from some other young man who really wanted to dedi-
cate himself to the Navy. But I found later out there were others like
me — who found themselves at the Academy for reasons other than
a Navy career, and sometimes for reasons beyond their control.

I do consider myself very fortunate to have gone to Navy. But, at the
end of my senior year of high school, it seemed like I was suddenly

basking in some undeserved glory, though it only lasted for a few weeks. Then it was off to a strange new world.

Sometimes when I look back on it, it all seems surreal and I cannot help but think that attending the Naval Academy was part of God's plan for me.

My mother took me to the Naval Academy. We went out to dinner the night before, near Annapolis. She was sad and serious. She was saying goodbye to her child, knowing that as the service had forever changed her from a Kentucky farm girl, it would change me as well. I was sad too, but more out of fear of the unknown. I knew that plebe year (i.e., the first year) was supposed to be tough; and although I was sure I could take the physical and emotional challenges, I was not so sure about the academics, especially because I didn't seem to have any choice in the subject matter I'd study. I had no idea what to expect.

My mother did give me the advice I have mentioned many times since, which was: "**Never volunteer for anything!**"

I do, indeed, consider myself very fortunate to have gone to the Naval Academy. I met some great guys there, some of whom went on to be leaders in our country in many different professions. However, only a few of them have remained lifelong contacts; I don't know if that is unusual or not. There is an alumni association and a class of 1966 group, and although I receive letters and now emails from both groups, I am not active in either. I think it's because I never really identified with the Naval Academy or the Navy. I wanted to survive the Academy, put in my four years of obligated service, and return to Sandusky to coach and teach math. Or at least that's what I thought at the beginning.

I know now that I could never have achieved academically what I did at the Academy had I gone anywhere else. In addition to the standard engineering curriculum, I also had dual majors in math and nuclear physics. I attended class almost every hour of every day and carried 26 credit hours each semester for my final three years. There were no distractions, like girls or beer, to compete with studying, and studying took my mind off the things I didn't like about the Academy — like the treatment of plebes and the rigors of learning to be a Naval officer. I think most of my attitude toward those obligations was due to my immaturity at the time.

I consider the Navy experience as a true blessing as well. I know of no other area of endeavor where a young man gets so much responsibility at such an early age. The training was rigorous and difficult. The duties were demanding on the men and their families. But it was truly an honor to be in the Navy, and especially in the nuclear submarine force.

I know of no other area of endeavor where a young man gets so much responsibility at such an early age. The training was rigorous and difficult. The duties were demanding on the men and their families. But it was truly an honor to be in the Navy, and especially in the nuclear submarine force.

Memories of the Academy

There are so many memories and anecdotes of the Academy that they alone could fill a book. So let me just share a handful that I think you'll find useful in understanding the philosophies and approaches I adopted in civilian life — the "where the rubber meets the road" insights in this book, which I think you can apply to your own life and career. And, for fun, I'll share a story or two whose merits might simply be that they're interesting or humorous.

As I said, I got to the Academy by sheer luck, or fate, or by the hand of God. I surely didn't approach my time there as maturely as I should have, probably because I never had the goal to go there. I worked hard academically and I tried hard at sports. I made some good friends, but only a few that have lasted me a lifetime, which is about what I can say for high school, work, and other activities.

Plebe year may have been my best year at the Academy because it was supposed to be tough, and I treated it as a challenge to be met head-on. I wanted to prove myself. Additionally, there was a fellow two years ahead of me at Sandusky High who received an appointment to West Point (the Army's academy) and quit after only six months. I remember what people said about him. Whether those comments were fair and appropriate or not, I was determined that I wouldn't fall into that category. I wasn't a quitter.

Plebe summer was physically, emotionally, and academically rigorous. The upper classmen ran us all the time, with the intention of tiring us out physically. Stamina was an "ingredient" they looked for in plebes as they were trying to see if we had the right stuff. It was also a tough time emotionally because many of us were away from home for the first time and, therefore, homesick (when we had a few moments to ourselves). We were, frankly, scared. And that first year was an academic challenge as well because we had to learn new things, like navigation, which was a chore for me (because my immaturity told me I would never use that skill set). Because I had no intention of making the Navy a career, I didn't see why I should apply myself. I was dumb!

I made some friends that first summer. We spent what few moments we had to ourselves, usually Saturday nights when many of the second-class midshipmen who were "in charge of us" headed for DC or elsewhere for a night of their own, out on the town. We would reminisce about our hometowns and our high school achievements. We would talk about how much tougher it was bound to be when the Brigade returned in September and the odds changed (not in our favor). Of course, we would talk about the second classmen and who was fair and who was not.

My roommates during the summer were not inclined to engage in this activity. They were both "service brats" and we simply didn't get along. That animosity boiled over into an actual fight shortly after the Brigade returned, before we got our "permanent" roommates for the academic year. The firstie assigned to our room was not sure what to do when I ducked a thrown punch, which resulted in my roommate breaking his hand on the locker behind me. I should have learned from that mishap that sometimes the puncher gets the worst of the bargain in a real fight. Tensions were high, and stress was sometimes manifested in ways that had nothing to do with the stress risers.

Sometimes the puncher gets the worst of the bargain in a real fight.

Things got even tougher when the Brigade returned, because now the upperclassmen outnumbered the plebes, instead of the other way around (as it had been during plebe summer). As the year progressed, I told myself that I would never haze plebes, failing to see the purpose behind that discipline and rigor (when appropriately done, of course, which was too frequently not the case).

When the Brigade returned, we received our permanent room assignments and roommates for the year in the company to which we were assigned. I was lucky that I was able to room with three guys I really liked from the summertime. Their names were (Jack) Connolly,

(Kevin) Clancy, and (Joe) Kinsey — three Irish Catholics from the Boston area. All had been high school football players brought to the Academy like me. As it turned out, only Jack ended up playing on varsity, and he lettered three years as one of the starting guards on offense. He was clearly the best football player in our class. My Irish Catholic roommates used to tell me, the Episcopalian, "Dave, it's like this. We Catholics are playing baseball, and you Episcopalians are watching the game through a hole in the fence. No one else even knows where the game is." This analogy seemed to make sense to them, so it went unchallenged by me. I guess, in some foolish way, I felt like it was a compliment.

The first really impactful thing that happened was winning the plebe summer wrestling tournament. I beat the two-time Oklahoma state champ in the championship bout. I am sure Coach Ed Perry wondered where this kid came from who beat someone he had recruited heavily. With that accomplishment and seeing all the great athletes brought in to play football (those were the Roger Staubach years when Navy was ranked high nationally in the football polls), I decided to stick with wrestling. I sent a note to the coach who had arranged my appointment, and he responded that he understood. I think a lot of the recruits fell by the wayside and some even left the Academy. At least I stayed. Wrestling was a real respite for me during plebe year. We had training tables, where the athletes of a particular sport sat together for meals apart from the company tables where the plebe hazing took place, through the football season, as well as the wrestling season, and that provided some relief from the hazing that went on at mealtime.

Also, when the Brigade returned, plebes were assigned "firsties" — first classmen or seniors who were to "help" us through the year. Some firsties turned out to be brutal to their plebes for much or even all of the year. Others were indifferent to the responsibility. Some were protective and even "spooned" their plebes right away. "Spoon" is when an upperclassman shakes a plebe's hand and tells him he can call him by his first name instead of "sir." After that, they are considered on equal footing and probably friends from then on. As I mentioned, I had won the plebe wrestling tournament, and I knew that Mike Harmon, two-time Eastern wrestling champ and captain of the wrestling team, was in our company.

When I got back to my room the day the Brigade got back, there was a note to go to Mr. Harmon's room. I didn't know what to expect. I entered his room, after first asking permission to enter, and then braced up, standing at rigid attention looking straight ahead ("eyes in the boat"). I heard, "You Amerine?" and, out of the corner of my eye, I could see this little red-headed guy shaving. He had small arms and a little paunch, probably from drinking beer all senior cruise. (You learned to see a lot out of the corner of your eyes.) I thought I was in the wrong room. When I answered, "Yes, Sir!" the little redhead said, "Carry on," which meant to relax or, in Navy lingo, stand at ease.

He said, "I am Mike Harmon, and you are my plebe." I soon learned that when that little red-head got in shape, he was faster on the mat than anything I had ever seen, and those little arms were wire tough and strong. He won the Eastern championship again and placed second in the NCAA finals.

Mike and I became friends, and I never took advantage of the relationship. After that year, we didn't see each other again until many years later, when we were both married and each had two kids. He lived in Portland, Oregon, where he was the president of some trucking firm (he got out of the Navy after his four-year obligation), and my family and I were living in Richland, Washington, about five hours away. We got together a few times, the most memorable being a three-day raft trip down the Deschutes River.

Tough Moments and True Friends

The closest I ever came to quitting the Academy was when Coach Perry asked me to wrestle off for a junior varsity match after the plebe season was over. I won but found out I had to lose 12 pounds to make weight the next morning, which was Saturday. I lost those 12 pounds by not eating or drinking anything and getting up at 0400 (4:00 a.m.) and going over to the boxers' locker room and turning it into a steam room with the showers on steaming hot. I worked out in there in a rubber sweat suit until it was time for breakfast formation. However, doing that and then going to class all morning, except for the weigh-in, left no time to memorize the daily items plebes were expected to know. When it was time for lunch, which I was desperately looking forward to, I didn't realize that I could still go to the training tables, even though the plebe wrestling season was over. As a result, I sat with the rest of the Brigade at a table with upperclassmen I did not know. When they started grilling me, I failed miserably on the "practical factors" ("prac facs") I was supposed to know.

To make matters worse, they started calling me stupid and then asked me what my grade point average was. At the time, it was 3.75, which was probably higher than what any of those bozos could aspire to reach, and that seemed to really piss them off. They also asked me what book I had read most recently, which was Thomas Mann's *Magic Mountain*. One of those jerks said that book must be a fairy tale. At least one of them acknowledged that it was heavy reading. The bottom line was that I got nothing to eat and was directed to "come-around" to their room before evening meal with every "prac fac" known, or else.

That afternoon, I wrestled for the junior varsity against Bloomsburg State and totally ran out of gas in the middle of the second period. Needless to say, Coach Perry was not too happy with my

Academy wrestling team photo, Dave second row, second from right end, 1964

performance. And I had the come-around to look forward to, so I was not having a very good day. I decided, for the first time, to go to Mike Harmon and ask for his help. He was furious that his plebe had been treated that way and told me to forget the come-around because he would take care of it.

A few days later, I bumped into one of the upperclassmen from the Saturday lunch experience as I was on my way to class. He glared at me but didn't say a word. Mike must have put the fear of God in those guys. I never heard a thing from any of them, despite that fact that missing a come-around was usually tantamount to suicide.

Over the next four years, my roommates and I did a lot of things together at the Academy and away from the school, both on our summer indoctrination cruises and on our own time. Clancy ("the Clance") and I seemed to identify most closely with each other because we both had a philosophical inclination. Sadly, the Clance was killed during flight training when he missed the catch wire, which is supposed to stop the plane when landing on the aircraft carrier, and then when he did not restore power in time, his plane was actually run over by the carrier. The day before the accident, a girl he had met in Sandusky and I had talked to him on the phone. He didn't sound like his normal self. I often wonder how our friendship would have developed over the years had he not died at such an early age.

Jack, Joe, and I stayed in touch for a while after graduation, and I have seen Jack three or four times over the years, usually initiated by me at our mutual convenience. Joe's first wife, Lisa, who met Joe when he and I and a bunch of my Sandusky buddies went to the Jersey Shore together, died of cancer after about 20 years of marriage. I have never met Joe's second wife, who I think he met after his Navy career was over (he stayed in for more than 20 years).

Jack's first wife was his high school sweetheart, Frannie. They married right after graduation and had two children. They ultimately got divorced and, as far as I know, neither ever remarried. Cindy and I saw them occasionally when both couples lived in Virginia Beach on our first tours after nuclear power school for me and flight school for Jack. He and Frannie had a tumultuous relationship even then.

On the Mat and in the Classroom

As far as wrestling goes, the plebes had a team and I wrestled in a few matches. I could usually beat Andre Rivermonte, who was the Virginia state champ; but then Tom Grim, the Pennsylvania champ, and I would trade wins with Bo Wiley, the fellow I beat for the plebe championship. I had a long way to go to catch up to these guys who had been wrestling since junior high or even before, and I just had the two years at Sandusky. But I loved the practices and the camaraderie and the opportunity to get away from the hazing. I feel good about the fact that I helped Tom Grimm with his math courses, with which he was struggling, even though he kept me out of matches when he would beat me. We were pretty evenly matched, but he was plenty smart on the mat, probably from all those years wrestling in Pennsylvania.

The next year, we all moved up to varsity. I was getting better and worked my way up the ladder to the number-two spot at 165 pounds behind Dave Carey, the team captain. I even beat him occasionally, but Coach Perry had a rule that if someone challenged the number-one guy and beat him, then the challenger had to beat him a second time to replace him on the ladder. Dave never let that happen. I feel good about pushing him because he was Eastern champ that year. He later was shot down flying in Vietnam and spent a few years as a prisoner of war.

The next two years for me were impacted by knee injuries, which necessitated operations. So, I had to recover from surgery each year, get back in shape, and try to work my way up the ladder again. The first injury occurred before the season started, when a wrestler from my company and I went over to work out on a Sunday afternoon. I caught my heel on a wrinkle in the mat when he went in for a double leg tackle and I tried to throw my legs back to avoid the takedown. I heard something snap and it hurt like hell. When I woke up the next morning, I could not move my leg, and my roommates carried me down to sickbay to see the doctor. Because it was Monday, and that was the day we practiced marching at the parade ground in front of the commandant, the doctor thought I was faking and would not write a chit for me to get out of marching. I limped through the day and was in a lot of pain. I barely made it over to the parade ground, where we stood in place for almost 30 minutes throwing our piece (a rifle) around in various positions. Then we passed in review in front of the admiral.

When my company took off, I couldn't move. Fortunately, being short, I was in the back row, (because we were lined up by height with the shortest in the back row), and I didn't get run over by my comrades. I finally got going before the next company ran me over, but I was a full 10 yards behind my company. When we passed in front of the admiral, I was not sure what to do, so I saluted him because I knew that was what the company commander did. I don't know why I didn't get in trouble for that little stunt. Maybe it was because I was operated on the next day. I felt vindication with the doctor who refused to give me the chit to get out of the practice marching! But that surgery sat me back for that wrestling season.

The summer between my junior and senior year at the Academy, I was on cruise on a destroyer out of Pearl Harbor. After six weeks in Hawaii, I returned to San Diego, where I went on leave for a month. I had arranged to meet the Clance in Los Angeles, where we were going to be the guests of my high school classmate, Carol Tomlin, who was an airline stewardess home-ported in L.A. and living in Manhattan Beach.

After about four weeks at Carol's, the Clance and I hitchhiked to Sandusky. We were to have a week there before we had to report back to the Academy for our senior year. The Clance and I were on the Cedar Point Chausee, skipping rocks into the Lake when my right knee, which had been bothering me all summer on cruise, locked up. The Clance had to carry me to the car and, when we got home, my dad said for me to sit in a hot tub of water with an ice pack on my knee and to alternate heat and cold. I guess he figured one temperature would loosen up the knee, and the other would keep the swelling down. When my mother got home from her nurse job at the hospital and saw what I was doing, she yelled at me, "Get your ass out of the tub.!" The Clance thought that was really funny.

My mother ended up driving me back to the Academy early so I could go right into surgery at the Naval Academy hospital. As such, I started my senior year in the hospital. Not unlike my senior year in high school, with respect to football, I figured it was my time to shine in wrestling. But here I was again, starting the year off recovering from surgery. Finally, after I rushed the rehabilitation, I returned to the team. Eventually, I decided I was just tired of waking up every morning hurting. I went to see Coach Perry and told him I just didn't feel like I could contribute and that I was tired of the pain. He seemed to understand. I had kept up with my studies in the hospital, so at least I wasn't too far behind academically. But what a way to start my last year.

To add insult to injury, when the Clance and I got stuck in Marion, Ohio, in the rain on our hitchhiking trip on our way to Sandusky, I called a girl who I had met my sophomore year in high school and who I had stayed in touch with off and on for the past few years. I looked her name up in the phone book and called her to ask if she would take us the hour drive to Sandusky, and she surprisingly said she would. Her sister, a college freshman, accompanied her, and the sister and the Clance hit it off really well on the ride to Sandusky. The Clance invited the sister to come to the Academy. Several weeks later, she did and brought a friend, but I was in the hospital at the time. So the Clance fixed her friend up with another buddy and they spent part of the weekend shacked up in DC. I heard about that for the rest of the year. As for my own romantic conquests, I did lose my virginity in my college sophomore year (what's called third class at the Academy). I will leave it at that.

Besides wrestling, which I consider one of the really positive experiences at the Academy (despite the injuries and overall lack of success), academics was another very rewarding experience. As I said, I decided to pursue majors in math and nuclear physics in addition to the standard curriculum. Most of the professors I had were excellent. I enjoyed my courses in those majors and did well in most of them. For some reason, I couldn't get the drift of matrix theory, but I really loved advanced calculus and had the highest score in the class on that final exam. However, it took a lot of work.

At night while my roommates, Jack, Joe, and the Clance were out generally screwing around, I was in the room studying. I would also study whenever I wasn't in class. It was a work ethic I had developed in high school, and it was to stay with me the rest of my life. In many respects, I felt I had to work harder to keep up with all these smart guys with whom I was going to class. That feeling only intensified when I entered the Navy's nuclear power program and then later in the nuclear industry. As I characterized it to others, I had jumped into the big pool with a lot of very smart sharks and had to work harder than they did to keep from being eaten.

I had jumped into the big pool with a lot of very smart sharks and had to work harder than they did to keep from being eaten.

In the basic curriculum, there were subjects across the four years to which I didn't give my full attention, somewhat in deference to the majors I had chosen. The truth is that my immaturity led me to think that I was going to put in my four years of military service and get out, and I didn't need to apply myself to the Navy studies. In reality, I needed that background for my time on submarines and many of the subjects would, in fact, be useful in civilian life. The result was that I hurt my total class standing and had to work that much harder to qualify on the submarines because I'd neglected some of the subjects that applied to operating a submarine or any Navy vessel. I regret those childish decisions but, at the time, I guess it was my iconoclasm coming through.

So Many Ways to Pass the Time

My parents didn't visit me during the plebe year, because I was only free on Saturday afternoons. But they did come to the Army-Navy Game, and we had a good time in Philadelphia. I did get to go home for Christmas for about a week, and it was good to be back in my room and see my friends from high school. I think I even helped my dad clean dog cages, for old time's sake. It was difficult to go back to the Academy after being with friends and family again.

I finished my plebe year with an academic standing of approximately 100 out of the 1,394 that started the plebe year (we graduated with a little more than 800, which is about the standard attrition rate for an Academy class). I had a good year wrestling, and I had made some good friends. Our summer cruise was spent going to some classes for a few weeks at the Academy before the new plebes arrived and then going to Virginia Beach Naval Station for an introduction to the Marine Corps experience. Each summer, the Navy sends its Naval Academy classes somewhere to introduce them to some aspect of the Navy, ostensibly to help them with their choice of assignment when they graduate.

The next three years went by agonizingly slow but, looking back, it seemed like they passed in a whirl. When I was in high school, I was a pretty straight arrow. In addition to never getting past second base with my girlfriend, and even that was an infrequent visit, I didn't drink or smoke. I spent a lot of time studying. The time at the Naval Academy, as it is for most guys (and girls) in college, changed all that. When we would get out of Annapolis (midshipmen were not allowed in bars within a seven-mile radius), usually to DC, we would drink our fair share of beer. I had always liked a cold beer on a hot summer day and would even help myself to one of the beers my parents kept in the refrigerator in the basement when I would come home from a hot August high school football practice. But I could never drink more than two beers or two glasses of wine without getting a headache. I never developed a taste for hard alcohol and can count on one hand the times I really got drunk. I hated the feeling the next day and came to regard heavy drinking as a waste of two days, each of which should be considered a precious gift from God.

Still, I did indulge when we were able to party, and the first year or so out of the Academy, I tried to make up for lost time, as did my buddies.

As I reflect on the highlights of my college years, I would be remiss not to mention my experiences with lacrosse. At the Academy, everyone is required to play a sport each season — either a varsity sport or a sport from the Academy's very competitive intramural sports program. Two of my seasons were occupied with wrestling but, in the spring, I needed to do something. I knew I didn't want to try track, even at the intramural level. However, this thing called lacrosse looked interesting. Lacrosse was very big at the Naval Academy, which was the NCAA lacrosse champion all four years I was there (as well as the year before I arrived and the year after I graduated). However, when I first joined our company team, the joke was that it took until my third game before I realized there was a ball involved. Before that, I was just out there, whacking guys with my stick.

When we weren't studying, training, or playing sports, we did find time for adventure. Two fun trips involved my Sandusky friends and my Academy roommates. The first summer between my first and second year, Wayne King, Dave Milne, Grant Healy, and I went to visit the Clance at his parents' Cape Cod cottage. Jack Connolly joined us one day on the beach and later that night to party. During that visit, we went up to Provincetown, on the very tip of the Cape, to catch up with another Sandusky High classmate, Kathy Dolan. Kathy was working as a chambermaid between her freshman and sophomore years at Northwestern University. She and two other girls lived in what can only be described as a shack on the beach. She showed us around Provincetown that day and said she wanted to take us to a popular bar later that night. Being underage, we had to sneak in through a window, but the patrons were very glad to help us. We had been in the bar a little while, and were having our second round of beers when Kathy asked me if I noticed anything unique about the bar. When I said "no," she told me to look around carefully. It was during that look that it dawned on me that the men were "with" the men and the women were "with" the women. Kathy had brought us to our first, and I might add my last, gay bar. When the light went on for me, I said, "Let's get the hell out of here." Kathy thought it was funny that we Midwesterners were so sheltered from a very different and, at that time, relatively unknown lifestyle.

The following summer, I took another trip with Sandusky buddies, heading to the Jersey Shore and bringing along my other roommate, Joe Kinsey. On this sojourn, we met a bunch of girls working as waitresses during the summer boom in tourists. They were college girls having a summer jobs interrupted by lots of partying. One of them turned out to be Lisa, Joe's future wife, so it was a very good trip for him. During this four-day excursion, one of our group had way too much to drink, and we put him in our car to sober up after he had thrown up and could barely stand. We came back periodically to check on him. The first time I came back, he was in the back seat praying, "God, please make me feel better, and I promise I will never drink again." The next time I came back, he was feeling a little better and the tone of his prayer had changed to, "God, I might drink again, but I promise that I won't get drunk." It seems like, sooner or later, we all bargain with the Creator of the universe for something, big or small.

It seems like, sooner or later, we all bargain with the Creator of the universe for something, big or small.

Although Jack and Joe each got married as soon as they graduated, and those weddings were another opportunity for some significant partying, the Clance and I were still bachelors. We had both bounced around the dating scene, sporadically dating after having ended our high school romances. I fixed the Clance up with girls from my hometown when he would come home with me. He met someone from the Cedar Point amusement park workforce, which was made up mainly of college coeds, whom he really liked. In fact, as I said earlier, I later bumped into her at Cedar Point, and we decided to give the Clance a call together. He was at flight school in Pensacola at the time, but we did manage to get through to him. It was the last time I got to talk to him.

As for me, I dated a number of girls while at the Academy, as well as in Sandusky when I would come home on leave. Nothing seriously developed, although I did have a good time. When I graduated, there was no steady woman in my life, and I was just as glad about it. It seemed to me, at the time, that getting married right after the Academy was going from one rather inhibiting relationship right into another. I wonder how so many of those marriages lasted and did well.

When I graduated, there was no steady woman in my life, and I was just as glad about it. It seemed to me, at the time, that getting married right after the Academy was going from one rather inhibiting relationship right into another.

The Final Year

Carrying 26 credit hours almost every semester for my last three years at the Academy proved to be challenging, and my grades slipped a little bit. However, I finished with slightly over a 3.2 average and felt like I accomplished a lot. I could have had a higher GPA if I had worked at the Navy courses. I think the study discipline I developed stood me in good stead for the rigorous nuclear power program I entered right after graduating.

My dad had agreed to buy me a Pontiac GTO as a graduation present, and he delivered it to Annapolis himself. We snuck my dad into the Academy to show him around and then went to a bar, which was inside the seven-mile limit, for a few beers. My dad then dropped me and my roomies off at the Academy. The next day, I took my dad to the airport so he could fly back to Sandusky, leaving me with my new car (ahead of the time we were allowed to have them). I pointed out to my dad how many demerits we would have accumulated had we been caught at any of the activities of the past two days. I don't think my farm-boy dad (or my farm-girl mom, for that matter) were all that goody-two-shoes themselves when they were in the service in World War II and away from home for the first time.

During my senior year at the Academy, my parents sent my brother Phil and one of his wrestling buddies to come visit me. Phil and his friend were able to stay at Coach Perry's house, but one day we decided it would be fun to sneak them into formation and into dinner. So, we dressed them up as third classmen and had them fall in with dinner formation. Needless to say, if we had been caught, we would have been in serious trouble. We were lucky not to be caught because Phil had, relative to our midshipmen haircuts, long hair. He and his buddy were also not much good at marching. I'm not sure why we thought we'd get away with it, but we did. And while they were on campus, Phil had the experience of wrestling with my teammates. For what it's worth, I think that stunt also convinced him he did not want to go to the Academy.

My new car — the GTO — was useful for getting to DC on the weekends and for dates (or looking for dates) and parties. One week our senior year, we received notes when we came back to class that told us to report to dental the following day. These trips were for dental exams and teeth cleaning. However, when I sat in the chair, the officer dentist announced, "We are going to have a few extractions today." When I asked if he meant me, he could tell he had a wise guy on his hands. He explained that I had two wisdom teeth, and because I was going into the submarine force, the teeth needed to be removed so they didn't become a bother while I was on patrol. I inquired if he was also going to remove my appendix for the same reason, confirming his wise guy suspicion. At this point, he reminded me that he was an officer and I was not, so I had better open up. With my wisdom teeth removed on that Friday, my face looked like a chipmunk that had just stuffed two nuts into his mouth. It was a little difficult to go on my date and be cool looking like that, but I went anyway and she thought it was funny. Nothing like a "wise guy" date, but I guess turnabout is fair play for the trouble I gave the dentist.

Six weeks before graduation, something happened that put a damper on the end of my senior year and "June Week" (graduation week) activities. I was in DC with a classmate named Rich and we were doing some drinking near the George Washington University campus. We met some girls who joined in the fun. I thought the one on whom I was focused looked like Sophia Loren. We went to some other bars with them, and then it came time, actually past time, for Rich and me to head back to the Academy. For some reason, "Sophia" decided to come with us. On the way, Rich pointed out that we were going the wrong way on the DC beltway, which I thought I would correct by cutting across the grassy center divide. It was V-shaped, and I ended up stuck in the bottom of the V. Rich bounded out of the car and said he would hitchhike back to the Academy and sign us both in — a definite infraction — but, hey, it sounded good at the time. I was more worried about all the state troopers, who began to converge on the scene.

I told the troopers my situation, which was the standard line we used back then: "I am about to graduate from the Naval Academy, I am going to Vietnam, and I am going to die." They arranged for a tow truck to extract me from the ditch and sent me on my way without a ticket. In the meantime, Rich spent the night riding around Bowie, Maryland, with some drunks who had picked him up. Both of us missed our curfew and ended up getting the maximum penalty, called a Class A infraction, which results in a ton of demerits and six weeks of free-time restriction.

However, when I got back to the Academy, I told Sophia to take my car back to DC and then pick me up the next day. (My Class A restriction would not be in effect for another week.) I figured she had sobered up, but still it was not the greatest idea to let a stranger have my precious GTO.

The next day, I waited and waited with growing trepidation when she did not show up. Finally, I found the number of her George Washington coed friend and called. Her friend confirmed my worst fears, which was that Sophia had been in an accident on the way back to DC and was in the hospital. Fortunately, all she had was a fairly serious concussion, but my car was toast. First, I visited the car in the wrecking yard and next I visited the girl in the hospital. Even given that she had been in an accident, it was obvious that she was not exactly Sophia Loren. Lesson learned there. I then went back to start my restriction (forced mustering — periodically lining up in front to the duty officer for inspection — and staying in Bancroft Hall over the weekends), which would carry me into the first two days of June Week, which was usually filled with celebration and merriment.

I contacted my insurance company, and they agreed to reimburse me for the car, but I was $500 short for the purchase of a new car. I wrote my parents (in red ink representing my last ounce of blood) to explain my situation. They said I was on my own as far as replacing the car, and they were coming to enjoy June Week whether I was free or not. So while on restriction, I would dress plebes up as upper-classmen and send them out into town to get submarine sandwiches, which I then sold at a profit to others on restriction. I sold all my books back to the Academy and did some other things to get the $500 I needed for the new car.

My parents and both grandmothers came for graduation. It was a proud day for them and a happy day for me. My parents rented a cottage, of which a few of my underclassmen friends took advantage. They may have spent more time there than I did, but they enjoyed my parents' humor and my parents seemed to enjoy my friends. I had to stick around Annapolis for an extra day after everyone had left before my replacement GTO was ready. Then I drove to New Jersey, where I stayed with the parents of Jack's wife, Frannie, one night before heading up to New London for submarine school and the start of the next phase of my life.

A Bridge to a New Life

Let me sum up the four years I spent at the Naval Academy. First, I consider it a privilege and a stroke of good fortune to have attended the Academy. I learned a great deal there that goes beyond academics. I don't think I would have had the same growth experiences at a typical college, and I know I could not have achieved what I did academically anywhere else. I am disappointed that I did not do better in sports, but I had a good time and got to learn from one of the best coaches in college wrestling at the time, Ed Perry. And I know I could have done better in terms of my grades, but my overall class standing, somewhere around 300, was not bad considering the workload and the immature approach I took to some of the required courses. I met some very good young men from a variety of backgrounds, all of whom graduated with a sense of dedication to our country and to each other.

The Academy unquestionably prepared me for life and set my life on a course that has been fulfilling and challenging. I remember my company officer talking to me about my attitude toward the Academy at the time. He remarked that I had worked hard and had a lot of promise as an officer, but I didn't seem motivated to be a midshipman. I told him frankly that all I had wanted to do was study and wrestle and would get out of the Navy as soon as I could. He then told me a truth that I have come to appreciate, which was that he guaranteed me that, someday, I would come to value my time at the Academy. He was correct.

The Academy unquestionably prepared me for life and set my life on a course that has been fulfilling and challenging.

So how did I end up going into the submarine force after graduation? Because of my grades and my courses, I was directed to go to DC to be interviewed by Admiral Hyman Rickover, father of the nuclear Navy. Like other interviewees, I was made to wait in a small cubicle until two prospective commanding officers (PCOs) came to get me. They practically carried me into the Admiral's office and plopped me in a chair in front of his desk. My impression of the Admiral, as I sat there in some amount of severe trepidation, was "white." There was this little old man sitting behind the desk with a shock of white hair and skin that was so white as to be almost luminescent. Before my butt bounced off the chair, he asked, "Why did your grades go down?"

I said, "Because I was carrying 26 hours, Sir."

He replied, "You're a fucking liar!"

I thought, *"This is not going too well."* Then he said without looking up from his desk, "Do you like to go to sea, Amerine?"

I replied, "Oh, yes, Sir!"

Once again, he said, "You're a fucking liar!"

I thought, *"Got me there, Admiral."* But I kept my mouth shut.

Then he said, "Are you going to get married?"

I said, "No, Sir."

Then he looked at me for a brief second and said, "Get the fuck out of my office!" I thought, as the PCOs picked me up to carry me back to the cubicle, *"Navy Air, here I come."*

Later that week, I was informed I would be going into the nuclear submarine force. The interview was apparently just for the Admiral's entertainment.

I mentioned Vietnam above and in not a very reverent way. This conflict was underway for most of my time in the Navy, including the Academy and submarines. Although submarine duty was considered hazardous, it was definitely safer than the jungles of Vietnam. I lost some friends from both Sandusky and the Academy because of their tours in that war, which was not very popular and another example of how politics interfere with the waging of war, to the detriment of the young men and women who actually enter the battle. I was surprised at how moved I was when I visited the Vietnam memorial and saw names of young men I actually knew. Our soldiers were not treated very well by our nation when they returned. I am encouraged that, as a nation, we seem to have matured in the treatment of our service men and women in recent years. I am, however, unhappy to say that our politicians don't seem to be doing any better at determining where and when to engage in war and, when we do, allowing our military to do what they have been trained to do — win.

SECTION II

MY CAREER

THE NAVY YEARS (1966-1973)

With the Academy officially behind me, I was off to new adventures. I was in a group that was assigned to the submarine (sub) school in New London, Connecticut, and we had only a few weeks off after graduation before we were to report for duty. I stayed in Annapolis for two days, waiting for my new car, and then drove to New London by myself. There, I met up with my buddies as prearranged. There were seven of us who had decided to live off base in a rented house, as well as have our room on base in the Bachelors Officers Quarters (BOQ). We were all bachelors, most without a serious girlfriend and all determined to make up for lost time when it came to the partying that we imagined our college counterparts had enjoyed.

The house we rented was on River Road, which was one of two choices when exiting the Naval base. One choice was to bear hard left and go up to the road that took you to Interstate 95 or to downtown Groton. The other choice was to angle slightly to the right to a narrow road that ran along the Thames River. The road was cut into the side of a hill that ran down to the river. Our house was perched on the river side of that road, on one of the few spots that offered enough room for a house to be built on that side of the road.

Between the house and the river was a single railroad track that led to and through the Naval base. It passed right by the Navy housing area, and the early morning train was called the "fertility train." When it woke couples up, it was too early to get up and too late to go back to sleep. So, what to do with that time?!

Directly across the river was the Coast Guard Academy, but we were more interested in the school across the road from the Academy, Connecticut College for Women — or as it was commonly known, Conn College. It attracted us Navy guys like bees to honey, and eventually we knew a number of girls who came to enjoy the parties we threw at our house, pretty much every Friday and Saturday night for the duration of sub school. We were fond of clearing out the refrigerator, turning it on its side, and filling it with grape aid or some similar kind of base juice. We would then "charge admission" to the party by accepting some sort of alcoholic drink from our guests, then dumping those bottles of alcohol into the prostrated refrigerator. It didn't matter what the liquid was — in it went and then we drank all evening from that batch, convinced it tasted like the "nectar of the gods." It didn't take long to separate the Conn College coeds who liked to party from those who did not, given the nature of our parties. The whole scene kind of reminded me of my favorite movie, *Animal House*. When I first saw that movie, it was in Spokane some years after Cindy and I got married, and she was disgusted that I was practically rolling in the movie theatre aisle, laughing. Go figure. I guess Cindy may not have come back after her first party at the "House on the River."

With our off-base party house rented, my buddies and I were ready to begin sub school, a six-month introduction to submarines. This introduction included classroom academics ranging from submarine engineering to weapons tactics. It also included simulator time in a computer-driven control room. We also went to sea for a day or two at a time on a World War II vintage diesel sub.

Sub School, Nuclear School and "Prototype"

A submarine is a complicated machine with a lot of interdependent parts — not the least of which are the officers and sailors who operate and repair the equipment. A submariner has to know his job and, to some extent, everyone else's. Although the submarines of today are larger and more sophisticated than those of my era, I am sure that interdependence is still true. The idea of submarine warfare is, first and foremost, to stay undetected. Second, the aim is to fulfill your mission, whether that's serving as a deterrent to nuclear war or spying on the enemy. Finally, of course, it was important to keep water out of the "people tank."

A submarine is a complicated machine with a lot of interdependent parts — not the least of which are the officers and sailors who operate and repair the equipment.

Sub school was an introduction to those relationships. For me, it was the first time I had to think about the practical application of principles I had learned at the Naval Academy and actually try to understand how machinery worked. There were other activities, such as navigation and weaponry, that made me wish I had studied those classes more diligently at the Academy. As it turned out, while I was in the Navy, two nuclear submarines, the *Thresher* and the *Scorpion*, "went down." They were lost at sea, and the reasons were never fully known, even though their remains can be seen by deep-diving robotic subs. There's a reason why submariners, like aviators, receive additional pay — known as hazardous duty pay — for their service. It was exciting, challenging, and scary, all at the same time.

There's a reason why submariners, like aviators, receive additional pay — known as hazardous duty pay — for their service. It was exciting, challenging, and scary, all at the same time.

While at sea for the first time on the WWII training sub, I was introduced in short order to the head (that's a toilet for you landlubbers). I took my first bowel movement and then turned around to figure out how to flush the product of my efforts. There were myriad valves and pipes. What seemed so easy on land became a challenge of significant proportions, especially considering others wanted to get into the commode. I failed to realize that there was a slight pressure in the sanitary tank that needed to be relieved before I opened up the valve to allow my excrement to slide down the pipe into said tank. So, when I opened the commode valve, the pressure in the sanitary tank blew my poop back into my face and onto my uniform. I quickly closed the valve, but then had to figure out how to hide my embarrassment of not being able to successfully conduct this most basic function correctly. Fortunately, I had a change of clothes, but for the next day and a half, I didn't use the toilet. When we returned to the base, while my classmates were running back to the BOQ to clean off the diesel smell, I was squeezing my butt cheeks while hoping I could make it to the first available BOQ john (bathroom) in time. My dirty laundry bag didn't smell any too good either.

While at sub school, "accidents" came in all forms, like when I broke my right thumb. I did this in a bar fight on a Wednesday night before Thanksgiving weekend, as a result of hitting some guy hard enough to knock him out. When I woke up on Thursday morning, my hand was swollen and hurt like hell. I went to sickbay and they ended up putting my right hand in a cast and gave me some medicine for the pain. I spent the rest of the holiday weekend teaching myself to write with my left hand. (I throw left-handed but write right-handed.) I took left-handed notes and exams for the next two months while my right thumb bone healed. Sub school lasted a total of six months, so we finished just in time for the Christmas holidays.

From sub school, my group headed to Mare Island Naval Base in Vallejo, California. This put us close to San Francisco, which — in addition to being a beautiful city — was a very interesting place in the mid-1960s, at the fore front of the burgeoning free love and drugs culture. Although the academics during this portion of our training were focused on nuclear theory (rigorous and fast-paced in nature and presentation), we still found time to party on most weekends. For me, with my majors in math and nuclear physics, the school was right in my sweet spot, so to speak. I did well but still put in tremendous hours studying to make sure that I did. The competition was fierce because the guys in this program were both smart and competitive. Also, it's my nature to work hard and study diligently. I attribute that not only to my Ohio upbringing, but also to a persistent lack of confidence that I would do well without a heroic effort.

As it turns out, another life-changing event occurred during this six-month period, and it was the best thing to ever happen to me. I met my wife.

As it turns out, another life-changing event occurred during this six-month period, and it was the best thing to ever happen to me. I met my wife. Cindy Brigandi was an Army brat in her sophomore year at Dominican College, an all-girls Catholic school in San Rafael. We both learned of a party at an apartment in Sausalito. I went there with some of my classmates, as did she with some other girls from Dominican. She had just turned 20, and I was a year out of the Academy and 22. She was very pretty with long dark hair, an olive complexion, and a dazzling smile, a very Mediterranean look. She was short, which made me feel tall, and she laughed at my jokes, which made me feel witty. I am neither tall nor witty, so she must be telling the truth when she says I "had her at hello." We made a date for the next weekend, and I picked her up at the house of one of her friend's parents. (Her father, Colonel Joseph Brigandi, had been reassigned from the Presidio in San Francisco to the Pentagon. Her family had moved back to the D.C. area, and she was to follow at the end of the school year.)

San Francisco was a great place to court, and we had a lot of diverse, eclectic fun. Cindy was an immediate hit with my classmates, and her best friend started dating one of my good buddies at the same time. We double-dated a lot. Cindy was beautiful with a killer body and a great sense of humor. She was adventurous and liked to have fun. On one of our dates, we drove down to Carmel. We had our picture taken at the lonely Cyprus. (Little did we

Dave and Cindy, 1969

know that, years later, we would have our photo taken there again, first with one child, Erin, and then even later with both girls, Erin and Alyssa.) Although I liked her immensely from the very beginning, I wasn't looking for anything long-term at the time, and didn't fall head-over-heels for her as she said she did for me. But there was definitely something there that I hadn't ever felt before. It was enough that I ultimately wanted to see her again when we both found ourselves back on the East Coast, Cindy after finishing her sophomore year and me after the six months of nuclear power school was finished and I received my assignment for reactor prototype training. However, for reasons explained below, Cindy's father was far from enamored with me in the beginning (and for quite some time even after Cindy and I got married).

Nuclear power school ("nuke school") was followed by another six-month training experience known as "prototype." Once a person made it through nuke school successfully, they went to a prototype reactor, which was an actual Navy submarine reactor in a land-based setting. At that time, those reactors were in Idaho and upstate New York. I was sent to the S3G reactor, which is located at the West Milton site outside of Saratoga Springs, New York. The experience was a six-week school on the reactor design followed by a five-month, in-hull shift assignment where the trainee had to accomplish a book of practical factors to the satisfaction of the training staff, which consisted of both officers and enlisted men. These practical factors, or "prac facs" as they were known, ranged from starting and shutting down certain machinery, to taking readings, to standing the maneuvering room watches from where the reactor and the turbine and main generators were operated just like on a real sub. The main generator went to a steam dump instead of turning a propeller, but the effect was the same. More power or less power could be demanded of the reactor by adjusting the rate of steam flow to the steam dump, acting just like increasing or decreasing the speed of the submarine.

For me, prototype was not unlike sub school in that I had to learn how things operated. I didn't bring a background in mechanics (or mechanical or electrical acumen) to either endeavor. To my detriment, I was not interested in those kinds of things growing up. Fortunately, I met several enlisted men and one officer who seemed to take a liking to me and went out of their way to help me. One of them, Herb Coulter, a chief on the training staff on my shift, was a particular help. He hadn't even graduated from high school before joining the Navy, but he had a superb mechanical acumen and a gift for explaining things. Little did we know that our lives would intersect several more times in the future.

Once all the practical factors were successfully accomplished, there was a comprehensive exam followed by a final oral board. Although the exam was tough, the board was scary. While all of us had taken difficult exams, very few of us ever been required to answer questions from a three-person board, who mostly wanted to see if you could think on your feet (as you would have to do in actual situations at sea). There was one of my classmates who was extremely smart and finished at the top of sub school, nuke school, prototype classroom, and even finished his prac facs first. However, he failed horribly (what we called "failing open" in the Navy) on the oral boards, even after three tries, and was discharged from the nuclear program and sent to the regular Navy. It was serious business.

In the meantime, we were on rotating shifts, which meant that we had four days off every four weeks. Sometimes, those days were spent catching up on things. At first, most of our free time was spent in the Saratoga Springs bars, chasing Skidmore girls. Skidmore was a women's college full of girls, most of whom came from wealthy families. Our joke was that you had to have "two heads and both of them ugly" not to get lucky on the bar scene those days.

After a few months in New York, I got up my courage to visit Cindy and face her father. We hadn't gotten off on the right foot ever since Cindy missed the plane home from San Francisco after she finished her sophomore year at Dominican and ended up staying with me that weekend. Fortunately, I was able to meet Cindy's mother first, and she became an ally. Additionally, I think Colonel Brigandi at least admired my courage in coming to their home outside of DC. However, Cindy and I were not permitted out alone. As I recall, Cindy's sister, Donna, and her fiancé, Mike, always had to accompany us, which didn't please any of us very much.

My mother-in-law was the first member of the Brigandi family to extend herself to me under what were the trying circumstances that Cindy and I had created. In retrospect, I understand the misgivings Colonel Brigandi had about me. No man is ever quite good enough for a father's daughter, and providing any justification for that feeling is what a good son-in-law should avoid. Fortunately, Mrs. Brigandi could see through my immaturity, and saw that Cindy and

I loved each other and were going to be good for each other. She had that gift. I am sure she became my strongest advocate and waged a convincing pillow-talk campaign on my behalf. For that, I will always be grateful.

No man is ever quite good enough for a father's daughter.

I'll always remember the first time Mrs. Brigandi invited me to a family dinner. Fried chicken was served and, when I used my utensils to scoop the chicken from the serving bowl, it bounced off my plate and onto the floor. I am sure Colonel Brigandi was wondering, *"Where did Cindy get this bozo?"* However, Mother Brigandi came to my rescue and said, "The dog will love you for that gift." Being a veterinarian's son, I spent the rest of the meal worried that the dog would choke on the chicken bone, and Colonel Brigandi would shoot me for killing his dog.

I started to go down to DC almost every time we had four days off. I enjoyed being with Cindy so much that I finally realized that I was in love with her. So I proposed. We were in Georgetown one Sunday afternoon before I had to go back to New York. I had traveled to New York City to buy a diamond ring from an Academy math professor with whom I had stayed in touch and who had inherited his father's diamond business. I remember going to his Fifth Avenue office, where there was row after row of chests with small drawers. Each drawer was about two inches tall and a yard square.

When he pulled out a drawer, it was divided into little two-inch cubicles, each of which contained a small, folded piece of white paper. When he removed a paper and carefully opened it under a special light at a desk, it contained approximately twenty diamonds of a certain size and quality. He took several hours to give me a tutorial on diamonds, and finally we found the one that was the best deal for what I could afford. I am sure he gave me a good deal because it had the best of the various characteristics he had explained. He had it mounted for me, and later I presented it to Cindy on that sunny day in Georgetown. Many years later, when bigger diamonds had come along, Cindy had that original diamond reset into a pendant.

There was only one problem — well, two problems. The first was to get permission from her father, who was in the midst of trying to control costs on Donna's pending wedding. The second was the timing, which was a function of me having successfully passed the prototype oral board on the first try and needing to get to my first duty station soon. Cindy's father reluctantly said yes when I asked him for Cindy's hand, probably due to the pillow-talk campaign Cindy's mother waged on my behalf. Once I knew when my board was scheduled, we settled on the date for a small wedding. Cindy and I would have been just as happy to elope, but we understood that weddings are only in small part for the couple being married. Our wedding was meaningful to our families too. The wedding was to be at Fort Myer chapel in Arlington, Virginia. The reception was at Cindy's parents' home, which was a far cry from Donna's elaborate wedding and reception just six months prior. Years later, when I sponsored the weddings of my daughters, I began to have more sympathy for the Colonel.

But first things first: I had to complete my prac facs, pass the comprehensive exam, and finally pass the oral board. I worked hard at the first, and studied relentlessly for the second, and accomplished both in fine fashion, thanks in part to all the enlisted staff who helped me on the prac facs. I am glad I never became one of those officers who looked down his nose at enlisted men. I had avoided bringing that trait with me from the Naval Academy, where I had opted out of "running plebes." I also discovered that the enlisted men were very bright, probably given to the fact that they wanted to escape being drafted into the Army during the Vietnam war and due to Admiral Rickover's rigorous screening for only the best and the brightest.

However, it was an officer I barely knew who took me under his wing to prepare me for the oral board. We spent countless hours in preparation, with a few mock boards thrown in for good measure. I passed the board on the first try. However, that kind of preparation (and later lack thereof for the engineer's exam) led me to always make sure people under my charge were thoroughly prepared for oral boards. With those milestones behind me, I was off to the wedding. I hate to think what would have happened if I had not passed (on the first attempt).

No Longer a Bachelor: Getting Married and Really Getting Started on My Military Career

I invited a few of my closest, which meant rowdiest, friends to the wedding. Wayne King from Sandusky was my best man. At the rehearsal dinner, Colonel Brigandi made his reservations about me known, which my parents seemed to take in stride, but that, understandably, really upset Cindy. I can still remember my father comforting her when she was crying afterward. Colonel Brigandi really got my mother's dander up, but she uncharacteristically held her tongue. I think that event caused my mother to warm to Cindy more slowly than she might have otherwise done. Eventually, both sets of parents could see that we loved each other, had wonderful offspring, and a marriage that lasted and flourished. Years later at a parents' weekend at Alyssa's sorority, I said that I thought Lis got her determination from her maternal grandfather and paternal grandmother, but I was sure her sweetness came from Cindy's mother and my father. The same could be said of Erin.

Cindy and I didn't have time for a honeymoon. We headed for my first duty station in the real Navy, a submarine undergoing maintenance in dry dock at the Norfolk Naval Shipyard. Cindy and I found a two-room apartment that fit our budget of $17,000 per year as a lieutenant junior grade. It was in the same civilian apartment complex in which several of my Naval Academy classmates lived, including Jack Connolly. He was attached to an aircraft carrier, which was docked at the Navy shipyard for retrofits and repairs before going back to the Far East for deployment in support of Vietnam. The Navy officers in the area were all young and still partying, even though most were married with at least one child at home. We had some good times.

I was assigned to the job of first lieutenant on the sub, which meant I reported to the weapons officer for all the SLJs (i.e., shitty little jobs). My real job was to qualify as engineering officer of the watch (EOOW) and as forward officer as well. There were advantages and disadvantages to doing this in dry dock in the shipyard, but it was basically a repeat of what I had just gone through at the prototype. It was complicated by real work doing maintenance, repair, or modification on a variety of things, no equipment actually operating, and having to learn things in the forward part of the boat, which took me back to sub school. I was putting in some long hours while Cindy was stuck in our small apartment. Cindy had worked in the war room at the Pentagon after returning home from her sophomore year at Dominican College. She was figuring out married life with some help from other Navy wives in the area. I would get home late and want to go work out. Sometimes I would take her with me to watch me play basketball. Great fun for her! In retrospect, I don't know how she put up with it. I did have most weekends off, and we made the most of that time together, visiting the surrounding area and friends and going to parties.

Then something happened that changed everything. We were invited to go on a sailing trip with another wardroom officer and his wife on his 24-foot sailing boat called a yawl. I knew very little about sailing, despite growing up on Lake Erie and having to take a course at the Academy. **I assumed (never a good thing to do)** the owner of the boat knew what he was doing, seeing as he actually owned a sailboat. The first night on our 50-mile trip up the Chesapeake Bay was beautiful. The couples took turns at the helm, staying on certain heading that would take us to our goal. The stars were out, and we had a portable radio playing. Very romantic! We arrived at our destination sometime late morning, had lunch, and prepared to sail back to Norfolk. That night, on the way back, a sudden storm came up, for which the Chesapeake is famous. I do not remember anyone thinking to check the weather before we embarked on the trip.

We were easily in state-four seas, which means very rough waters with high waves, and taking on water. Then we lost electrical power and the little hand pump we had was not keeping up, including the fact that the hose ended about an inch inboard. It was demoralizing to see the last cup for every effort fall back in the boat. My buddy told me to take down the jib and we would sail on the main, just the opposite (I learned years later) of what should be done in those conditions. I told Cindy to go below in the cabin, where she promptly fell asleep. I then went out on the bow, which was moving up and down about four feet and dipping under water on the downward stroke. While holding onto the mainstay with one hand, I pulled in the jib with the other hand. I could have easily been swept overboard, but I was following orders from the boat owner. Finally, when that job was done, I returned to the futile pumping effort.

Off in the distance, I saw a large dark shape, which turned out to be a Dutch freighter. I used our only flashlight to signal an SOS, and the freighter pulled alongside and let down a huge rope ladder. The four of us climbed three stories to safety while the captain signaled the Coast Guard. No one on the freighter spoke much English, but we could tell they were not happy about picking us up or waiting for the Coast Guard to come tow us to port. It was probably costing them a lot of money, but they had no choice. They did give us some candy bars.

When the Coast Guard finally arrived some three hours later, the sun was just coming up. The girls rode in the Coast Guard boat back to port while I was in the sailboat, pumping the hand sump pump, fighting a losing battle. By the time we got in port, there was virtually no free board, meaning the top deck of the boat was almost even with the water level outside the boat. Cindy and I said goodbye to the others and hitchhiked back to Norfolk. The first thing we did was go to church to thank God for our lives. The next thing we did was procreate (while we still could). Erin was born nine months later.

The lesson learned from this sailing event was the tried and true **"never assume anything."** Whether it is visiting the doctor, discussing matters with your financial advisor, talking with a sales representative about a major purchase, managing a project, or embarking upon an adventure with a friend, always (diplomatically) ask a few pertinent questions, and don't assume anything. It's your money, your health, your career, and your life.

Whether it is visiting the doctor, discussing matters with your financial advisor, talking with a sales representative about a major purchase, managing a project, or embarking upon an adventure with a friend, always (diplomatically) ask a few pertinent questions, and don't assume anything.

When Cindy found out she was pregnant, we could not have been happier. But I still had a few things to learn about being a jokester with your pregnant wife, and I am afraid I was not as sensitive as

I should have been. My ears were cauliflower from all the wrestling I had done. I told my young wife that cauliflower ears were hereditary. She was worried her child, especially if it was a girl, would be deformed from the get-go. She ran down to the nearby apartment of a doctor to see if there was anything that could be done. The doctor's wife was home and assured Cindy that there was no need for worry. The doctor's wife came back to our apartment to give me a lecture on how sensitive a pregnant woman can be and for me to be more considerate.

Approximately seven months later, I was inside a ballast tank on the submarine in dry dock doing an inspection when I heard a voice coming from above me. It was a sailor yelling through the open tank vent to tell me my wife needed to speak to me urgently. I crawled out of the tank and went to the barge, where our offices were located, and answered the phone. Cindy was at the hospital and crying. She had gone there for a checkup, and the Navy doctor told her the lab results indicated she was "abnormal" and left the exam without any word of explanation. (Sort of reminded me of my experiences with medical at the Naval Academy.) I borrowed a car and tore over to the Portsmouth Naval Hospital and basically made an ass of myself, demanding to see this doctor. Finally, an admiral pulled me, in my dirty tank inspection outfit, into his office and calmed Cindy and me down. He was patient and kind and obtained Cindy's records. He informed us the abnormality was that Cindy was borderline diabetic, not an unusual analysis for a pregnant woman, but one that needed awareness in diet and care. I never found out whether the admiral counseled the doctor on his bedside manner, but I suspect that he did.

When the day came for Cindy to deliver, I was at work when she called to tell me it was time. I raced home, and for some reason I still cannot explain, jumped in the shower while Cindy waited with her packed bag. I then informed her that I knew a short cut, which led to us waiting on the longest train ever to pass in front of us while Cindy's labor pains were coming more frequently and intensely. Finally, the train passed, and we continued our rush to the hospital. At the hospital, they told us Cindy was only slightly dilated, and we had some time to kill. I thought it would be a great idea to go to McDonald's for a couple of hamburgers. I guess my neighbor's lecture about paying care and attention to my pregnant wife had not been taken as well as it should have. By the time Cindy and I returned to the hospital from McDonald's, Cindy was in quite a bit of discomfort. When the nurse examined her again, she said that they needed to get Cindy into the delivery room right away. I was not allowed to follow, so I went to the expectant father's room and watched *The Bill Cosby* show. Soon the nurse came out and announced that I was now the father of a healthy baby girl. The next phase of our life, parenthood, had begun. And now Cindy and I were no longer a couple; we were a family!

Erin was born in April. Cindy and I met in April and were married a year later in April. We liked to say that we had a true "April love."

Erin was born in April. Cindy and I met in April and were married a year later in April. We liked to say that we had a true "April love."

I soon joined Cindy and our baby as they were brought out of the delivery room. I cannot describe how good it was to see them. I thanked God on the spot that both mother and daughter were in good health. However, Cindy and I didn't have a clue how to manage a baby. Everything was an experiment! Fortunately, both of our mothers visited in quick succession. Cindy was exhausted and told her mother she didn't know if she could manage this new responsibility. Her mother firmly told her, "You can! And you will!"

I always tell Erin we got her name from *Playboy* magazine, which was featuring girls of Ireland the month she was born. The truth is that we were so sure that we were having a boy, we hadn't bothered to pick a girl's name — not seriously anyhow. We had decided we would name our son Clancy after my deceased roommate, Kevin Clancy, the Clance. That led us to an inclination toward Irish names, reinforced by the fact both of our mothers were of Irish descent. Looking at a list of names for Irish girls, we soon settled on Erin.

Coming out of dry dock, I had responsibility for making sure the submarine lifted off the blocks evenly with the correct positive buoyancy. That meant weighing all the net changes to the submarine since it was last on the surface, making sure the various tanks had the correct amount of fluid in them, and ensuring that the correct pressure was applied to the main ballast tanks. I sweated over this assignment, figuring and refiguring the loads and the changes. There were formulas to follow and a procedure on how to accomplish this task, but it was indeed my first big assignment. The bottom line is that it went well. Then we were off to our new home, New London, Connecticut.

One funny thing that occurred as we were getting ready to flood the dry dock was my search for a component for one of the cleats. It was basically a metal block that secures the cleat, which is how the boat is tied to the dock via lines (ropes). I was calling all over the shipyard looking for that piece. Finally, I located a place that had some but would not release one to me. So, I screamed into the phone I was Commander Amerine, and that component better show up at the dry dock within the hour or heads would roll. At the time, I was a lieutenant junior grade, one notch up from the lowest officer rank, and several notches below a commander. When the truck pulled up alongside the dry dock, I had to convince the executive officer (XO) to go down to the truck and pretend he was Commander Amerine. He said he would do it one time and one time only, and he did. We got our component, and I got a funny look from the XO, who said I owed him big time.

Another amusing thing in relation to flooding the dry dock is that we had a huge scale to weigh the equipment as it was brought on board. We were also getting a lot of visits from the feared Naval Reactors (NR) personnel, Rickover's henchmen who wanted to make sure we were ready to operate the reactor. One particular seaman, the lowest level enlisted rank, who was kind of a wise guy, told the visiting NR folks they had to weigh in to get on the boat. Never mind that they would get off the boat before we even got under way and individual personnel weight was insignificant relative to equipment weight. It was funny to see these academically very smart (but not so street-smart or submarine-smart) men lined up to have their weight checked.

Cindy, with baby Erin, drove our GTO to her parents' home and then came to New London where I met her, having ridden the sub from Portsmouth to New London. We set about buying our first house, as so many of my classmates had done once they got married. We found a great realtor who specialized in helping submariners find homes, and we soon found a three-bedroom house with a large yard on a quiet cul-de-sac. I asked my parents about the wisdom of buying a house and they advised against it, based on the fact that the Navy was bound to move me again. We bought the house anyway. I am fond of telling people the story of our first house when explaining that a manager/leader should consider input from those they manage or lead, but the final decision and responsibility rests with him or her

Dave, Cindy, and Erin in Mystic, CT, 1969

alone. I call this "participative management." If the decision is good, success is shared all around. If not, the manager/leader takes full responsibility and regroups around lessons learned.

I am fond of telling people the story of our first house when explaining that a manager/leader should consider input from those they manage or lead, but the final decision and responsibility rests with him or her alone. I call this "participative management." If the decision is good, success is shared all around. If not, the manager/leader takes full responsibility and regroups around lessons learned.

Later, when I asked my parents for advice on another matter, they responded by asking me why they should bother ... because I had ignored their advice on buying the house. I told them that I had considered their advice carefully and greatly respected it, but had decided to go another way. I would always consider and respect their input in any decision. By the way, I had to borrow the $600 needed for the down payment from my father, which I repaid at 10 percent interest. The house cost us $18,000 in 1970; how times have changed!

The sub to which I was attached, the USS *Pollack*, was a "fast-attack" sub, which during the Cold War meant that it was used for spying on the Russians. However, it was designed to wage war with other subs if the situation ever turned hot. It was deployed all the time and, even when we came into port, the hours were long and hard in the rush to get ready to go again. I remember one time we came in after a long patrol only to pick up an examining board and head back out to sea to be tested. Even when we got back from that three-day excursion, one shift of the crew did not get to go home in the first three days, as we addressed the findings from the exam.

There were a few exciting occurrences while on the fast-attack sub. One night, we were on the surface coming into port when a Russian trawler started to harass us. It was the late 1960s and in the midst of the Cold War. Their "fishing" trawlers were loaded with spy gear, and they probably wanted a closer look. They also probably just enjoyed giving us a scare. It would not be good to have an open-sea collision. I called the captain as the trawler closed, but then I had no choice but to turn the sub facing into the direction from which the seas were being blown and increase speed to get away from the Russians. As I did, the sub, whose hull was designed to be submerged, lowered into the water as the relative speed of the water over it increased. The cockpit, where the lookout and I were strapped onto the boat by a single rope line from our safety belts, flooded with water as we hung on for dear life. The captain called up to tell us to secure the bridge and lay below, which we were only too glad to do as he "took the con" (i.e., took control of the sub) until I could get into some dry clothes.

Not all my memories of that era were harrowing. Some were downright funny. It was another cold and rainy night on the surface when I had the watch on the bridge. The lookout asked permission for a coffee to be brought to the bridge, and I said yes. Now, even though I had not developed a taste for coffee, I knew in the Navy it only came one way: strong and black. When the cup was brought up to bridge, it smelled great, and the lookout seemed to be warmed by huddling over it. So, I called down to the grizzled old chief on the panel and asked for a hot chocolate to the bridge. Back came the rasping response, "Yes, Sir! And would you like to have some cookies too?" I could hear the whole control room laughing in the background as the chief put this whippersnapper in his place in "This Man's Navy."

Time for a Transition

As I was nearing the end of my four-year obligation and as I had planned from the beginning, I submitted my resignation, but now not only because I had never planned to make the Navy a career, but also because I wanted to get off that submarine and spend some time with my family. Unfortunately, the Navy had other plans. You see, at that time, my whole group (i.e., those of us who started our service during the same year) was extended for a year. We served at the discretion of the President, and it was decided that too many submariners were leaving the Navy at an important time. I was told that if I would withdraw my resignation, I would be sent to graduate school before the next patrol. I didn't have to think about it twice and accepted the offer, even though I knew that a year of graduate school would cost me two more years at sea. I thought that, if those two years were assigned to a Fleet Ballistic Missile (FBM) Submarine with its alternating crews splitting the time away from home, that would be better than another year on the fast-attack submarine that seemed to be at sea almost all the time.

While waiting for school to start, I felt more at ease on the submarine, knowing my time was short. One day we were going to take the Squadron Commander out for some exercises that were planned. Cindy and I had partied hard the night before we were to go out. She drove me to the pier where the sub was docked because I was busy hanging out of the car throwing up. When I got to the sub, I found out I was to have the con as we undocked and headed out to sea, what was called the maneuvering watch. It was a bright, sunny, and warm day. When we were underway, the squadron commander came to the bridge and greeted me with, "What a wonderful day to be going to sea, huh, Dave?" My reply was to lean over the side and throw up, at which time the Commander requested permission to lay below and did not wait for my response. Even though the Commander was a good guy, it was probably a good thing I didn't have a Navy career in mind. I was also beginning to realize my partying days needed to be put behind me. I needed to start growing up.

When it was time to leave Connecticut for the Naval Postgraduate School in Monterey, California, we were able to rent our house to a Navy chief. That lightened our financial burden, but we still didn't have a lot of money. So, we decided to camp our way across the country, something I would not even consider today. Of course, we stayed with our parents en route, but everywhere else we pulled into a campsite and pitched a tent. We slept in sleeping bags on inadequate air cushions. We ate food we cooked or bought from a fast food place. A few campsites, like one outside of Billings, Montana, were beautiful. We were also pulling a small motorcycle I had bought so Cindy could have the car when I was at work or at school. It was an adventure, to be sure. Our spirits held up, and we had fun and met some interesting folks along the way. We were driving our GTO with a crib in the back seat and our clothes hanging on a bar that held up the convertible top. We couldn't even see Erin unless we peeked through the clothes. We had no air-conditioning, so it was 4D7 (four windows down, 70 miles per hour) to keep cool. Of course, that was before seat belts.

At one stop, we splurged and decided to stay in a hotel. After we checked in, the three of us went for a swim. Now Erin was only a little over two years old and could not yet swim. Cindy and I played with her on the steps going into the shallow end of the pool. At one point, we decided to have a swimming race to the other end of the pool, and we admonished Erin not to leave the steps. When we got to the other end of the pool and looked back at Erin, she was going down under the water. We raced back to pull her up. She was crying at first but in no danger. I thought that I needed to take her back in the water so she would have no fear of it. Although I was able to coax her back into the pool, I had nightmares for some time about that incident. How stupid were Cindy and I to have left her alone for even a moment?!

When we arrived in Monterey, we decided that we wanted to live off site instead of in Navy housing. We found a very small apartment to rent for almost exactly what we were charging to rent our home back in Groton. But it was in beautiful Carmel, California, and we were a very short car ride from the beach. Downtown Carmel reflected the changing times and social norms of the late 1960s and early 1970s. I was a driving hazard downtown because the new no-bra look was in full force there. Finally, after several close calls, Cindy told me to keep my eyes on the road and she would find the next girl worth looking at and point her out to me for a quick look. What a great wife!

School was a great reprieve from the demands of fast-attack submarine life. I had some interesting classes in support of my master's in management science. I especially liked those classes, which deviated from the mostly hard science courses I had at the Naval Academy. The weather was wonderful, cool in the mornings and warm in the afternoons. I would ride my motorcycle up over the mountain that separated Carmel and Monterey, usually in the cold mist that covered the mountain in the early morning. I would go to class, usually continuously, until three or four o'clock in the afternoon. Then I would go work out, either in the graduate school weight room or, during the season, with the local high school or junior college wrestling teams. Then I would come home for dinner and hit the books for a few hours after playing with Erin after supper.

On the weekends, we usually had some adventure planned for Saturday, like going down to Big Sur, and Sunday was back at the books for at least part of the day. We would also visit parts of nearby California on Sundays. It was almost surreal, after the grind of the previous six years.

One of the things I started while at the graduate school was to become an important part of my life for the next three decades. I began officiating wrestling. The coach at Monterey Junior College, where I worked out with the team, asked me if I would be interested in joining their officials' organization. I said yes, and thankfully they had a good training program and introduced new officials to the lowest level of competition in the area, junior high school matches. That meant the first time a new official stepped on the mat, there was a lot less pressure to do well than at an important high school match or tournament, or at the junior college or college level.

Mark Kane, a USNA graduate five years after me, who came straight to grad school from the Naval Academy and who was also three-time Eastern heavyweight champion, started officiating at the same time as me. We had gone together to work out with the junior college, so the coach asked us both if we would be interested in officiating. Mark soon began calling to ask me to take his matches and later confessed that it was just too much pressure because he didn't want to make a mistake. I determined early that I would make mistakes, but usually no one other than me would know. If the error was egregious, most times it could be corrected. But, in any case, it was never a life-and-death situation. Before I left California, I had established myself as a very good ref, did some important high school tournaments, and was requested for some important dual matches. I enjoyed this activity a lot because I think wrestling is a wonderful sport, and this was a way to keep close to it as my competitive days and opportunities were numbered.

I did enter one tournament so Cindy got to see me wrestle for the first time. I cut my weight down to the 160-pound class and was becoming somewhat ornery. Also, the high school season was over, so I didn't have anyone with whom to work out. There was an enlisted man assigned to the Presidio Language School who was just a little bigger than me, and we worked out together, but that was it. Cindy was very afraid that I would lose and be upset. The three of us — Erin, Cindy, and I — traveled to Fresno for the tournament. Cindy covered her eyes for the first match, and I pinned the guy in 17 seconds; she never saw it. The next match, I pinned the guy in 27 seconds, and Cindy began to think this was a pretty easy sport. The next guy was a stud, but I beat him. I wrestled seven times that day, won every match, and was named the tournament outstanding wrestler. By the end of the day, Cindy was screaming at me what to do on the mat. It was her first wrestling tournament, but that didn't seem to inhibit her. After all, she was my wife. When I went to get my trophy, Erin followed me out on the mat; it was a real feel-good moment.

About half-way through the year, we were notified that the Navy chief renting our house back in Connecticut had received orders and would be leaving. His contract allowed him to vacate our house if that happened, with no penalty to him. However, for us, it was a financial nightmare because we had no margin in our budget to accommodate the mortgage and our rent at the same time. We had to put the house on the market and rely on the realtor long distance to do her best. It took almost to the end of school before it sold. In the meantime, we had to scrape by, and somehow we did. What little savings we had were soon depleted. We joked that one of the expenses we could eliminate was lunch, and we almost did. And yet, even though we had no money, it was a great time in our life and in our marriage. Having our daughter, Erin, made it all the better. When we had an event to which only Cindy and I could go, our next-door neighbor, who had a little boy Erin's age, gladly babysat.

When graduate school was just about over in the spring of 1971, I received my next assignment, a fleet ballistic missile (FBM) sub, the USS *Ulysses S. Grant*, out of Charleston, South Carolina. The sub was actually stationed at Holy Loch, Scotland, but the crew home-ported out of Charleston. Cindy, Erin, and I began another cross-country trip to start another phase of our life. We decided on our trip to go through Las Vegas for the first time. We stayed at Caesar's Palace, and the joke was that that was a good enough bathroom in which Erin became potty trained (which was a blessing for the rest of the trip).

Coming out of Las Vegas our retread tires, which I bought to save money, shredded. Fortunately, we didn't lose control of the car, but it did mean using for the first time our credit card to buy something, in this case new tires, which we could not otherwise afford. Doing this was against my personal pecuniary policy, which I inherited from my dad, but we were desperate. We stopped along the way to visit our parents, Cindy's in an Indianapolis suburb (her father was stationed at Fort Harrison) and mine in Sandusky.

When we arrived in Charleston, it was July and hot. Cindy set about to find a home, and I checked in at the base. Fortunately, we had sold our house in Groton, Connecticut, before graduate school ended, so we had enough money to make a down payment on a new house. We found a nice single-story brick ranch house in a developing neighborhood. We bought a dog for company and protection. He was a German shepherd puppy when we got him, and we named him Tag. He bonded with our three-year-old Erin. Cindy would send them out the door in the morning without a care. How times have changed! Tag grew up around children and was very good with them but also protective of Erin.

I met my new shipmates at the office building we occupied, and our initial focus was on getting ready to leave for Scotland. And what to our great mutual surprise did I find but Herb Coulter, the chief who had been such a big help at prototype. I was assigned to be the main propulsion assistant, so that meant Herb was my leading chief. He and I quickly decided how we would run the division together, built on mutual trust and our friendship. It worked really well. I think God was looking out for me, not to mention the rest of the submarine crew.

I qualified both fore and aft on the first patrol, which was not usually done but the work effort kept me busy and made the patrol go by fast. I was very fortunate to have a great engineer officer, Ted Del

Gaizo, who was a firstie at the academy when I was a plebe, number one in his class, and Brigade commander twice. Therefore, I knew who he was. To my pleasant surprise, he turned out to be a great guy, a wonderful teacher, and ultimately a friend. How a nuclear power plant really works finally came into sharp focus under his tutelage.

When we pulled into Holy Loch, Scotland, after that first patrol, I had the first watch in port. Ted called me from the gangplank on his way to the officers' club and told me to shut down the plant, put it on shore power, and go into "cold irons," which meant to start cooldown of the plant. Now none of these activities are trivial, but for a brand-new qualified EOOW, it seemed a little overwhelming. But it also demonstrated Ted's confidence in me. Fortunately, I had a good crew, including as the leading chief of the watch, my buddy Herb Coulter. It was quite possibly the most fun I ever had running a plant and a real confidence builder. I think Ted knew Herb and the rest of the crew wouldn't let me get into trouble.

My patrols were in the summer and in the winter, which saved me from the Charleston heat but had me away from home for two Christmases. It wasn't easy to transition between those two exis-tences — away from home and then at home — not for me, not for Cindy, and not even for Erin. Erin coped by saying she had a pretend Daddy who lived on a fictious Darrell Street (we never knew from where that name came). He would come home soon. I could not wait for this phase of my life to be over and to enter civilian life.

On the other hand, with Ted and Herb's patience and instruction, I got a good feel for real, practical engineering that would stand me in good stead later in my nuclear career. Cindy once again took up dance, which she had done as girl and teenager, and was asked to join the Charleston Modern Ballet Company. She was very good and I loved to watch her perform, especially when her long brown hair was flowing. Erin started a preschool class, which also allowed Cindy to work part-time in an interior design studio. When I was not on patrol, work was an eight-hour day, usually doing some sort of training or studying.

We loved Charleston. Overall, it was a good time in our life with one notable exception: the engineer's exam. The engineer's exam was the precursor to being assigned as the engineer on a nuclear submarine and the next phase in a nuclear Navy career. Not interested in a career and having submitted my resignation to be effective after my last patrol, I had no intention of taking the exam. Our captain, Tom Sisson, had other ideas. It was important for him

Cindy practicing with the Charleston Modern Ballet Company, 1971

to put officers up for the exam, and he ordered me to take the exam before that last patrol. I had no choice, so I studied as hard as I have ever studied using the bank of questions that the boat had assembled. These were questions assembled by sitting with someone who just returned from taking the exam and writing down every question they could remember. The question bank also had the answers developed by the crew and approved by the engineers. I answered every question in that bank (and there were hundreds of questions) over and over until I could do it in my sleep. However, Captain Sisson and the engineer, who had replaced Ted when Ted received a promotion, never thought to address the oral portion of the exam. Neither did I.

When I took the exam, there was not one written question I had not seen before, remembered, and understood the correct answer. I am confident that I aced the written portion of the exam. I went to bed after that part of the exam feeling pretty good but still nervous about the oral portions, because I hadn't really prepared for it like I had at prototype. The next day, the oral examiners were merciless, and their anticipation was for much more thorough answers than at the prototype oral board. As confident as I was about the positive results of the written portion, I was equally confident that I had done poorly on the oral. It turned out I had good reason to feel that way because at the end of the day, after an excruciating wait, I was told I did not pass the overall exam. I went home with my tail between my legs but determined never to put someone in the position in which Captain Sisson had put me — that is, unprepared. He made his quotient, but I felt like an idiot.

Farewell to the Navy, and Hello to a Brief European Adventure

After the last patrol, I went to the base administration building to get checked out of the Navy. A Marine sergeant looked at my medical history, saw that I had had operations on both knees at the Naval Academy, and advised me to file for a disability. He asked me if my knees ever bothered me while on patrol, and I answered that, honestly, they did a little, but I was used to it. He said, "You probably won't get the disability because they're really cracking down on granting them, but it will be in your record. If your knees ever do need attention, you will be able to walk into any veteran's hospital and receive treatment." So, I filed the disability and found that I would be extended in the Navy for approximately three months while my case was evaluated. It was May, and I had just accepted a teaching assistantship at Oregon State University (OSU) in its nuclear engineering department to help pay for my doctorate in nuclear engineering. School didn't start until September so I wasn't too worried.

Cindy and I sold our house, and we moved in with two other couples — the weapons officer and the executive officer (both of whom were getting out of the Navy at the same time) and their wives. It was almost a commune-type existence, which was in vogue at the time. The three of us officers decided to have a getting-out-of-the-Navy party, which was held on Isle of Palms, South Carolina. Rather than arrange for a keg of beer, we bought a truck of beer. Three days later, the truck departed empty. It was quite a party!

As things dragged on with the disability review, Cindy and I decided we would go to Europe. We would take Erin and Tag out to Cindy's parents, fly from Indianapolis to McGuire Air Force Base in New Jersey, and get a hop (free flight on a service-charted plane for servicemen and their families) to Germany, and wing it from there following the book *Europe on Five Dollars a Day*. It was an adventure, but it didn't get off to a good start. First, in Charleston, Tag got out of the yard where we thought we had securely locked him when we went for a bike ride. As he crossed a busy highway to catch up with us, he was hit by a car and killed. It was the first time I felt true grief. He had become an integral part of our family and now he was gone.

The next surprise occurred at McGuire Air Force Base. The Air Force didn't like the looks of my Temporary Assignment Orders, which allowed me to travel. They called the Navy at the Pentagon and, before I knew it, I was discharged from the Navy right there in the Air Force base lobby. This meant Cindy and I were no longer eligible for a hop flight to Europe. I needed to return to Charleston to close out a few things and pack a few belongings before returning to Cindy's parents' house in Indiana to pick up our car and our daughter, and head for Oregon. We had just about resigned ourselves to forget about the trip to Europe and head out to our new civilian life when I noticed a phone on the wall with a little typewritten sign under it that read, "If you want to go to Europe, pick me up." Feeling a little like *Alice in Wonderland*, I picked up the receiver. Without any ringing, a voice answered and asked, "When do you want to go?" When I answered "as soon as possible," the voice said, "Be in the basement of the TWA terminal at Kennedy Airport at 0200 tomorrow." I asked how much, and the voice said, "one hundred dollars," and the line disconnected. I turned to Cindy and told her what had happened. We were young and stupid enough to take a chance.

That night, at midnight, we found a crowd of people milling around in the basement of the TWA terminal. It turned out that there was a charter flight and as soon as enough people had shown up to fill the plane, it was going to take off. We found out that the $100 each was for a one-way flight, and we could not buy return tickets until we were in Europe. Again, it seemed perfectly okay to us at the time, so off we went. It was a great flight, with movies and multicourse meals. When we landed in Frankfort, we were eventually given an address in Munich where we could purchase our return tickets, so we boarded a train for that city. We found the address to be a second-story apartment in a suburb. When we knocked on the door, a voice behind the door asked me what I wanted. When I said a return ticket from Frankfort to New York, the voice asked, "When?" and I gave the date of our originally planned return. The voice said, "just a minute,"

and a few minutes later a young man opened the door and asked for $100 American from each of us. When we had our tickets, he closed the door, and we left. Sometimes it pays to be young and stupid!

We spent the next three weeks following the book as we went from Munich to Garmish, to Vienna, to Florence, to Rome, to Nice, to Paris, to Amsterdam, and finally to Frankfort. It was quite an adventure, sleeping on trains to save money, rarely eating out but shopping for food to make our own

Dave and Cindy on the beach, Nice, France, 1973

Dave and Cindy on the train between Paris and Amsterdam, 1973

meals, meeting lots of interesting people, and drinking a lot of wine. When we returned to New York, we had just enough money to fly back to Indianapolis, pick up Erin from Cindy's parents, and head out to Oregon for the next phase of our life. It was a little scary because now the service — the Army in Cindy's case as an Army brat and the Navy in both our cases — was no longer there to take care of us. We were on our own!

THE NUCLEAR INDUSTRY

As a reader of this book, you have just arrived at the pivotal moment — when the stories, experiences, and lessons of my upbringing, education, and service experience would shape the man and the leader I was about to become. Follow me now on an exploration of how these preparations shaped my philosophy, which guided the challenges I was destined to face in the nuclear industry. The techniques and approaches I used were based, in no small part on, these early experiences. I had a good foundation, but was open to adapting my attitude and methods to each new situation — based on what I had previously learned and how I had been taught to behave, think, and treat others. I had learned so much from my parents, teachers, coaches, Navy shipmates (officer and enlisted), and college professors.

Corvallis, Oregon (1973–1974)

Because we had so little money, Cindy and I decided once again to camp our way across the United States. This time, we had more gear but less heart for it. About half the time, we opted for a Holiday Inn, which meant we were pretty financially strapped when we arrived in Corvallis. When I checked into the university, I found out it would be a month before I would receive any pay. So, I filed for unemployment compensation. I hated doing it, but we had no choice. We had not yet received the settlement for our Charleston, South Carolina, house, which we had fortunately sold by the time we had returned from Europe. Cindy was able to get a job at the OSU Department of Information. I only received one unemployment check, and even though I still qualified, once Cindy started to work and Oregon State started to pay me, I didn't take any more money from the government. Now people are receiving unemployment compensation while they take cash paying jobs. I do not know how they rationalize it.

With the money from the sale of our Charleston house, we found another house outside of Corvallis on the edge of McDonald National Forest. It sat on a three-acre lot in the middle of a field, with a small brook running through the property. Our ride to work and Erin's day pre-school was about five miles through the country. Cindy had the GTO and I had the motorcycle, which was fine until the start of October, when it began to rain nearly every day and it turned cold in the morning. The bike ride was miserable — even more daunting than the one in the cold Pacific mist up over the mountain that separated Carmel and Monterey when I was at the Naval Postgraduate School.

Erin liked her school. Her teacher asked all the kids to make up a poem about Halloween. Erin's was the following:

> *The sky is dark.*
> *The windows are broken.*
> *The goat is dead.*
> *Black curtains.*

That poem actually scared us. We thought *"our little girl has dark thoughts of which we were not aware."* Maybe she was going to be another Edgar Allen Poe, God forbid.

Cindy liked her job at OSU and made friends quickly with her work mates, as she always did. We double-dated with one of her office workers and her husband, who was also pursuing an advanced degree, but in forestry. Erin took swimming lessons and dance lessons for the first time, as well as attended day school. We took in three kittens, who we named Gray Cat, Orange Cat, and Butchy — the first two for obvious reasons and Butchy because she had no tail.

Let me share three stories about those kittens, who quickly became cats. They loved living in the field where our house was and were always bringing their latest catches back to the house to show us. They slept in the garage. One time, I had to work on our washing machine, so I carefully disassembled it, putting the parts on a long piece of wrapping paper (which I had spread out on my workbench) and labeling each group. By the time I discovered the broken part, it was ten o'clock in the evening. So, I thought I would run into town first thing in the morning, buy the part, and return to easily assemble the washing machine with the new part. I had so meticulously arranged all the components that reassembly shouldn't have been difficult. I went into the house, rounded up the cats, put them out in the garage with a small nightlight, and went to bed. When I opened the door to the garage the next morning, there were parts everywhere. The cats had had a great night batting them around. I scooped up everything I could find, went to town for the defective part replacement, came back and began the laborious assembly job, trying to find the part from the big pile that fit the description on the diagram. When I finished my re-construction, I still had a handful of parts left over. The washing machine ran great for another 10 years. Go figure.

Another time, I came home from the university and I found Cindy and Erin beside themselves with worry. Butchy had part of her intestines hanging out of her anus. I called my dad, the veterinarian, and he instructed me to put some Vaseline on my index finger and shove the intestine back up the anus. Knowing my dad's sense of humor, I was skeptical, but he insisted that Butchy's condition was not unusual for minx cats. So, I did it. Butchy seemed to recover, but she never looked at me the same after that. The third cat story comes a little later.

As for my classes, I liked them and I was doing well, but I wasn't sure where the doctorate was going to take me. I had also learned that the school finances, (i.e., my teaching assistantship pay), might be in jeopardy. I really struggled with what to do. We liked Oregon, but I thought the one commodity that I had to offer was my Navy operating experience, and the further away from that experience I got, the less value it might have to a potential employer. So, I decided to put my resume and information in the University's placement office (i.e., career services) files. I never thought much would come of it. However, a Westinghouse recruiter came through the University and scoured the placement office files. He passed my information on to the management at the Fast Flux Test Facility (FFTF), which was being built on the Hanford Reservation in southeast Washington state, about a six-hour car ride up the Columbia Gorge from Corvallis. Bill Moffitt, the FFTF operations manager, gave me a call and asked me to come to Richland, Washington, for an interview. Cindy and I talked it over, and we decided to investigate the possibility.

The one commodity that I had to offer was my Navy operating experience, and the further away from that experience I got, the less value it might have to a potential employer.

Westinghouse flew both Cindy and me over to the Pasco, Washington, Airport and provided a rental car. When Cindy went to get in the rental car, she was attacked by a giant tumbleweed, so her initial impression of the Tri-Cities was not a good one. On the other hand, it had been raining for three straight months at that time in Oregon, so it was good to be in a dry climate. We just didn't know how dry it really would be. My interview went well, and I really liked Jay Powell and Bill Moffit, the head of operations and Jay's deputy, and some of the other staff I met. There was a lot of building going in the Tri-Cities at that time, in anticipation of increasing activity at the Hanford Reservation such as FFTF. Therefore, there were lots of new homes for Cindy to see.

Richland, Washington (1974–1981)

We returned to Oregon with a lot to think about and yet the decision was easy. I was no academic and the FFTF technology, a liquid metal breeder reactor, intrigued me and seemed to hold a bright promise for the future of civilian nuclear power, at that time barely 30 years old. As much as we liked the atmosphere of Corvallis and living out in the country, we made the decision to take the job in Richland. I informed my boss, Dr. Bernard Spinrad, of my decision and he was very understanding. I left for Richland right after the New Year to begin the first operator class in January. Cindy stayed behind for another month to complete her obligation to the OSU administration group and to rent our house. I bought her a used Datsun sedan and drove the GTO pulling my motorcycle to Richland. I rented a small apartment near a shopping mall. As it turned out, the apartment was kitty corner from the grade school Erin would attend and only two blocks from the home we would buy on Wright Avenue, which was under construction at the time.

Before I left Oregon, Cindy and I made the decision, after a three-year study of nutrition, to become vegetarians. We also pledged to each other we would stop eating ice cream. The first decision was an easy one to make based on the information in the book *Diet for a Small Planet* by Frances Lappe. The second one was more difficult because I really loved ice cream. Frankly, I was also fascinated by the idea that we would be different from most people with respect to our diet habits. During the first seven years in Richland, we were serious with our balancing of amino acids and eating as much whole food as possible. It was made a little easier by living in a Mormon community and soon we were following their lead with respect to storing wheat, grinding it for our own flour, and making all our own bread products from that flour. We had decided to be lacto-ovo vegetarians, which meant we could eat dairy products and eggs. Years later, I was to find out that might not have been a wise decision due to cholesterol concerns. We also occasionally had chicken and turkey as well as fish in our diet. Cindy made her own bread, yogurt, and grape juice, as well as other things. We tried unpasteurized milk but my Dad, who thought the whole thing was a silly fad, threw a fit and advised us on the risk we were taking. This was one time I listened to him.

After arriving in Richland, I met with my fellow classmates for introductions. Most, but not all, were ex-Navy nukes, both officer and enlisted. We held classes in the basement of an old Federal Building in downtown Richland, with occasional trips out to the FFTF site to see how Bechtel was doing with construction. The academic competition was intense because we knew down the line how we did in class would be a major factor in determining who would be selected to be one of the first four shift managers. However, just a block away from the Federal Building was a Baskin Robbins Ice Cream shop. The fellow with whom I walked to work each morning loved ice cream, too. The Devil's handy work was all over the situation.

Before Cindy drove herself to Richland, after finishing her obligations at the University, she gave away Gray Cat and Orange Cat, but no one seemed to want Butchy. So, she drove down the Columbia River Gorge in her little Datsun with Erin, her belongings, and Butchy. The winds were blowing hard as they are given to in the Gorge and it made fierce sound against the car. Butchy was so scared that the only place she felt like she had any refuge was on top of Cindy's head. If Erin would try to take Butchy off her mother's head, Butchy would dig her claws in. Therefore, Cindy accepted her passenger's perch. I wish I could have seen it. Not long after Cindy and Erin moved into the apartment, we heard some terrible screeching outside after we had put Butchy out for her constitutional. We looked out our apartment window and there was Butchy, hauling down the street with three larger cats in pursuit. We never saw her again. The trip down the Gorge was for naught.

As soon as Cindy and Erin arrived, Cindy said to me, "I have a surprise for you." When she told me she was pregnant, I was ecstatic. I was just learning how to be a father to Erin and now there would be four of us. (No longer could we sing the song we sang as soon as Erin could talk, which was "The Three of Us, There Will Always be the Three of Us.") I said to Cindy, "To celebrate, let's forgo our vow to not eat ice cream and see if we can find an ice cream shop." She agreed, so I wandered around Richland until I "stumbled" across the Baskin Robbins store. However, when we walked, in the owner, who usually was there just in the daytime and with whom I had many conversations about sports and politics as I consumed my double scoopers, was working the evening shift. He announced in a booming voice as we came in, "Dave! This must be the family." I was exposed. Cindy said, "I knew you couldn't do it."

After the final exam (there was no oral board just yet, though it would come later), we moved to a building on the Hanford reservation in what was called M Area. There we began to write the procedures we would ultimately use to run the plant. We were also closer to the site, so we could travel out there to actually see the components of the systems to which we were assigned (if they had been placed yet). We also began a process of receiving completed systems from Bechtel, the construction contractor. Our task was to have our procedures ready to receive the system, take it through acceptance testing, fix problems discovered by testing or turn the system or component back to Bechtel for fixing, and document final acceptance. At the same time, we needed to set up required maintenance schedules for our new system. All of this was done under the watchful eye of the

Atomic Energy Commission (AEC). The AEC ultimately became the Energy Research and Development Agency (ERDA), and was later separated into the Nuclear Regulatory Commission (NRC) and the Department of Energy (DOE).

The systems for which I was assigned to write the operating procedures were the Radioactive Argon Processing System (RAPS) and the Cell Atmosphere Processing System (CAPS). I decided I would write the prototype procedure for all to emulate. I based my procedure format on the Navy's Reactor Manual we had used to learn the systems on a submarine. This book covered the system from design to operations to maintenance. I researched the systems thoroughly and even visited the vendors for the gas compressors, the main components of each system. I was proud of my final product and others did use it as a guide for their procedure efforts. However, as I used to tell people as an example of **"not letting perfection get in the way of progress,"** when I left FFTF seven years later, modifications were still being made to my "perfect" procedures as we learned more about the systems during actual testing and operation.

During this time period, as part of our training, we were sent in small groups to the Federal Idaho Site for nearly three months to qualify on the EBRII reactor. "EBR" stood for Experimental Breeder Reactor and "II" indicated it was the second one. This reactor plant was a sodium-cooled reactor like FFTF would be, so it was considered a good experience. One of my classmates owned a house in Idaho Falls (which he had vacated when he was hired by Westinghouse), so I lived there with two of classmates during this training experience. Cindy and Erin stayed back in Richland during those three months, which were in the summer. Cindy was experiencing her first summer in the high desert of eastern Washington and it was hot, and she was pregnant and getting more so each day, obviously. Not a good time for me to be away.

At the same time, I was sitting in the classroom at EBRII looking out the window on a mid-June day, watching three inches of snow come down. I really missed Cindy and Erin, but we treated the separation like a submarine patrol. I had to work hard to accomplish the qualification in the three-month period we were assigned there and that made the time go by quickly.

While I was staying in Idaho Falls for the EBRII training, the guys with whom I was staying and I decided to take a raft trip down the Snake River. It was in early April and the guides who took us down the river were doing it for the first time that year. The river is different every year and varies during the year as well. And it was cold. However, it was exciting and there were plenty of rapids. At one juncture, the guides knew we were coming to one of the largest standing waves on the Snake at a place called "Lunchbox." We got out on the national forest side of the river and walked up the rock jetty, which created the standing wave. If we had gotten out on the roadway side of the river, I would not have gotten back in the raft. I was scared. As we approached Lunchbox in our raft, the raft ahead of us completely disappeared. I was more scared. It was a wild ride and thrilling. Once we got through it intact, I wished we could go back and do it again. That was my first rafting trip but definitely not my last.

In fact, there soon came an opportunity to go rafting again — this time with an old buddy from the Academy. In March of 1975, the NCAA wrestling matches were held in Corvallis. Cindy and I went down for those matches, and there I bumped into my firstie from the Naval Academy, Mike Harmon. We exchanged phone numbers and, a few months later, we visited Mike and his family in Portland. By this time, our second daughter, Alyssa, had been born and was already six years old. We were now a family of four. Mike was working as an executive for a major trucking company, married, and had two boys who were just a few years older than Erin and Alyssa. We got together a few more times and then Mike invited us to raft down the Deschutes River with him and a few of his friends. Alyssa was too young to go but Erin made the trip as well as Cindy. We were on the river three days and camped under the stars two nights. It was fantastic fun! We visited Mike and his family in Portland several times. Mike's boys, besides, of course, being wrestlers, also played the violin. That sparked an interest in the violin for Alyssa and she began to take lessons. She and her friend from across the street actually put on a concert at the grade school, but then she lost interest and the violin was history ... as Erin's ballet was soon to be.

But in sharing stories of rafting adventures, I've jumped ahead a bit. Let me return to that late summer in 1974, when I was finishing up three months away for training, and Cindy was pregnant with Alyssa. At work, things were getting busier and more intense. As more systems were turned over at FFTF, around-the-clock operation and testing soon became necessary. This required the operations group to be divided into crews or shifts, and a manager had to be chosen to lead each shift or crew. There were four crews, which meant there needed to be four Shift Operations Managers selected. I was one of those first four chosen and it was quite an honor. This position was my entry into management as a civilian. My experience as an officer in the Navy helped in most ways, although civilians were not sailors and that difference required an adjustment. As I recall, most of the people, all of whom were carefully selected by Bill Moffitt, were good people — hard-working, smart, and folks who took their responsibility seriously. I was in this position about three years and on shift work (working different hours/shifts from week to week) the whole time. Shift work is hard on the individual and on his/her family. It requires several adjustments, not all of which are pleasant.

During this time, Cindy and I found and purchased a house. It was the biggest house we had owned yet, on a corner lot of a new development. At the beginning, we still had the house we had bought in Corvallis, so we were "house poor." However, it was a nice house with a big room for Erin and a nice size room for a nursery on the second floor. It also had a full, unfinished basement, which I ultimately finished myself. I was quite proud of that job, even though there were lots of imperfections. Cindy was in her element decorating the house on a limited budget. She did a very good job.

On September12, 1974, I took Erin across the street to neighbors and took Cindy to the hospital for the delivery of our second child, Alyssa. Erin was born in a Navy hospital at the Portsmouth Naval Base and I was not allowed in the delivery room. That was not the case with Alyssa, and I held Cindy's hand as she delivered another baby girl. After the delivery, I went to work — such were the demands of the job. I still remember later in the day picking up Erin and taking her to the hospital to see her mother and new sister. On the way, I told her that while I would love her sister as much as I loved her, she would always be special as our first-born. Given her age at the time (5 years old), I doubt that she remembers that.

Because Erin was born while we were in the Navy, her expenses were covered by Navy medical benefits. Westinghouse Benefits Department informed me that they had done a calculation that indicated Cindy was pregnant by two weeks before I accepted employment with Westinghouse. Therefore, that was considered a pre-existing condition and the expenses of Alyssa's birth would not be covered. That seemed to set the tone for the next 20+ years … in that Alyssa was always a more expensive child with more expensive tastes than Erin.

Cindy nursed both children, but Erin had been in a crib in our bedroom in the small apartment we had in Virginia Beach when we were first married. Alyssa's nursery was upstairs in our three-story house in Richland. When she would wake at night for a feeding, I would go upstairs to get her and then take her back upstairs afterward. After six months, I was turning into a zombie at work and informed Cindy I had done my husband duty and she could now get Lis. When Alyssa woke that night, I shook Cindy and covered my head with the pillow. Cindy did the same thing, and Alyssa slept through the night from then on.

Despite how busy I was with my career and my family, I still found time to help the local high school wrestling programs and officiate at both the high school and junior college level. I found that I could do a good job of officiating and was in demand for important matches and tournaments. One such occasion was when I was asked to officiate

Dave officiating wrestling, 1975

the dual match between Sunnyside and Othello. They had finished one and two in the state tournament the year before, were undefeated prior to the upcoming dual match, and had six returning state champs between them. The place was packed to capacity and the wrestlers were introduced in a darkened gymnasium under the spotlight before each match. I was nervous to start with but probably did one of my best jobs ever. The lead changed hands several times and came down to the final match. Othello was the home team and their heavyweight had to pin the returning state champ for Othello to win the match. The two wrestlers were evenly matched, but the Othello wrestler pinned the Sunnyside kid in the final period. The place went crazy. After the match, both coaches came up to me and thanked me for a good job. The coaches, the wrestlers, and the fans were very well behaved. It was sports the way athletics were meant to be.

I loved officiating but still missed competing as an athlete. I still had it in my mind to compete in some AAU (Amateur Athletic Union) tournaments; I couldn't help but feel that injuries and circumstances had always prevented me from reaching my full potential as a wrestler. Unfortunately, once again injury — this time a serious neck injury suffered while working out at Columbia Basin Junior College — ended the wrestling once and for all. The result was a very close call because a nerve was pinched in my neck, which resulted in a partial paralysis of my right arm and hand. Fortunately, a local coach was able to get an appointment for me with a renowned sports medicine doctor in our area.

When Cindy took me to Yakima to see the doctor, his office was in a trailer complex. Cindy stayed in the car reading while she waited for me to return. The doctor, an orthopedic surgeon, decided he wanted me to see a neurosurgeon in the same trailer complex. This doctor, who happened to be from Pakistan, was somewhat callous and recommended surgery as the only course of action. The original doctor decided he wanted to confer with his partner, another orthopedic surgeon. All of these doctors were in different trailers and we had to parade in front of the car and Cindy, with the line of white-frocked doctors who accompanied me growing larger each time we walked past. After the last doctor, it was decided for me to see another neurosurgeon back in Richland. When I got in the car, Cindy asked me what they said. I said they had decided to take my head off and repair my neck, and then put my head back on. Cindy was stunned and it was several minutes before I had to start laughing, at which point I thought she was going to take my head off for them. Fortunately, the doctor back in Richland said that the fact that I was regaining feeling in my hand meant that there was healing in progress and we should wait. He did have me wear a neck brace, which immediately relieved my pain due to relieving the pressure on the nerve. I eventually recovered completely. Again, thank God!

I never did attempt wrestling again but I did start to run and lift each day after work. A neighbor noticed me running past his house each day and asked me if I ever thought about running in a marathon. I thought I would try it, so he gave me a book to read on how to train for a marathon. I set a target for a race that was just six weeks away. I followed a tough training regimen, increasing my distances carefully. However, I overlooked the need to stay hydrated. One particularly hot Sunday morning, I set out to run 20 miles for the first time, but I didn't take water. At 18 miles, I literally could not take another step. I crawled about two blocks to my home, where Cindy wrapped me in a blanket because I had chills, and she began to force all kinds of liquids down me. I remember swallowing a whole can of peaches. Cindy called my mother, who said that I probably had an electrolyte imbalance and if I didn't lose the chills, I should go to the hospital without delay. Fortunately, things got better rather quickly but it made me doubt that I could continue with the marathon, which was in two weeks. Cindy and I talked about it and we agreed that I should just take it easy.

As it turned out, I did run in that marathon and finished in 3:26. Not a real fast time, but at 20 miles, I knew I was going to make it. So, I picked up my pace and started to pass people and caught one guy right at the finish line. Cindy and the girls were there to see me finish. Later when Cindy and I were asked to recount the times we felt the closest in our marriage, we agreed on two of the three. One was in the delivery room for Alyssa and the other was that first marathon.

Later in life, I would have two hip replacements, which were probably due at least in part to all the running I did for about two years. However, I really enjoyed it and almost broke three hours my last marathon. Not long after that marathon, I wore through the articular cartilage of my left knee (you might recall that I had the medial meniscus removed from both knees while at the Naval Academy). Because she was becoming a runner's widow, Cindy, a sprinter by nature, had even started running and actually finished a 10-mile race. We both ran in the Spokane Blooms Day Race with 15,000 other runners. However, when I had to quit running, Cindy quit the very same day. I then decided to swim for cardiovascular exercise and have been doing that on and off ever since.

I started running at the beginning of the running craze that seemed to sweep our nation in the late 70s and into the 80s. I remember finding a shoe advertisement in *Runners* magazine for New Balance shoes. Back then, the only way you could get a pair —because they weren't yet sold in stores — was by tracing your foot on a piece of paper and sending the tracing into the New Balance company. Now, of course, it is one of the most popular brands in the world.

Sports figured largely into the lives of my entire family. When Erin was in the third grade and walking home from school one day, she noticed some boys in her class playing soccer. She watched and they asked her to join them. Soon, she was asked to be on a third-grade-age coed soccer team. She was one of only three girls on the team. I was very busy at work and knew nothing about soccer, even though one of my roommates after the Academy, Jim Burger, had been an All-American soccer player for Navy. Nonetheless, I would go to her games on Saturdays when I could and watched a bunch of kids chase a soccer ball. Erin got to play a little and seemed to enjoy it. I figured it was good exercise. The winter after that fall season, I received a call asking me if I would like to be a coach in the girls' recreational league that they were forming the upcoming spring season and, in a weak moment, I said yes. In that first season, I had no idea what to do and we lost every game. I didn't think that was fun for me or for the girls and, frankly, I didn't teach them much. So, over the summer, I read several books, attended a few seminars, and talked to several veteran coaches. In the fall, I put those things I learned into practice. I also learned to treat the girls as athletes, not little girls. We won or tied for the league title the next three years.

Erin became a very good soccer player. She just seemed to have a good head for the game and put up with me as a father/coach insisting she practice the techniques. She was the team's leading scorer and, in one game, scored six goals. Cindy and I got sucked into the adult "over 30" soccer league and had a good time. Cindy's athleticism really showed during those games. Me, not so much. Because of my knees, I played goalie on a men's team. One time, when we were playing a team made up of Mexican-born players who were truly talented on the soccer field, Alyssa, probably five years old at the time, walked behind my net and commented, "Dad, your net looks like the other team's ball bag." Nice vote of confidence from my daughter. I told her she did not need to bother getting up Christmas morning. Also, in that adult league, when I came out of goal to race an opponent to the ball was the only time in all my athletic endeavors that I was actually knocked out.

While I was learning to work with girls for the first time in an athletic environment, I was experiencing women in the workplace for the first time as well. Like wrestling, which was an all-male endeavor at that time, my college and my Navy service had been in strictly all-male environments. Now I was suddenly interacting with women engineers and technicians at work. My experience with the girls' soccer team helped because I quickly realized to treat the women as professionals, just I had learned to treat the girls as athletes. In general, that approach made things go better.

During this time in Richland, Cindy got involved in community theater. She was a very talented dancer and a good musician but never liked the spotlight. But she enjoyed being part of the chorus or supporting players and "putting on a show." She had roles in several plays and other light opera shows while we were in Richland, including *Pippin* and *Finian's Rainbow*. The girls and I were proud of her, and she had a good time.

Earlier in this chapter, I mentioned that we had no oral boards right after we finished our schoolhouse phase and before our EBRII experience. However, by the time we had two more classes of operators, our management knew that they wanted to emulate the Navy requirements and commercial utility requirements for obtaining a reactor operating license. So, they planned to have another comprehensive exam followed by an oral board as a requirement to become qualified. I learned a lot from my experience taking the oral boards in the Navy. I also determined I would not let my engineers and operators go into their oral boards without extensive preparation and coaching (which I, unfortunately, did not receive for taking the Engineers Exam in the Navy). Being ready for the boards requires not just learning all the expected knowledge, but there are also various techniques for taking control of the board. Those techniques are based on time management and understanding what you do know versus what you are unsure of. I would use Erin's wall mounted chalkboard in her large closet to drill my crew members to make sure they were ready. Some dreaded that experience, but we had the highest scores in all crew classifications and, in many cases, the second highest score as well.

During my time at FFTF, I was making the adjustment to managing in the civilian world. It is definitely different from the Navy.

During my time at FFTF, I was making the adjustment to managing in the civilian world. It is definitely different from the Navy. For one thing, civilian employees aren't necessarily a "captive" group of workers, like the sailors and junior officers are in the Navy. As I will explain in the Section III of this book — in the chapter entitled, "What Have I Learned from these Experiences?" — the authoritative style of management was not the acceptable norm in the civilian world and became even less so over the course of my career. Coming out of the Navy and into lower levels of management seemed to offer more success (or at least less potential failure) than coming out of the Navy as a Captain or an Admiral and being inserted at a high level of management and visibility into the civilian world. While I made mistakes as I went through my adjustment period, they were not of the potential consequence and visibility as they would have been at a much higher level of management. That is why I think so many Navy Captains and Admirals don't do particularly well in the transition. They aren't afforded the adjustment period that those of us who came out at lower levels had. Although the Navy and other branches of the service offer tremendous opportunity for responsibility and leadership growth at a young age, that experience, in my opinion, is not immediately and exactly transferrable to the civilian world. While I made mistakes as a first-level manager, I also had successes. For me the most telling and gratifying indication of that success is in a statement one of the technicians on my crew made in an interview with the head of Operations, Bill Moffitt, which Bill later passed on to me. The technician said, "Crew C [my crew] may not have been the best shift, but Dave made us feel like we were."

"Crew C may not have been the best shift, but Dave made us feel like we were."

All this time, we were still living in our house on Wright Avenue in Richland, Washington, and in writing this book, I'm reminded of two stories about that house. The first is quick. When Alyssa first learned to walk and then graduated to a big-girl bed from her crib, she also saw the movie *Jaws* (which may not have been the wisest parenting move on our part). She would wake up to go to the toilet and pass the bathroom between her bedroom and Erin's bedroom to wake up her sister so she could accompany her to the bathroom. That way, *Jaws* would not come up through the toilet, or if he did, at least her older sister would be there to save her. To Erin's credit, she would dutifully shoulder her big-sister responsibility until this fear of sharks passed for Alyssa.

While we were on a vacation to Cannon Beach, Oregon, (its coast line was beautiful!), that same toilet overflowed when the Tidy Bowl man became stuck between the float and tank wall, preventing the float from shutting down the filling of the toilet tank after evaporation had lowered the level. Our neighbors discovered the cascading water when they came in to water the flowers for Cindy. They called us to tell us about the event and that they had cleaned up everything. However, after the event, one of our technically challenged neighbors, trying to make sure the event did not happen again, opened the supply valve to the toilet, thinking he was shutting it. (It had been shut by one of the fire department personnel who had been called to pump out the basement.) The whole event occurred again and was not caught as soon. Fortunately, USAA insurance covered all the repair costs, but Cindy almost went into shock when we arrived home to discover all the damage.

In all, we lived in Richland for seven years, and that time marked the entire grade school career for Erin and saw Alyssa enter kindergarten. Jason Lee Grade School was a real blessing — with many of the teachers being spouses of the technicians, engineers, and managers who worked on the Hanford Reservation and many having advanced degrees themselves. Richland was very much a family-oriented town, having been incorporated in the mid-1950s, coming into existence as a result of the Manhattan Project and the nuclear work that was done at the site. There were two other cities in close proximity: Kennewick, a farming community originally, and Pasco, on the other side of the river and originally a railroad town. The area was known as the Tri-Cities and was near the bend in the Columbia River, where it turns westward from its southerly path from Canada to head toward the Pacific Ocean, passing through the Columbia Gorge. That area is also where the Snake River and the Yakima River flow into the

Columbia River and was part of the Lewis and Clark Trail. We traveled around the Northwest whenever we could to see that part of the country where Cindy and I had never been before. I took up backpacking and even climbed Mt. Rainier.

Although, as a family, we have been blessed with good health and we have tried to support that with a healthy diet and a dedication to working out, there were several medical situations that occurred during this time in Richland. One was Alyssa suffering a hernia. It took four grown men to hold her down when she had a bad reaction to medicine given at in the hospital. And when she had her operation, they glued her shut, rather than using stitches or staples. We referred to her "glues" ever after.

Similarly, Cindy had to have an appendectomy, and she was stapled together afterwards, a new approach at that time. For the rest of her beautiful life, she had one staple in her abdomen that was never removed.

Once Alyssa was born and all her fingers and toes accounted for, I decided to have a vasectomy. In those days, we were into the environmental movement, which was in its infancy. One focus of concern was the world population expanding beyond the world's resources, so we decided to do our part by limiting ourselves to only two children. Today, the wisdom of that action might be questioned, in light of a sustainable population and the present demographics in our country. Nonetheless, that was our decision at the time. My operation was performed on an outpatient basis. I went to the doctor's office with more than a little trepidation, based on tales of other men's experiences and the sensitivity of the area on which the procedure would be performed. I was lying on the table in my surgical gown when the doctor walked in, trailed by a good-looking nurse. He proceeded to throw the gown over my head, which in retrospect was a good thing because then I couldn't see the nurse's face as she gazed upon my "shrinkage." The doctor numbed the area and began the procedure. When he pulled on the cords to be severed, it felt like he was pulling on the top of my brain. He kept a running dialogue, but when he said, "Whoops!," I was more than a little apprehensive about how things were going. When the operation was over, however, I felt fine, probably due to the painkiller not yet wearing off. When I got home, I decided I would work out, which was at that time proceeded by jumping rope to warm up. I was in mid-air on the first jump when I realized that idea was not a wise one. However, Sir Isaac Newton had me by the balls, so to speak. When I hit the ground, it was painful. I crawled into my room and pulled myself into the bed, where I stayed for three days, nursing a very uncomfortable set of testicles.

While we lived in Richland, there were two other near misses that were much more serious and, I thank God to this day that we did not suffer what *could* have happened. The first was the incident that I mentioned earlier that ended my wrestling. I believe poor form, lifting significant weight, when doing the bench press as part of my workout at the Naval Postgraduate School distorted the fifth and sixth cervical discs and put them closer to the nerve. When I was twisted while working out for an AAU tournament, I could have been paralyzed. It was a close call and would have changed life dramatically for me and for my family. That realization made it easy for me to walk away from the sport I loved.

The other incident occurred right out in front of our house on Wright Avenue. When Alyssa was four or five, she was on one side of the street, and Cindy and I were on the other. We were motioning for her to stay put, and she thought we were calling her to cross the street. She stepped into the street without looking and was just missed by a speeding car. I can't even think about all we would have missed if every parent's worst fear had been realized that day. Thank you,

God, for sparing us the agony either of those two events would have brought to our family.

During this time in my early civilian career and our family's young, vibrant years, we also had our house in Corvallis, which we needed to rent. We interviewed prospective renters and chose a young couple who presented themselves very well. After six months or so, their rent payments came later and later until they stopped coming altogether. Phone calls resulted in empty promises until finally their phone was disconnected. We had no choice but to drive the six hours to Corvallis. What we found was a disaster! The couple had abandoned our house and left the garage door open. A strong wind had come through the valley in which the house was located and blew the chimney and part of the garage roof off. We needed to arrange for insurance and repairs, all on a three-day weekend, as well as clean up as much of the house as we were able.

In the middle of all that, Cindy talked to some neighbors who told her the name of the moving trailer the couple had obviously rented to move their effects out of the house. Cindy then drove into Corvallis and explained things to the man who owned the rental company. He said he had to honor the confidentiality of his clients. However, having sympathy for Cindy, he told her he needed to go down the street for a while to get some coffee, and his files would be left unattended. Cindy found the address to which the couple had moved. They were very surprised when they answered the door to see us standing there. They owed us three months' rent and an explanation. We received one month's rent and a bunch of empty promises, which they never honored. So much for our ability to judge character. Luckily, we were able to sell the house within six months and make a profit.

Another investment we made during our time in Washington state was the purchase of property in Cle Elum, Washington, which was to be developed. It took quite some time, but that investment finally did pay off, even though the final lot sold after we moved to our next home in Arizona. One of my favorite photos ever is of the girls when we went to visit the property, which shows Alyssa amazed by a large cocoon of some type. Like that cocoon, there were many things to marvel at while we lived in the Northwest, like hearing Mount St. Helens erupt, experiencing a total eclipse of the sun, and seeing the northern lights. With respect to Mount St. Helens, I have a photo in my study taken when I climbed Mt. Rainier with some friends. The photo is of me and Lonnie Pierson, the Richland High School wrestling coach and a good friend, on top of Mt. Rainier. In the background of that picture is Mount St. Helens. That same photo taken today would look very different, as it has taken decades for the land around the volcano to begin to recover from a massive eruption in 1980. Richland was on the edge of the plume of ash from the volcano, which moved toward and engulfed Spokane. I was in the backyard doing some gardening when the eruption occurred and I heard what sounded like a sonic boom, which is honestly what I thought it was because there was an Air Force base about 60 miles north of the Tri-Cities, and sonic booms were not uncommon.

Soon, the sky began to darken and the radio informed us of what was happening. The dark sky turned into what I can only describe as a collection of clouds that looked like a head of cauliflower. As the ash began to fall, conflicting directions were provided over the radio with respect to how to how local residents should protect their cars if they couldn't be put in a garage. It was actually kind of funny: "Brush it off. No, hose it off. No, blow it off. No, leave it alone." Our daughters brushed the sidewalks and collected the ash in several canning jars. Later, when we went to Ohio to visit my parents, my dad gave the girls empty medicine vials of different sizes, which he had cleaned. They parceled the ash into the vials and set up a stand in the driveway to sell the ash to my dad's customers. They made about $50!

Like the volcanic eruption, the solar eclipse created sensory memories for us all. The eclipse of the sun was truly spectacular. The radio played the theme from the movie *Space Odyssey 2001*, and we looked at the sun for Halley's Beads, created by the sun shining through the craters on the facing edge of the moon, when the moon completely covers the sun. There were some magnificent photographs taken on top of Rattlesnake Mountain during the eclipse. However, those photos were government property, and we could only look at some that a neighbor had brought home to show everyone.

In Washington, Mother Nature rarely disappointed. The Northern Lights were fascinating. They looked like an undulating purple curtain hanging in the sky.

During this period of my life, I tackled another "first" — redoing the bodywork on my GTO and then rebuilding the engine. Fortunately, I had friends who helped guide me through that adventure, but the crux of my education in this regard was reading books on how to do it. Besides savvy friends, the key is to have the right tools. I bought or rented those tools under the supervision and with the advice of those friends. I was quite proud of the finished product and hated to sell the car a few years later when we were preparing to move to Arizona and when gas prices had skyrocketed to 75 cents per gallon. That experience gave me the confidence to do other major repairs on cars — that is, until cars became so electronically sophisticated, which essentially ended the days of backyard mechanics.

Alas, we were on to the next big step in our lives — leaving Westinghouse and Richland and joining Combustion Engineering (CE) as the startup manager for the Palo Verde Nuclear Station in Arizona. But to set the stage for what I'm about to share with you about my time at CE, I need to first tell you a bit more about the work situation at FFTF. I had been there for three years as the shift manager for C Crew when there was a major problem that occurred during the calibration, grooming, and alignment (CG&A) phase of testing. One of the three in-vessel handling machines (IVHMs) was run up against the stops and then the hoist chain, which supported the machine, broke. That IVHM then freewheeled down to the bottom of the core, where it came to rest in a broken state. The IVHMs were used to insert and remove fuel assemblies from the core. They were very large, robust machines that could be accurately positioned over an assembly in the in-core storage position after the fuel assembly had been lowered into that position from outside the reactor vessel. The IVHM could then lift the fuel assembly and transport it to the desired position in the core, then lower it down into that vacant spot and disengage. It could also retrieve a spent fuel assembly and transport it from the core to the in-vessel storage, where it could be retrieved by the external handling machine and taken to a special cell for examination or out of the reactor containment for subsequent storage and disposal.

When the mishap occurred, the CG&A was taking place in air. In other words, the reactor vessel had not yet been raised in temperature using hot air, or inerted (i.e., the air environment replaced with hot argon gas) or loaded with sodium, which takes place after the inerting.

This incident was a major upset to the startup program. It was decided that I would take over the Refueling Group to lead the recovery from that situation and lead Refueling for the rest of the reactor startup. This turn of events set the stage for the rest of my life and was the first of eight times when I was called in as a member of the new management team or as the leader to recover a severely troubled project, plant, or organization. In this case, the Refueling Group was on the critical path for the FFTF startup for the next two years. Besides recovering from the IVHM incident, Refueling was always on the firing line. We had to test the equipment in air, then hot air, then argon, then hot argon, and finally in hot sodium. Many pieces of equipment had to be developed or modified to accomplish the task. Once this was done and the plant was ready for power ascension, Refueling had to accomplish the initial core load. Then once the core was loaded and power ascension started, the reactor was very slowly raised in power level. As each new designated power level was achieved, the reactor would be shut down and the core shuffled to some extent, and old experiments removed to be replaced with new experiments. Fortunately, I had a good group of engineers, some older, some younger, all very competent and dedicated. I could also relate to the operations organization, having come from there myself. It was a tough two years with the Refueling Group on the FFTF startup critical path, but we bonded as a group and my reputation as a problem solver grew in the Westinghouse organization (which served me well at later junctions in my career).

This turn of events set the stage for the rest of my life and was the first of eight times when I was called in as a member of the new management team or as the leader to recover a severely troubled project, plant, or organization.

One thing that bears mentioning — which I did not appreciate or understand at the time — is that Cindy suffered her second bout of depression, which lasted almost a year. (Her first episode was in Charleston, of which I was also not aware.) Fortunately, she lived out the rest of her beautiful life without ever being again in what she referred to as "that dark place," even during her courageous ALS odyssey. One of the things that contributed to her depression was my job. As refueling manager on FFTF, I was on a critical path for two years with seemingly one crisis after another. Cindy could tell when I was on my way home because the phone would start to ring (that was before cell phones), and it would ring all night long — with colleagues needing my input with time-sensitive problems. Even when I wasn't at work, I was always at work. I finally got smart enough to move the phone out of the bedroom, so Cindy didn't have to listen to the conversations, some of which were relatively heated.

During this era, my daughters were feeling the pressure too. I needed to help them understand it wouldn't last forever. So one day I came home with two pieces of paper to show them. One contained a single-line schedule for putting the reactor together and then putting fuel in it. The other piece of paper was a drawing of the reactor core. I told Cindy and the girls when we got to a certain point on the schedule line, my responsibility would be fulfilled, and things would be a lot less hectic. That "light at the end of the tunnel" speech, as Cindy likes to call it, helped her a lot and hopefully the girls as well.

After the FFTF startup was complete, it was obvious that there was an overabundance of highly qualified managers, engineers, and technicians. I began to wonder what the future held for me, knowing that competition was going to be heavy for the next level of management, and I had accomplished all that I needed to as the refueling manager. Fortunately, it's all about who you know. One of the startup engineers with whom I had developed a good relationship was contacted by a classmate of his from the Naval Academy, and that former classmate was looking for a startup manager for the Palo Verde Nuclear Station in Arizona. My friend wasn't interested but he suggested that I would be just right for the position. That recommendation led to an interview with his classmate and subsequent interviews back in Windsor, Connecticut, where the corporate headquarters for Combustion Engineering (CE) were located.

CE was the designer of the System 80 plant and provider of the fuel for that reactor design. They were known as the Nuclear Steam Supply System (NSSS) supplier, and they needed to have a strong presence on the Arizona site for construction and startup of each of the three nuclear reactor power plants. The plants were being built by Bechtel Corporation for Arizona Public Power Supply (APS), which would be the operator. The plants were also being funded by Southern California Gas and Electric (SCG&E). My job would be to assemble and lead the group that would represent CE, and advise both Bechtel and APS through the construction, initial fuel receipt, fuel load, and startup of the three reactors. By the way, Palo Verde, which served California as well as Arizona, is the largest generator of electricity from nuclear power in the United States. With its three 1,350-MW plants, after Chernobyl in Russia was shut down, Palo Verde became one of the largest-capacity nuclear generation sites in the world.

I was quite excited about the prospect of this responsibility. I was also more than a little intimidated. Professionally, my thinking was that I had liquid-sodium cooled, fast-breeder reactor experience, and the job at Palo Verde would give me commercial nuclear experience. Those two experiences, if I was successful in this new job, would put me in the catbird seat for the first commercial fast-breeder reactor designated to be built at Clinch River, Tennessee. Was I up to the job? Did I have enough experience gained from FFTF and the Navy? Could I win over the new people with whom I would be interfacing? What were the relationships like between and among APS, Bechtel, and CE? (I had certainly seen tough management negotiations between Westinghouse, Bechtel, and the AEC at FFTF.) These were the questions running through my mind.

Was I up to the job? Did I have enough experience gained from FFTF and the Navy? Could I win over the new people with whom I would be interfacing?

Personally, the decision was even tougher. As a family, we were very happy in Richland. Erin had close friends she had developed over the course of her grade school days. Jason Lee had proved to be an excellent school for her, and we anticipated the same for Alyssa. Cindy was active in the community with the Parent Teacher Association (PTA), with the church vestry, in community theater, and soccer. She had developed a close network of friends during the seven years we had lived in Richland. I had also made many friends both through work and through activities in the community, mainly wrestling coaching and officiating. We enjoyed the Northwest lifestyle and the Columbia River. There was a lot to consider.

At the time, we had a round kitchen table made out of Tiger Oak, and this table was the scene of lots of family decisions, birthday-cake cutting, homework, and other projects. I had learned the decision analysis tool at work, which was basically giving relative weights to the desired outcomes of the decision and then determining how well each alternative option satisfied those desires. Cindy and I involved the girls in this process, even though they could not fully understand it. The involvement did make them feel like they were part of the family decision process and their concerns were being taken into consideration. **I think that helped them feel like they had a modicum of control, which always helps people in any situation.**

Cindy and I ultimately decided that life is an adventure, and we were ready to try something different even though we were very comfortable in Richland. So, I went to my Westinghouse management and asked for their advice. I figured if they got upset with me for considering this obvious opportunity, that action would help me with the decision. **This practice of talking to one's management before making a financial and emotional decision is a practice I have suggested to others throughout my career.** Something very gratifying happened then, which was that various levels of Westinghouse management tried to talk me out of leaving. They were courteous, professional, and helpful, and did give me some things to dial into my decision process. Ultimately, we decided to take the plunge, but I burned no bridges at Westinghouse, sending all levels of management a very complimentary letter of resignation.

Richland had been our first experience in civilian life, and it was rather idealistic. Richland was a very family-oriented community, and it was a good time for our family. We were as close as we ever were and did a lot of things together. Erin's grade school years were very good for her and provided a sound base upon which to build. For me, it may have been captured in a school performance when she was in the fourth grade, and her class sang "You Light Up My Life." That innocence and tranquility would never be the same. It was a time when the parent-and-child relationship was one of unadulterated love, and when our parental direction and values were not challenged. (Erin did, however, put her foot down ultimately on taking ballet, which, to her mother's dismay, she hated.)

I don't think Alyssa had quite the same experience in her grade school days in Phoenix. On the other hand, I think Alyssa's school experience in Port Clinton, Ohio, which was to come, may have been better than Erin's junior high and high school experience in Phoenix. Would Erin and Alyssa have had different and better experiences if we had stayed in Richland? It's impossible to know, but we were fortunate to have been there at the time we were. My only regret is that maybe I didn't relish those years enough.

While we were in Richland, Cindy and I had decided to capture — in a little memory book of sorts —the things the girls said and did. Even though the book reflects mostly our time in Richland, the girls — grown adults with children of their own now — still love to read that book when they visit. Here are two examples of things we captured. One such saying came from Erin when I hopped out of my car when returning from work, and she was playing in the driveway. I said, "Hi, Erin. What do you know?" not really expecting an answer, just a greeting. However, she replied, "I know snakes do not crawl in wet cement." I still have no idea where that came from!

Another time, I was studying for my graduate class when Alyssa came into my den and asked if we could go get some ice cream. I said no, that I had work to do. About 15 or 20 minutes later, she came back and asked again. This time, I was a little firmer, frustrated at having been interrupted from my concentration. When she did this a third time, I spoke harshly that if she interrupted me again, she was going to get a spanking. She thought for a moment and then, with her hands on her hips, said, "I guess I will keep my shoes on in case we go somewhere!" I wilted under that determination, closed my book, and took her to Baskin Robbins. When she graduated from college, we gave her a plaque with those words, "I guess I will keep my shoes on," engraved on it.

Phoenix, Arizona (1981-1986)

I joined CE and immediately entered into indoctrination on the company, the System 80 plant (which was the design of Palo Verde), and commercial startup. This entailed making trips back to Windsor, Connecticut, to meet my new management and the project management team for whom I would actually be working. The startup group warned me to be leery of the project management group, but I instantly took a liking to Chuck Ferguson, who was the lead for the Palo Verde project. He and several of his direct reports have become lifelong friends.

Of course, I had to go to Palo Verde to meet Ron Ahearns, who was one of three test engineers who constituted the group I inherited. Over the next several years, I grew that group to 60 engineers and technicians. I also spent three months at the San Onfre plant near San Diego, learning the CE plant there.

While I was doing all this traveling, Cindy was busy getting ready to move the girls and working to sell our house in Richland. We were fortunate that the house sold quickly. At the time, we had four cars and we needed to sell two of them. We decided to keep the Volvo station wagon and the Fiat Spider, and to sell the Datsun and the GTO. Selling the GTO broke my heart. Not only was that car a reminder of the initial GTO gift my dad gave me when I graduated from the Naval Academy, it also represented my youth before the responsibilities of family. I'd also put a lot of work into that car. But gas was expensive, and I was now the "responsible" adult and family man. So, it was station-wagon time.

When it was time to leave Richland, we decided to make a vacation of the trip to Arizona. We went down the Columbia Gorge for the last time, introduced Alyssa to Corvallis, and then took I-5 into California. We stopped to see the Redwoods and visited San Francisco. We stopped in Carmel and had our picture taken at the Lonely Cypress. That photo and the earlier ones taken there showed the evolution of two young people into a family of four. We visited my friend from the Naval Academy, Chris Manger, and his family in Los Angeles. We went to the beach with his family, and the girls got to put their toes in the Pacific Ocean.

Then we headed to Phoenix. It didn't take Cindy long to find a house that seemed to fit the Arizona lifestyle. It was in an established neighborhood with the requisite swimming pool and good schools nearby. Within a year, we became dissatisfied with it for a variety of reasons and found a wonderful house in a newer neighborhood, nearer to work, and in an even better school district. That home became the model for a house we subsequently built when we moved to Cliff Road on Catawba Island in Ohio.

I had learned a lot about CE in the first three months, but now I had to learn the System 80 plant in-depth and, at the same time, represent CE in negotiations with APS and Bechtel management. Ron Ahearns initially resented me because he thought he should have had the startup manager job because of his CE startup experience. But I eventually won him over. We ultimately made a pretty good team. We also needed to interface with the CE construction manager, who needed to turn the responsibility for CE systems over to startup as construction completed. As usual, that process had a built-in conflict; construction was motivated to turn the systems over and startup didn't want to accept something that wasn't ready for testing and operation. The real transfer of responsibility rested between Bechtel and APS, but that meant CE was frequently caught in between the two, as they argued about who was responsible for what.

As our responsibilities and credibility on-site increased, I needed more help. I decided some of the best people for the job were back at Hanford, so I began to recruit the best of the best. It didn't hurt that they were also friends. I was able to convince Herb Coulter, Dave Gerkensmeyer, Larry Daggert, Phil Parker, and Dick Getz to come join me. I would have gone after a few more, but Bill Moffitt called me and suggested I might not want to completely burn my bridges to Westinghouse and, therefore, should stop taking their (best) people. He was right, and so I did stop. However, I am honored that these men followed me to Arizona. **I also learned that the real key in getting someone to join you in an endeavor, besides your credibility with them, is your credibility with the spouse. The spouse should be wooed as much as, if not more than, the candidate.** The fact that these families agreed to take a chance, based on their faith in me as well as in themselves, makes me feel good to this very day. Herb, Dave, Larry, Phil, and Dick added incredibly to the value APS and Bechtel had for our team.

Not long after we arrived in Arizona, I learned that a friend of mine from the Naval Academy had come back to his hometown of Phoenix after getting out of the Navy and started his own construction business. His name was Bob Gosnell and he had built large resort complexes known as the Point Resorts. Bob was obviously an astute businessman, but also still a party animal like he was back when he was a year ahead of me in the same company at Annapolis. We had a lot of fun with Bob, and there are a number of stories to tell. The best one I only vaguely remember was one New Year's Eve at the North Point, when I met a couple vacationing from Kansas at a swim-up pool bar where you sit on underwater barstools. They were in their bathing suits, and I had entered the pool in a three-piece business suit. I don't know how I got there or how I got home, but I do remember coming down the stairs the next day with a tremendous hangover and announcing, "I am not a low-grade man," which was a line from a Mickey Rooney movie.

Once Cindy got the girls settled in the neighborhood and their schools, she started to investigate her own interests. Erin soon found her way onto an elite girls' soccer team, and from that contact Cindy and I found ourselves on several over-30 adult soccer teams — in Cindy's case, both indoor and outdoor. Cindy also began playing tennis and made some good friends. One of the tennis friends, Kathy Sullivan, became Cindy's partner in selling real estate. (Cindy and Kathy had decided to get their real estate licenses together.) Cindy also got her first Jaguar, in which she enjoyed driving prospective clients around to look at houses.

When I tried to help Cindy prepare for her real estate exam, which had a little math in it, she ended up in tears. The same thing happened when I tried to help Erin with her math when she moved into high school. Some years later, the scene repeated itself with Alyssa. Getting a little ahead of the story, the funny thing was that this pattern repeated again and again, of me tutoring math and leaving my students in tears. Down the road, as to the new corporate director of nuclear services at Davis-Besse in Independence, Ohio, I ended up sharing an apartment part of the week with a guy I knew from Sandusky. His name was Bobby James and he was a former small college All-American football player. He told me his boys were struggling in school with math and science. Bobby had the great idea, based on my engineering degrees, that I would teach him math and science before the weekend when he had the boys, and then he would pass the information on to them. One night, I called Cindy to tell her that Bobby was in tears, just like she and the girls were earlier. More recently (February 2014), I tried to help my grandson, Carson, with his math over the telephone, and he ended up in tears as well. So much for being a teacher.

Math might not have come naturally to my entire family, but sports did. Erin made the select girls' soccer team for the west side of Phoenix. She was not the best athlete on the team but, as a result of the Richland experience, could dribble, pass, and shoot with either foot equally well, something most of the other girls could not do nearly as well. She had a good head for the game and just seemed to be in the right place at the right time. She did well for the time we were in Phoenix, especially indoors. She also played for her high school, but it was difficult for me to get to her games because my work was over 70 miles from her school. (Although we lived in a west side suburb of Phoenix, it was still a long trek into the desert to get to the site of the Palo Verde nuclear station.)

As I said, Cindy and I both played in over-30 adult indoor leagues, some same-sex leagues and some coed leagues. Cindy played outdoors as well, and her skills continued to improve. We played on the same indoor coed team. During one breakaway, I passed the ball to the player on my left, who touched it back to me. I touched it to Cindy on my right, who was wide open for a shot because the goalie had not yet recovered, but she passed it back to me. I was covered and we lost the opportunity. As we were trotting back to our end of the arena, I said, "Sweetheart, when you are open, take the shot." To which she replied, "Shut your fat mouth!" We never again played on the same line after that exchange. ("Sweetheart ..." may not have been my exact words. Too long ago to be sure.)

Alyssa, unlike her sister Erin, didn't enjoy soccer much. She wanted to try her hand at every sport that came across her horizon. She was in swimming, soccer, softball, tennis, volleyball, and even high jumping for track. It was obvious she had the same ability to anticipate in tennis that Erin had in soccer. To prepare her for her track meet, I set up a high-jump pit in the garden compost pile and tried to show her how to do the Fosbury Flop (the dominant style of high-jumping, popularized by Olympian Dick Fosbury). Despite my instruction, somehow she caught on and placed well in her meets.

Work was proceeding well, and I was able to build the billable (to APS) staff up from the original four (counting me) to about 60. We had our hands full with three units in various stages of construction, preparing for fuel receipt and eventual fuel loading, and testing the equipment as it was turned over from Bechtel to APS. CE had to support both companies in all phases and answer questions about all the equipment we provided, which was essentially the primary plant equipment and instrumentation. The System 80 plant was designed around the European version but with larger components to achieve an increase in power output. Unfortunately, scaling up equipment can lead to unforeseen problems.

Things were going well until we took the reactor head off after pre-core load hot functional testing of Unit 1. This testing is to check out all the primary equipment before fuel load. The fact that there was no core loaded significantly decreased the resistance the primary pumps experienced. The additional flow rate had several ramifications.

When we took the reactor head off and peered inside the core, we saw chunks of the reactor coolant pump impellers lying in the bottom of the core. As we lifted our gaze up to the top of the upper guide structure, even from approximately 20 feet away, we could see cracks in the structure. I went back to my office to report the findings to the project lead in Windsor, Chuck Ferguson. After that phone call, I sat in my office saying to myself, *"It can't get much worse than this."*

In a few minutes, I found out I was wrong. While we were finishing unit 1 pre-core hot functional testing, we were also testing the Unit 1 low-pressure safety injection (LPSI) pumps that CE provided. The lead test engineer came into my office to inform me that, every so often, the pump would not start but instead tripped on electrical overload. He could not explain why.

Needless to say, APS was not very happy, and I was on the firing seat. Carl Andognini, who was the vice president of operations, was screaming at me almost daily in the planning meetings to get this equipment fixed. (We later became pretty good friends.) Luckily, CE back in Windsor did a good job of analyzing the problems. With their insights, we determined the impellers came apart because the welded design could not handle the larger size and associated greater force on the welds. We went to a completely forged impeller to solve that issue. The upper guide structure was just a matter of eliminating the harmonic vibration, which was set up during pre-core functional high flow rates. We could have just calculated that this would not happen with the core loaded but decided to weld a few blocks on the structure that would eliminate the harmonic vibration at all flow rates possible to be experienced under all conceivable conditions. The LPSI pump issue was more elusive but we finally determined that the larger size of the motor and increased length of motor/pump shaft caused the shaft to bend when starting up. Sometimes, the bending shaft would seize on the ware ring (which supported the spinning shaft) and the motor could not overcome that restriction and would trip on overload (drawing too much electrical current). The fix was to make the shaft stouter.

These problems cost the startup about six months, they cost CE considerable money, and they cost APS potential loss of revenue. But we endured. As a team, we demonstrated dedication and resiliency, as well as some superb engineering analysis. At the conclusion of this exercise, it was decided that with the three plants in various stages of construction completion, turnover, acceptance testing, integrated testing, fuel receipt and load, and power ascension, CE needed one person who could speak for all aspects. I was chosen to be the CE site manager and have the CE construction manager report to me, as well as the nuclear engineering analysis and test groups. It was a significant increase in responsibility, and I am sure the opportunity was offered to me, in part, because APS and Bechtel appreciated my tenacity during the preceding problems and their resolutions. I had to win the construction manager over, but he came around and we worked well together.

As the startups proceeded, we ran into an issue with parts. To some degree, you have to expect that components might not survive ship-ment, construction, and/or testing. And it's a challenge to main-tain the right kinds of spares, in the right numbers, stored in the correct conditions. Too many spare parts represent wasted money and storage. Too little and things can come to a grinding halt while replacements are located and shipped. This situation has become exacerbated in the nuclear industry, due to the extremely stringent and frequently unique quality-control requirements. The number of vendors willing to meet those requirements has dropped to less than a third of the number when nuclear was in its heyday in the 1960s and 1970s (before Three Mile Island and Jimmy Carter). For Unit 1 and then Unit 2 startups to proceed on schedule in the face of these challenges, parts were sometimes "borrowed" from Unit 3 (because its startup was considered further in the future and there was assumed time to obtain replacements for the confiscated parts). Well, what is done in the dead of night in the name of expe-diency is not always done correctly. There were times we would go to a Unit 3 instrument cabinet and find a handwritten note that simply said, "Thanks." We ultimately inventoried the entire plant and placed replacement orders as far in advance of the potential need as possible.

What is done in the dead of night in the name of expediency is not always done correctly.

When Unit 1 was online and Unit 2 was nearing power ascension completion, I began to think about my next job. The one thing I knew was that I didn't want to become the CE site representative after Unit 3 startup was complete. I would have liked to have been appointed site manager on the plant that CE was selling to South Korea, but that deal had not yet been finalized. There was no guarantee the deal would go through or that I would be chosen as the site manager, despite the fact that the plant would be identical to the Palo Verde units.

While these thoughts were on my mind, I came across an article in *Nuclear News* about Davis-Besse (D-B), a nuclear plant about 30 miles from Sandusky, Ohio, my hometown. D-B had been shut down by the NRC for operational issues. I called the man who had been brought in to lead the recovery of the plant, one Admiral Joe Williams, Jr., U.S. Navy Retired. I explained who I was and that I grew up in Sandusky. He said to stop by to see him the next time I visited my parents. I quickly arranged a trip back to Windsor and scheduled a stop to see my parents on the way back. I then scheduled a meeting with the Admiral, as he liked to be called. He hired me on the spot. However, there were some little obstacles yet to overcome — like a formal offer and a negotiated salary. More important, it was family decision time.

This decision was complicated by the fact that Erin was just finishing her junior year in high school. However, she had more than enough credits to graduate and we encouraged her to apply for college. She did. She applied to Arizona and Arizona State, and we applied to Ohio State, Ohio University, Miami of Ohio, and a small college in Kentucky. Erin, who was a good student, was accepted to all of them. I told her she could go wherever she wanted; I would pay for Miami University, Ohio. She went there, got a good education, loved the college, and ended up being placed in her first job through the school.

Once again, I was leaving one company to go to another company. I was determined to not burn any bridges with CE, especially because I really liked the project team from Windsor corporate, for whom I had worked, as well as the team I had assembled at Palo Verde. My replacement had to be chosen as CE site manager and that led to a little consternation because I didn't recommend the construction manager who thought he should have been chosen. CE corporate went with my recommendation, which made me feel good. Many of those same people are friends today, even in retirement.

The Palo Verde experience was a good one. Not only did I have to learn a new nuclear plant system and how to lead a nuclear startup, I also had to learn how to negotiate at the executive level because I was the senior CE person on the site. The experience was made even more challenging because CE was frequently between Bechtel and APS, and those could be treacherous waters to navigate. But I must have done something right, as many of my colleagues from APS and Bechtel remained friends and references for years to come.

Phoenix was the first metropolitan area in which Cindy and I had ever lived. At first, it was invigorating and exciting. But five years later, we were ready to leave. In a big city, there was a certain anonymity that seemed to breed indifference. Many of Erin's and Alyssa's friends' parents were divorced, at a time when divorce was relatively rare in other regions of the United States — like Richland

and, as we were about to find out, Port Clinton, Ohio, and Catawba Island as well. Given the choice, Cindy and I preferred smaller communities where people may know your business sometimes a little more than you desire, but they also seem to care about you and your family a lot more. Kids have a lot more trouble getting away with mischief in a smaller community. Still, Phoenix was a unique experience in our lives and, overall, I am glad we had it. While living there, we made time to get away from the city when we could. We spent every Thanksgiving at the Grand Canyon and we all unexpectedly fell in love with the place. We loved the stars at that altitude and the grandeur of the Canyon. Cindy and I hiked to Havasu Falls near the bottom of the Canyon with some friends, which was a memorable trip. As a family, we also loved Bryce Canyon and other western spots.

As I recount my favorite memories from our time in Arizona, I'm reminded of a morning when I was traveling along the two-lane country roads, which have deep irrigation ditches on either side and cotton fields beyond the ditches. It was very early in the morning and still dark outside. I came upon a car with its back wheels in the ditch, and I stopped because there was a black lady waving me down. I judged her to be in her late 30s or early 40s and, from the smell of her, I also guessed she had been drinking. Her situation, however, was sobering her up fast. She asked if I could help. I thought that if the back end of the car could just be lifted a little, the tires might be able to get traction. Fortunately, there was very little water in the ditch, so I instructed her to get in the car, roll down the window, start the motor, and on my command, put the car in gear and give it just a little gas. I jumped down in the ditch, told her to start the car, and then I lifted the back end with a military press. With the car's back end raised so the tires were resting on the edge of the ditch wall, I told her to put the car in gear and gently press on the gas pedal. She did, and it worked. In retrospect, it may not have been the wisest approach to the situation, but it worked.

When I got out of the ditch, she thanked me profusely and offered me some money. I said no but asked her to pass along the ability to help someone if she had the opportunity in the future. It was a time in America when many white people would not have stopped to help a stranded black motorist, and I like to think that maybe my gesture helped race relations a little.

While most of my Phoenix stories that didn't involve work were ones like random situations on the way *to or from* work, Cindy had several interesting experiences and new hobbies during this period of our lives. She not only played soccer but also worked out at the local gym, where she one day met a guy who was training for the upcoming Mr. Arizona bodybuilding contest. He asked Cindy to be his choreographer for his posing routine. At the same time, I was injured, could not work out, and felt like the Pillsbury doughboy. When I met her "student," even I had to admit he was gorgeous and nicely muscular. When I asked him how he got interested in bodybuilding, he said he started lifting weights when he was in prison! But Cindy was fine with her hours in the gym with him in his tiny performing jock. In the end, he won the Mr. Arizona contest in Tucson (to which Cindy took several of her girlfriends) and he also got first place in the best poser category. Cindy had suggested the theme song for his posing, which was "Chariots of Fire," so she was very happy.

During this same period in Phoenix, Cindy was working at an art gallery selling art and, while on a plane ride back from the Dallas Trade Center show, met Arthur Court, the designer of beautiful metal gifts and tableware. He invited her to come stay in his condo in San Francisco or, as Cindy would say, "His beautifully appointed apartment, which he provided for guests, right across from Ghirardelli Square." There they could discuss opening a showroom in Phoenix. Of course, I stayed home to babysit while she went on this trip.

Cindy was fearless about traveling, even without her family or when alone. She once went to Hollywood with a girlfriend and ended up going to a producer's mansion to "see his etchings." He later sent her an original poster of a movie he produced, *Invaders from Mars*, one of my favorite childhood movies. Once again, I was at home, but I trusted her implicitly. I would later find out that she wasn't as comfortable with me traveling with other women.

Catawba Island, Ohio (The First Time; 1986-1990)

While Cindy was dealing with all the aspects of moving again, drawing once more upon her Army brat experience, I was returning to my parents' home as an adult. Although it resulted in a 40-mile drive to work, it did save on lodging expenses. It also afforded me an opportunity to get to know my parents a little better while I waited for Cindy and the girls to join me in Ohio. After I left for the Naval Academy, my visits home became less and less frequent. At first, they usually entailed entertaining a Naval Academy buddy or partying with former high school friends, with my parents taking a backseat to those activities. Then it was opportunistic visits as Cindy and I passed from one side of the country to the other with our children. Now it was just the three of us at home every night because all my siblings were out of the house by now. We had some good conversations and got to know each other on a different level, for which I am still grateful.

While I was staying with my parents, my dad brought me over to Catawba Island, part of the Ottawa County peninsula, which extended into Lake Erie. Growing up in Sandusky, the name of the "island" was vaguely familiar to me. As a teenager, we used to go over to nearby Gem Beach to meet girls at a teenage dance hall. As I recall, we rarely made any connection with the fairer sex, but the pursuit

was exciting at the time. Anyway, my dad took me to Cliff Road, and
I was immediately thrilled. It was so beautiful I could not believe
I had never been there before. We rounded a curve in the road and
there, sitting back off the road, was a nice white ranch house with
a big sloping yard and a beautiful view.

I cannot believe I did this, but I asked my dad to let me out of the car,
and I walked up to the door and knocked. This huge man opened
the door, and I asked if he wanted to sell his house. He looked at me
like I had just dropped in from outer space and then said, "Sure." Of
course, that the price he gave me on the spot was astronomical. Little
did I know then that Tom Goebel and his wife, Mim, would ultimately
become our neighbors. Eventually, when Cindy and the girls arrived,
we rented a house on Cliff Road and bought two lots right next door
to Tom and Mim. We built a house there, the only one of the 17 we
owned over the course of our moving around in support of my career
that we actually designed (Cindy did the designing) and built (Cindy
supervised the construction). We met the owner of the lots, Vern
Hakes, through a realtor, and he thought we would make good neighbors. Vern and his wife, Evy, became friends of ours, and it was many
years later that Cindy and I would attend Vern's funeral after we had
retired to this very street, just a few houses down. But that story will
come later.

Living with my parents as an adult was a blessing. It was nice to be
able, each evening, to spend a little time talking as adults. I really
liked my parents and enjoyed that time. My dad took advantage of my
presence every time he had responsibility to provide the speaker for
his Kiwanis Club. He thought it was time they heard about nuclear
power, so I was always asked to come speak. Most of these older
gentlemen slept through my talks, including my dad.

When I would go for a drive with my dad, he would tell me to slow
down, that I no longer lived in Arizona. I got pulled over coming

home from work one night, and when I got to my parents' house, my dad said, "You have a little trouble coming home, Dave?" It turned out that Dad had a police monitor in his office and picked up the report of an Amerine being pulled over, and he knew it wasn't him.

Work was intense. Toledo Edison needed to address issues that had caused it to almost emulate the Three Mile Island reactor accident. The NRC had shut the reactor down and labeled D-B (my new employer) the worst plant in the country. The Admiral, who had a reputation for no-nonsense, had been brought in to recover the plant as quickly as possible. He, in turn, hired some of the most alpha-type males imaginable as his direct staff. These guys were all smart, aggressive, hardworking, and, in many cases, hard-drinking as well.

The Admiral was not worried about building a team; he was concerned with action and mostly action that complied with his will. Fortunately, he knew what he was doing, and most of the NRC commissioners at that time were ex-Navy captains and admirals who had worked for Admiral Williams when they were in the Navy.

Admiral Williams was a firebrand who didn't suffer fools kindly. He was old-school authoritarian on the management style continuum. He wouldn't hesitate to chew out anyone who disappointed him, and it didn't matter who heard it or how embarrassing it was. Because I was on the receiving end more than once, I got up the courage to ask him whatever happened to the axiom "praise in public, chastise in private?"

He said, "Look, when I'm chewing someone out, I'm not attacking him personally. I'm addressing [a loose use of that word] what he did or did not do. At the same time I am calibrating him to my expectations, I am also calibrating everyone within earshot."

I observed him the next time he was in a tirade and his description of his approach was, more or less, accurate if one listened closely. However, **the problem was that his underlings tried to imitate him without that subtle understanding and usually attacked the person and made them feel horrible.** That behavior may have contributed to the reluctance of people to bring up issues that eventually led to problems D-B experienced over a decade later. There were suspected issues that were not raised and, therefore, not pursued that resulted in the reactor head having to be replaced. The corrective action program (CAP) labyrinth may have contributed, but the reluctance to go outside the system for possible fear of reprimand also contributed. **By the way, I later called an unresponsive CAP system "hierarchical suffocation."** It was not intimidation by retaliation, but it could be just as deadly.

As I said, the staff the Admiral had assembled was very good technically and dedicated to the task. However, they were all vying for position because they knew the Admiral would retire once D-B was back on line. They looked for any opportunity to practice one-upmanship and embarrass each other. I was still learning the ropes of a new position but also a new reactor plant technology. I had to find ways to exert the authority of my position without invoking outright hostility. Many of my colleagues were win-lose personalities — that is to say, you had to lose for them to feel they had won. They didn't necessarily look for win-win possibilities.

One very intimidating person was the new maintenance manager. I had been there less than two months when he called me up and, using loud, foul language, basically said I was no better than the guy I replaced. I slammed the phone down and went into the Admiral's office to say I was going to kick the maintenance manager's ass, to which the Admiral said, without even looking at me, "Don't do it on site." By the time I got to the maintenance manager's office, I had calmed down, but I closed the door and said, "We can either address this issue like gentlemen and find a mutual solution, or I will be glad to meet you behind the Barn (a nearby bar) to settle it with our fists." Now the maintenance manager was about twice my size, but he knew that I had been a wrestler. Thankfully, he opted for diplomacy. The story circulated rapidly and, for that time and place, seemed to gain me some measure of respect in the workforce. Steve and I became good friends.

Although Cindy ultimately grew to love Catawba Island, it turned out not to be an easy transition for her. She was jerked out of the cosmopolitan atmosphere of the big city of Phoenix and plopped down in rural northern Ohio. Although not an actual reoccurrence of previously mentioned depression, she was in a deep funk for about three months. Additionally, she was sad that Erin had left for college a year earlier than what Cindy had anticipated. She was in a period of mourning and was in bed three days crying after we returned from taking Erin to Miami University in Oxford, Ohio.

I was not too sensitive to Cindy's general malaise and, for once, that insensitivity may have worked for us instead of against us. After about three months of moping and complaining, I finally told her to get over it. We were here, and I had a tough enough job without her adding to my stress. Well, she seemed to snap right out of it. She wrote a poem to herself describing her sadness at not being able to appreciate the beauty right outside her window and how she was determined to once again find joy in beauty. I think it helped when we agreed to buy a property to build a house, an endeavor many of our friends warned us not to do, but an activity to which Cindy dedicated herself. She also started her own interior decorating business while she was also serving as general contractor on our new house. Alyssa started school in the sixth grade so the duties of motherhood and community that came with that enabled Cindy to find her old energy and enthusiasm. Her beautiful smile returned.

Back to work and the Admiral. Although we were making good progress in the eyes of the NRC, every day was a struggle. I asked the Admiral if we should consider some sort of team building for the senior management. His reply was, "I am not interested in harmony. I am only interested in progress." He practiced what I later characterized as the Pol Pot approach to culture change. Pol Pot was the notorious 20th Century leader of the Khmer Rouge in Cambodia who forcibly changed a 700-year culture in less than a year after seizing power. He did it by the following practices:

He changed the language. No more French or Cambodian; only Khmer.

He changed the icons, tore down all the churches and temples.

He moved people — country to city, city to country.

He killed all the intellectuals.

In a manner of speaking, the Admiral took an analogous approach. Everyone learned acceptable behavior, everyone was clean-shaven, the smoking lamp was out on the whole site, accountability was the new language, and people were assigned to new jobs. He assessed who was going to align themselves with him and he moved those who would not to jobs with corporate (his form of "killing" people; I do not recall him firing one person). Still the atmosphere was tense, but it was also an atmosphere of getting things done on time and on budget and done right the first time.

I had the unenviable task of grading the Admiral on an emergency drill. He was such a take-charge guy that in the Emergency Operations Center (EOC), where he was assigned by the emergency plan, he was doing everyone's job for them. Part of getting our operating license back was demonstrating to the NRC and Federal Emergency Management Agency (FEMA) that we could successfully handle a plant emergency of significant magnitude in a way that would protect the public, the environment, and to the extent possible, the co-located workers (i.e., the on-site work population). D-B's last grade in emergency planning was dismal, and, in the new organization, it was one of the activities for which I was directly responsible.

Anyhow, the Admiral called me into his office after the first drill and said. "Okay, Dave, tell it to me straight. How did I do?" Talk about being in a tight spot!

So I said, "Admiral, you were a running back in high school football, correct?"

"Yeah," he said, looking at me a little quizzically.

"Well," I continued, "what is the worst thing you could do on a screen play as a running back?"

Starting to show just a little impatience but after a little thought, he said, "Get out ahead of your blockers?"

"Bingo," I said.

He looked at me for a moment, smiled, and said, "Get the hell out of my office, wise guy!" I knew I had made my point and survived.

In one way, the Admiral was like every boss I had ever had: he loved Cindy. We were out to dinner with him and his wife, Margaret, a saint who visited for a weekend or more, every so often, from their home in Mystic, Connecticut. Cindy was "yes sir-ing" the Admiral up one side and "no sir-ing" him down the other, when he turned to her and said, "Cindy, honey, you can call me Joe." And without taking a breath, he turned to me and said, "And you can continue to call me Admiral!"

Around this same time, I was receiving a lot of literature in the mail about my upcoming 20th Naval Academy class reunion. Unlike my high school reunions, which were held every five years and to which I always looked forward, I had never been back to an Academy reunion. I stayed in touch with a few Academy buddies and really didn't have a desire to return to Annapolis — perhaps another sign of my lingering immaturity toward the greatest undeserved break of my life besides Cindy. Anyhow, Cindy went behind my back and told the Admiral, who did not go to the Academy but worked his way up from an enlisted man during World War II, that she wanted to go and I wouldn't take her. He subsequently called me into his office and ordered me to go to the reunion. And so we went.

I have to admit that we had a good time at the reunion, but maybe the most telling story is about our initial arrival. We came into Annapolis from the far side of the Severn River, which is up on a hill providing a panoramic view of the whole Academy grounds. Where there were once fields for athletic team practice and intramural competition, there were now several new buildings. I turned to Cindy and said, "This place has really changed." We crossed the bridge and drove in the gate near the hospital, where I had the two knee surgeries that essentially ended my collegiate wrestling career. We wound our way through the beautiful Academy grounds until we were at the parking lot by the field house.

As we were coming around the corner of the field house, headed for the Midshipmen's Store, there were six or seven female midshipmen warming up for a run. Again, I turned to Cindy and said, "This place has *really changed*!" As we wound our way through the young ladies, one was bent over touching her toes when she let out a loud fart. I turned to Cindy once more and commented, "It really hasn't changed that much."

While it had been 20 years since graduating from the Academy, my career itself was an ongoing education. While I was at D-B, the union went on strike, basically for increased pay and other benefits. As usual, the rank and file didn't want to do it, but the union leadership had its own agenda and did it anyway. It was quite an experience, preparing to be in lockdown for as long as it would take to break the strike. These preparations included training exempt employees to do union jobs and bringing in supplies so we could minimize the times we had to cross the strikers' barriers. When they went out on strike, there were definite rules about how the site could be accessed and what the strikers could and could not do. The police were involved to make sure the picketers didn't get out of hand.

As usual, there were only a few ardent union people who wanted a confrontation; most were very civil and would have rather been working (as they told us in phone calls). For the exempt people, morale was sky high because we were determined to show the union that we could handle activities without them, and we did. Of course, many of our other tasks had to be set aside as we assumed the union's critical jobs and our paperwork was piling up. But we were getting a lot of work accomplished and having fun doing it. The union gave in just about when the fun had worn off and everyone was getting tired of the experience. The union didn't gain a thing. The experience gave me some insights that helped me deal with unions in other settings.

One weekend, the Admiral had gone home to Mystic, with plans to return to Ohio on Monday. On Monday, he called me to synchronize our watches and told me to have security go out and take down the barriers in 19 minutes. From my office window, I could see him barreling down Route 2 from Port Clinton where his condo was. He arrived at the barricades just when the security forces pulled back the barricades, and he did not slow down. Strikers were jumping out of the way and signs were flying in the air as they did. I think that move, dangerous as it was, broke the spirit of some union strikers.

So, remember when I regaled you with stories of Cindy making trips to visit with male artists and movie producers, all while I trusted her implicitly to do so? Well, fast forward to life in Ohio, when the tables turned and the Admiral directed me to go to an emergency planning seminar in California and to take our emergency director with me. Her name was Jennifer. When I told Cindy about this trip, she hit the roof. She would not hear of me going off to California with some woman named Jennifer, regardless of the business appropriateness. The argument was dropped when the trip was canceled. It was some time later when I introduced Cindy to Jennifer and, without maligning Jennifer in any way, Cindy could see that I had let her stew in her own jealousy juices for naught. Compare that with my support of Cindy's adventures in Arizona, and it seems there was a definite double standard. Or maybe it was a Sicilian woman thing.

While I'm on the subject of Cindy, there is one story that has obtained the status of legend in the Amerine folklore. Cindy wanted a baby grand piano, and we had been looking at a privately owned used one in Sandusky. (In addition to being a talented dancer, Cindy played the piano and guitar.) Cindy had been lobbying to buy it, and I was choking on the $9,000 price tag. One bright sunny Sunday afternoon, Cindy had returned from a meeting just when I had finished working out. She was in high heels, a skirt, and a blouse, and I was dripping wet with sweat. I asked her to walk with me down to the Catawba Cliffs beach, where I was going to jump in the water. When we got there, I told Cindy that if she would go skinny-dipping, I would buy her the piano. We were at a public beach on busy Cliff Road in the middle of the day, so I felt pretty secure that she wouldn't do it. However, I failed to notice there was no one else on the beach, and we were at the end of the beach where the cliff and trees did provide some sense of privacy. Her clothes came off so fast and she was in the water before I knew what happened. I owed her a piano. I did buy it for her, and we dragged it around many moves before we gave it to her sister when we decided to retire to our small cottage on Cliff Road, where it simply wouldn't fit.

Meanwhile, back at work, there was constant change. When it came time for the Admiral to retire, he brought in a retired Navy captain to take his place, so all the in-fighting and maneuvering was for naught. At the same time, Cleveland Electric and Illuminating Company (CEI), who had acquired Toledo Edison but kept its distance while Davis-Besse was in the recovery mode, began to assert its corporate authority.

On the nuclear side, the two utilities had gone from each having a single reactor (CEI had Perry Nuclear Station) to being one utility with four reactors because together the new utility had controlling ownership of Beaver Valley and its two operating reactors. The new utility was called Centerior and had corporate offices in Independence, Ohio, about 120 miles from Catawba Island. They were looking for synergy and cost savings from this merger. I was asked to become the director of Nuclear Services, whose mission was to promote the cooperation between the nuclear plants and the sharing of resources to achieve this desired synergy.

The Nuclear Services department also absorbed some distinct functions, like nuclear quality assurance and contract negotiation. It was a demanding and interesting job. Of course, the nuclear plants guarded their autonomy and resources with a vengeance, but that attitude, which I could understand, made the job more challenging and called to task my negotiation and persuasion skills, which I basically had to develop on the job. I was able to assemble a good team and made good progress.

We had no intention of selling our home on Cliff Road, which we loved, or moving Alyssa, who was in a good school system with close friends. So, I rented a small apartment in Lakewood, Ohio. Eventually I bumped into the aforementioned Bobby James, and we decided to share the two-bedroom apartment and associated expenses.

After about a year as director of Nuclear Services, I went to lunch with the CEO of Centerior, Bob Ginn, who told me he appreciated the job I had done at D-B and was doing at Centerior. He told me I had a bright future with the company. A month later my boss, Murray Edleman, the VP of Nuclear Generation, called me into his Toledo office and basically told me that all vice president promotions would be going to former CEI personnel and that I would probably be stuck in my grade for the foreseeable future. He was basically telling me I had no future with Centerior. I think Murray was just being honest that the future belonged to CEI personnel as CEI had really acquired Toledo Edison. Bob may not have been as candid.

However, it was a shock and as I drove back to Independence from Toledo, pondering my future, I noticed Cindy and Alyssa in our car going in the other direction on Route 2. I was tempted to turn around and go home, but instead went to my office and finished the day. I had a sleepless night in Cleveland, and that weekend Cindy and I did some real soul searching. I am proud that we decided to look for another job even though all of us were very happy on Catawba.

This was the first and last time I had to actively seek employment. Up to this point and for the remainder of my career, people came looking for me. I contacted a person who was a recruiter but also a friend. He advised me to get the book *Rites of Passage* by John Lucht. John was a retainer recruiter, and the book was about how to find a job at a high salary. I followed it religiously and, within six weeks, I had six substantial job offers at an increased salary. So, it was time to sit around the family table once again. We loved our home on Cliff Road and had made some good friends outside of work. It was nice to be near my parents after 25 years away. Alyssa was very happy with her friends and school. She was doing well in school and very well in athletics, lettering as a freshman and sophomore in tennis and showing great promise in both volleyball and basketball. Erin, due to graduate from Miami, was thinking she would head to California to teach, so her opinion, while valued, didn't weigh much on our decision. What was pretty clear was that if I stayed with Centerior, it was pretty certain I wouldn't go much further with my career.

Ultimately, we decided to leave. I had narrowed my job options down to two offers, both with Westinghouse. One was a program manager for the Replacement Tritium Facility (RTF), a troubled project on the Savannah River Site (SRS) outside of Aiken, South Carolina. (The SRS contract had been won from DuPont by the Westinghouse subsidiary, Westinghouse Savannah River Company (WSRC), about a year earlier.) The other opportunity was as the deputy manager at the Waste Isolation Pilot Project (WIPP) near Carlsbad, New Mexico. Westinghouse flew Cindy and Alyssa out to New Mexico, and their trip was not pleasant. When they returned and saw me waiting at the terminal window (in those days before the 9/11 hijackings, you could meet the plane at the gate), they both stuck their fingers into their mouths. I knew Carlsbad and WIPP were toast.

Still the job at WIPP was in the executive ranks as the number-two man on the site. So, I called John Yasinski, number-three man in all of Westinghouse at the time. I had met John when I was the refueling manager for the FFTF and on the critical path to FFTF startup for nearly two years. John was president of Westinghouse Hanford at age 38 and a very sharp guy. We got along well, so I thought I would seek his advice. He didn't hesitate to recommend the job at the SRS. SRS represented a bigger site, more opportunity, and was more important to Westinghouse. Also, Aiken and Augusta were considered much better places to live than Carlsbad. I took his advice and accepted the RTF job.

As usual, Cindy would stay behind to sell our dream home and get Alyssa through her sophomore year. Lis was actually very supportive of the move even though she hated to leave her friends and the area. I broke the news to my parents, who were also supportive. Basically, they said "You have to do what you have to do." Even though it was difficult, I couldn't stay with a company that told me I had a bright future and then a week later told me just the opposite. It was clear to me that CEI personnel had the upper hand on promotions and pay increases going forward with the new company. It was definitely more of a takeover than a merger. Additionally, I was hired by Toledo Edison as an Assistant Vice President and took the job at Centerior as a Director because it was an important position for the new consolidated corporation and I felt that it would lead to an executive position with the new corporation. Murray Edleman informed me that was not true and to have stayed under those conditions would have been to settle (and I was never complacent about my career).

I was proud of my effort to find a new job once my mind was made up. I felt good about telling Murray Edleman that I had a position of some importance (the RTF was to be the sole source of tritium for our nation's nuclear weapons program) and had a substantial pay raise to boot. This experience helped me advise people in the future about career change — what to do and what not to do at critical junctures in their careers.

Aiken, South Carolina (The First Time: 1990-1997)

It was decided that I would take Cindy's car, which was a small Toyota, and leave my larger one for her to transport Alyssa and her friends to events. She was also more likely to need to transport large items for the house, so leaving the larger car with her only made sense. I can still remember driving down Cliff Road, leaving behind Cindy and Alyssa and the only house we had built, which was situated on a cliff overlooking Lake Erie. I also knew I was leaving good friends I had grown to really like and leaving my parents again. It was heart wrenching, but it was necessary. **As I mentioned earlier, to have stayed would have been to have settled.**

I was excited to take on a new job and to rescue a project that was faltering. Once again, I would have to learn a new technology while meeting new people and learning about a new organization. Westinghouse had only had the contract for a year after winning it from DuPont, who had been the only other contractor since the beginning of the site, when the Manhattan Project needed a place to process weapons-grade nuclear material. I am sure Strom Thurmond, the venerable South Carolina senator, had some influence along with Georgia politicians to get that federal money coming into their states. The history of the SRS is interesting and is much like that of Hanford, Oak Ridge, Los Alamos, and other locations that supported the nuclear weapons program during the Cold War with Russia. We were engaged in an arms race that had its beginning in World War II, and avoiding the threat of mutual destruction could only be preserved if we had as strong a nuclear arsenal as Russia (and later China) had.

I will address the approach I took to turning the project around in some detail in the second half of this book. Suffice it to say that I approached the RTF with a modified version of Admiral Williams's Pol Pot philosophy. I rarely reprimanded people in public, but I did let the group know that we were going to turn things around, and they could join the effort or go elsewhere. The Westinghouse management, many of whom knew me when I was at Hanford, gave me a pretty free hand.

I was living in a motel until Cindy could come down and find a temporary residence in which she and Alyssa would be comfortable while Cindy looked for a new house. The lack of creature comforts at the motel didn't matter to me, because I was spending most of my time at work anyway. After going through orientation to obtain my site access badge, I spent the first three or four weeks just walking around getting to know the personnel, both Westinghouse and DOE. My predecessor was going to still be there as my assistant program manager. This situation could have been awkward, but the first thing I did was to tell him he should keep his current office and I would move into the much smaller office across the hall. I think this act of humility by me and saving of some face for him won him and a lot of his comrades over. He was a good man and well liked, perhaps a little too well liked. Holding people accountable to their commitments does not necessarily gain popularity.

I spent the first three or four weeks just walking around getting to know the personnel.

I knew I needed to establish a more aggressive atmosphere and some people would need to adjust their attitudes or move on. As usual, **I found that most people just wanted some direction, some support, and some recognition when they met their commitments. The best vehicle for that, on a daily basis, is the Plan of the Day (POD).** The POD is a meeting in which the constituents of the schedule to some ultimate goal, like a plant startup, are reviewed and the commitments to achieve those schedule constituents are "statused" and assessed. It is an accountability meeting.

I knew I needed a project schedule, and I needed a good project controls manager. Ebasco, a large contract services company, had a support services contract for Westinghouse at SRS, so I asked them to send me some project controls personnel to interview.

That is when I met Bill Pettigrew, and when I began a professional relationship and personal friendship that was to last the next two decades. Bill was a quick study, and we set up a team dedicated to constructing a challenging schedule and a new project completion cost. I presented these to management and then to the client. Fortunately, the senior DOE person was a former commercial nuclear executive and former Naval officer. He had once worked for Admiral Williams, so we had that experience in common as well. We hit it off right away, and he defended my new schedule and budget to his superiors. I also needed a new construction manager and Bechtel sent me Bob Pedde. Our paths would cross a few times at SRS, but we were a good team from the start.

Bill ran the POD, and I added emphasis when necessary. At first, it was sometimes bloody, but people began to understand accountability and commitment. They soon learned to bring problems to me and Bill early, rather than sit on them and hope they would get better. When they brought them early, we could marshal our resources to overcome the situation. If they reported that their work was on schedule each day but then needed more time when the deliverable was due, there was nothing we could do to recover and it was a bad day at the office. Even though people were going through a significant change in acceptable behavior, we **softened the blow with humor whenever we could.** One day, a new test engineer was introduced at the POD, and I quickly turned to Bill and said loud enough for all to hear, "Fresh meat!"

As a result of our deliberate changes in process and culture, we began making great progress and upper management started sending others to observe our POD and Plan of the Week (POW). Bill and I conducted daily critical path analysis to determine how we could pull the schedule back to gain float (i.e., time between forecasted completion and the original schedule's target completion) to the committed milestones. Critical path is that list of activities that must be achieved on time to make the committed schedule. The schedule was developed with a bottom-up (i.e., worker input) and top-down (i.e., management input) analysis of activities and the estimated time to complete those activities. We analyzed the probabilities of untoward impacts, which later became known as risk assessment management plans (RAMP), and then folded those determinations into the schedule. We also challenged the owners of schedule activities to bring us a true estimate of the personnel and resources needed to achieve their activities. This approach became known as a work breakdown structure (WBS).

We also made it known that all "float" (i.e., number of days off the critical path an activity string was determined to have) belonged to Bill and me. These tools and their nomenclature for project management were in their infancy in the industry at that time but were approaches both Bill and I had brought from other endeavors. Eventually, these tools became codified in project management directives and nomenclature, and our use of some version of them was coincidental at the time. Again, **the key was team buy-in and commitment to *their* schedule and early problem identification. We also emphasized that safety trumped schedule every time.**

The staff members at our plant were mostly young and many were unmarried. We worked long hours together, but we also partied together. As such, it didn't take long to build a real esprit de corps with that approach. Of course, there were a few times when I realized that I was not as young as I once was and that going to work on a Saturday or Sunday with a hangover was not a good idea.

On one hot Saturday, the hangover created a tremendous thirst, which in turn drove me to a McDonald's drive-through where I ordered a large iced tea. As I pulled out of the parking lot, I took a big swig and learned for the first time that tea in South Carolina comes automatically significantly sweetened. I almost threw up.

While all of this was going on, I was trying to adjust to living alone. I was learning to grocery shop for myself to support a vegetarian diet. I found myself preparing and eating the same dishes every day, which made me appreciate Cindy more. After a few months, Cindy came down with Alyssa for a long weekend and immediately helped me find an apartment to her suiting. It felt good to move out of the motel. Her visit made me realize how much I missed her and Alyssa. At this point, our oldest daughter Erin was off on her own, teaching in California. As for Alyssa, she was about to start her sophomore year, and we hadn't sold the house yet, so Cindy and Alyssa went back to Ohio and I was alone again. But at least I was living in a nice place. I started working out again after laying off exercise for the first six months as I got settled in Aiken, an approach to new endeavors that was to repeat itself several more times over my career. However, I found that as I got older, recovery from the six-month exercise hiatus seemed more and more difficult.

Back at work, we were six months in, and the project was ahead of schedule and costs were on track. The morale was greatly improved, and the DOE was happy with our performance. Bill Pettigrew came to me and said his contract would be up soon, and he planned to return to his home and his family in Texas, where he planned to make a run at his computer business again.

So I needed to find a replacement for Pettigrew and I had just the guy in mind. I had met Chuck Spencer at Perry Nuclear Station when I was director of nuclear services for Centerior and when he was planning and scheduling manager for Perry. At the time, he was also going to school at night to get a law degree. When he obtained his degree, he was moved into Centerior as a member of the corporate law group. He and I worked on several tasks together, such as negotiating the agreement with the Ohio Emergency Management Agency. One bitterly cold day, we were on our way to Columbus when he said that if he ever had a chance to move south, he would jump on it. I remembered that in this moment, and I called him about taking Pettigrew's place. He said yes.

Not only did Chuck come south, but I also asked him to move in with me and share costs until our families could join us. He was in the same situation I was — with two children needing to finish school and a house to sell. As it turned out, his wife, Rose, sold their place and was ready to move south before Cindy. So Chuck came to me and asked me what I thought about moving me out of the apartment, which had three bedrooms and was just right for him and Rose, their daughter, and their son. Because Cindy had found the place and it met her expectations, I said "let me think about it." When I came home from work the next day, Chuck had moved all my stuff, which wasn't much, to a small two-bedroom apartment on the Aiken bypass highway ... with no furniture. I slept on the floor for the next three months until Cindy came down and rented some furniture. Oh, the things I would do for the benefit of a work project!!

I did break down and buy a folding chair so I could eat my cereal sitting down. When I told Cindy over the phone that I had bought a chair, she went linear, figuring I didn't have the interior design sense to make that kind of purchase without her. So I strung her along. She asked what color the chair was, and I said "green." She exclaimed that we didn't have anything that coordinated with a green chair. She was becoming more and more agitated, so I never did tell her it was just a folding chair. It seemed to motivate her to sell the house in Ohio and get down to Aiken before I made any more furniture purchases.

The apartment I was living in was a motivator for finding a house when Cindy and Alyssa did arrive, just in time for Lis to start school at South Aiken High. I had made an offer on a house that Cindy had not seen and that was a worse mistake than buying a folding chair. We had to back out of that deal, which required the help of a lawyer. Cindy did find a house to her liking in Woodside Plantation on a golf course. I liked the house but not the location. After living there for about five years, I could not take the golfers in my backyard anymore or the general lack of privacy. I told Cindy we could build in Woodside on a lot that was not on a golf course. She agreed, and we found and purchased a nice lot high on a hill overlooking a small lake (certainly not Lake Erie). We developed some plans and paid $2,000 for them to be made into builder's drawings. We hired a builder and were all set to start construction.

However, when I came home one night, Cindy said there was a house that just came on the market that she wanted me to look at. I asked why, but I knew I was in trouble. I had to admit I liked the house when I saw it. It was at the end of a cul-de-sac outside of Aiken at the end of a long driveway through three acres of woods. It was European in its design and had lots of possibilities. We told our builder we were going to buy this house rather than build on the lot on the hill, and would like him to convert the garage into a study and workout room, and add a new garage. Fortunately, Cindy had done some decorating work for him, and he was an Amish man from Ohio. So we were off the hook with the builder but still had a lot in Woodside, which was to be dealt with later.

Even though the RTF project was going well, the DOE was having budget issues. RTF was just about to start operations when the project was held in abeyance while overall budget concerns for the site were addressed. At the same time, another Savannah River Site major project — the Defense Waste Processing Facility (DWPF) — was in trouble. The facility was being built to process high-level nuclear waste from the nuclear weapons development program resulting from the Manhattan Project. This waste was currently residing in underground million-gallon tanks that were corroding. I was asked to lead a review of the project because the DOE was threatening to take it away from Westinghouse.

I rounded up a good review team, which included contracting Steve Piccolo from D-B and Bill Pettigrew, whose computer business in Texas was failing to prosper in the down economy. The DWPF was being managed by a good guy from the DuPont team, who, frankly, was just being too nice and not holding people accountable, not unlike the Program Manager I relieved at RTF. Our review team had several recommendations, which echoed the situation I had found at RTF but on a much larger scale. Ambrose Schwallie had just taken over the SRS presidency from Jim Moore, and he needed a win with his new management and the client.

Because RTF was stalled, Ambrose decided to take a chance and asked me to move to DWPF. I hated to leave the RTF team, but DWPF offered a bigger challenge and RTF was on the right course once the site finances were resolved. So, a little more than a year after arriving at SRS, I left RTF and took over DWPF. Fortunately, I was able to direct hire Steve and Bill and convince them to move their families to Aiken. I will address the approach to that project turnaround in some detail in the second half of this story.

I feel I left behind a good team at RTF with good momentum. They gave me a nice send-off party. They even wrote a Christmas poem about me and sent their colleagues at DWPF a letter on how to survive me. I did feel bad about leaving Chuck Spencer there but was told, in no uncertain terms, I could not bring any of the RTF folks to DWPF, and that included Chuck. He went on to have a stellar career, rising to the ranks of president of one of the subsidiary companies of the corporation into which Westinghouse Savannah River eventually morphed. I feel honored that Chuck consulted with me on a few major decisions he faced along his career path.

Meanwhile, my family was settling into life in Aiken. Alyssa seemed to adjust to her new school very well in her junior year. She was selected as the most valuable player on the tennis team, an honor that usually goes to a senior. Much like her sister Erin was when it came to soccer, Alyssa was a very intelligent tennis player with her head in the game at all times. She didn't seem to get rattled by any situation. She was also chosen as Miss South Aiken, beating out girls who had always assumed the honor would go to one of them. They called her "the drive-by beauty queen" — the girl who arrived seemingly out of nowhere. We were looking forward to her senior year and another round of vicarious achievement when she informed us she wanted to go back to the Midwest.

Like Erin, she had enough credits to graduate high school at the completion of her junior year. She determined that she wanted to go to a Midwest college. Cindy contacted the same counselor that helped Erin six years earlier and arranged a tour of five colleges across Ohio and Indiana. They went for the visits and called me after seeing each school. They felt Indiana University (IU) was very gloomy. I explained to them they had just lost in the semi-finals of the NCAA basketball tournament and that Indiana took basketball pretty seriously.

When they called to say they thought Dennison in Granville, Ohio, was the cat's meow, I told them to give IU one more chance, because I knew how expensive Dennison's tuition was.

Things at IU had cheered up when they returned to Bloomington for a second visit. However, when Lis went to talk to the admissions counselor, he informed her that it was unofficial IU policy not to admit high school juniors, feeling they were not mature enough. An hour later, Alyssa had convinced him to enroll her in the fall, which he seemed pleased to do if she would just leave his office. This is typical of her persistence when she sets her sights on a goal — shades of "I guess I'll keep my shoes on in case we go somewhere."

When Alyssa left for college, Cindy cried for almost a month due to missing her "baby." However, when Alyssa would come home, Cindy would cry when her perfectly kept house was in shambles within hours. It did seem that the period of time when both our daughters were in college was time accelerated. Maybe it was because we measured that time in visits and other events when we would see the girls or know they had gone on some trip or some other notable event. It was an era about milestones and memories, rather than about the day-to-day interactions of our family unit.

At DWPF, like RTF, after the first three to four months of walking and talking and setting a new paradigm, we had set our schedule and budget using the same tools that worked well at RTF. We had made the appropriate staff changes, as those who were going to sign up for the new approach became apparent, as did those who could not make the adjustment. There was a new sense of commitment that was soon followed by an equally important sense of achievement. We started to weave humor into our POD and other meetings. Camaraderie was building as we started to make more and more milestones and had appropriate celebrations at each new achievement. A real team was being developed, and you could almost feel a new spring in people's steps. We became the model for the site and felt good about it. We had serious technical challenges, which we met head-on and solved with the help of site expertise. We found workarounds and parallel paths to keep the project moving forward while issues were being resolved.

One of the first things I had to do at DWPF was to convince the DOE headquarters that I knew what I was doing. Prior to me coming to DWPF, Leo Duffy, the truculent head of the DOE Environmental Management (EM) division — which was charged with the responsibility of cleaning up the DOE sites from the residue of the Manhattan Project — had been threatening to take the DWPF project away from Westinghouse.

I was accompanied by my boss, Norm Boyter, to the Forrestal Building, the DOE DC headquarters, but the presentation to Leo was to be all mine. Norm was in high trepidation of the meeting, but I said to him, "We can always get another job. They will have trouble finding another us." I was a little full of myself, but we needed to have confidence. Leo sat there eating a huge sausage with some kind of green sauce he kept putting on the end of it before he shoved it into his mouth for another bite. Frankly, it was pretty gross and I should have said we would wait until he finished gorging himself, but I persevered because I knew our presentation time was limited. At the end, Leo said he was glad Westinghouse finally had someone in charge who seemed like he knew what he was doing. That was the vote of confidence I needed.

With Leo's blessing, our work continued. Another important thing we did at DWPF concerned the operator qualification. Before I arrived, the approach was basically a journeyman/apprentice approach. A new operator (the apprentice) would follow a senior operator (the journeyman) around at a certain station in the plant for a month or so, memorizing the job requirements. When the journeyman thought the new operator understood the job well enough to be on his own, he would inform management. Then the shift manager would sit down with the new operator and "quiz" him on the job station. If the shift manager was satisfied, the new operator could then stand the watch by himself. There was no written test, no verification of competence on the engineering basics behind the equipment operation. There was just rote memory.

It was my intention to change all that and institute an operator qualification that required understanding of the equipment and the principles of integrated operation so that the operators understood what to do in upset conditions rather than just call an engineer. This required instituting a formal training program with classroom time and tests along the way. In parallel, there would be performance of practical factors associated with the station as well as discussion of the principles that lay behind those "prac facs." At the end of the classroom phase, there would be a comprehensive test and an oral board. Then — and only then — could the operators become qualified to stand the station watch.

It was my intention to institute an operator qualification that required understanding of the equipment and the principles of integrated operation so that the operators understood what to do in upset conditions rather than just call an engineer.

There was a lot of trepidation on the operators' part because these requirements were all new. But what really lay behind their fears was the inability to read. We assessed the reading skills of our operators and found, on average, that they were below the eighth-grade level. So we instituted a remedial reading program. Some could not even pass the remedial program. We found them jobs that did not require the same reading and comprehension skills that being an operator required. Those who emerged from the remedial reading successfully entered the new qualification program. We still needed to do a lot of coaching to get the operators through and, different from my engineering exam experience, I made certain they had the best preparation possible. Soon, it became a badge of honor as operators began to pass the exams and orals. More importantly, the new reading skills had significant positive impact on their personal lives. I feel really good about that.

Along the way, there were personal milestones for our team members, and we all participated and celebrated or commiserated, as appropriate, when those events occurred. I had quarterly meetings with all personnel, where we mapped our progress, listed our challenges, and outlined how those challenges were to be addressed. These meetings were held in the large glass waste-storage building, which would eventually receive the highly radioactive canisters of glass. Unfortunately, the building had no heating or cooling, so sometimes the meetings were hot, and we brought in huge fans to create some airflow. In the winter months, we brought in heaters that weren't very effective. I remember one meeting, where I was shivering by the end of the meeting and had planned to say, "Go forward and have good success," but it came out "Go forward and have good sex!"The millwrights were all saying, "Yes!" and the secretaries were saying, "What did he say?" That faux pas was one I had trouble living down.

DWPF was essentially a project, a $2.5 billion dollar project with a vital mission to the Savannah River Site. We had succeeded in developing a sense of urgency but needed to capture our approach to things. We made sure everyone understood our priorities of SAFETY, QUALITY, SCHEDULE, and COST, in that order. We did that by example as well as emphasis in our meetings, signs, documents, etc. We rewarded stopping or holding work in abeyance when in doubt about the direction or outcome of an activity. However, we needed the whole team to understand we were about getting things done and that was not in conflict with the priorities listed above.

Our subprojects required to complete construction were under the management of Harvey Handfinger, who reported to me, and his right hand lieutenant, Rod Mohammadi. They epitomized Americans working together with a common cause as one was a Jew and the other a Muslim. Together they found work-arounds and solutions to keep critical path work moving forward at all times. To make sure their underlings understood what was expected, they came up with the phrase, "**You must push it to move it; and if you stop pushing, it will stop.**" Basically the message was not to let up or let things take their own course. Rather, be in control, find answers to keep the work moving, or get help. Soon the entire DWPF team adopted the slogan, "**Push it to move it**" and everyone knew what it meant. **We are in**

charge of our own destiny and we can make our commitments to get this vital project completed and in operation if we work hard, work together, and never let up. The success that will follow will be worth the effort.

Soon the entire DWPF team adopted the slogan, "Push it to move it" and everyone knew what it meant. We are in charge of our own destiny and we can make our commitments to get this vital project completed and in operation if we work hard, work together, and never let up. The success that will follow will be worth the effort.

After the DWPF achieved full operation, I was selected by Austin Scott, who had replaced Norm as the High-Level Waste (HLW) division vice president, to be his new deputy. Once again, it was difficult to leave the team I had forged. When I assembled them for my final quarterly meeting, I told them that we represented what is best about America. We were black and white, male and female, young and old, Protestant and Catholic, Muslim and Jew, Republican and Democrat. Yet when we focused on a common goal, setting those differences aside, there was nothing we could not achieve.

We represented what is best about America. We were black and white, male and female, young and old, Protestant and Catholic, Muslim and Jew, Republican and Democrat. When we focused on a common goal, there was nothing we could not achieve.

It was a double honor to have been selected as HLW division deputy because Austin — who selected me for the role — was a retired two-star admiral and because Charlie Peckinpaugh — who I was succeeding — had been my boss at Hanford when I was the refueling manager during startup of FFTF. Austin turned out to be a fantastic boss as well, truly one of the best bosses I ever had. Besides being smart with tremendous personnel insights, he was a good teacher. He had witty sayings that cut to the heart of the matter. Two of my favorites were the following:

- "Never pass up an opportunity to keep your mouth shut."
- "Call me 20 minutes before you're going to screw up so I can talk you out of it."

One learning event that sticks in my mind and helped me at other times in my career involved my old project, DWPF. We were experiencing high absenteeism on Mondays and Fridays, and I told the various plant and operations managers that I needed them to address this issue, especially because it appeared to be indicative of substance abuse (i.e., employees who were starting their weekend partying early and needing Monday to sleep it off). Mike Borders was the operations manager at DWPF and an excellent one. However, when he heard this directive, he decided to examine the medical records of his operators and mechanics, which was his right to do. (The company is required to keep medical records, including the results of random, periodic, and for-cause drug testing as part of the fitness for duty requirements on nuclear projects.) However, he sent those records to his various managers via emails for them to examine. His mistake was publishing that sensitive information on a quasi-public media (i.e., email). Austin told me I had to take preemptive action demonstrating the company's concern for employees' privacy and replace Mike.

I strongly argued against this action, saying we should circle the wagons to protect a good man. I went so far as surrendering my badge to Austin in his office. He handed the badge back to me and told me to think about it overnight, which I did. The next day I went out to Jim Wilson, the DWPF plant manager, and Neil Brosee, the program manager, and told them what I thought needed to be done and that I would talk to Mike. It was very difficult as I explained to Mike what had to happen and why. He would be moved to an administrative job elsewhere in the division, and he would be losing his management authority. At one point, we were both crying. I never said that it was anyone else's decision but mine, but I did tell Mike that Austin agreed with the decision (as did Ambrose), so there was no chance for appeal.

To Mike's credit, he did a good turnover of his previous role to capable relief and went where he was told. Eventually his career recovered, and the situation was completely diffused by the action Austin had instructed to be done. I thought about the whole situation for about a month, realizing that **one mistake can undo an otherwise stellar career**. There are many reasons for that truth, as difficult as it seems. A month later, I went to Austin and apologized. I told him he was right, and I was wrong. I told him I understood why we had to do what we did, and I thought Mike did as well.

While Cindy, Alyssa and I were in Aiken for seven years, we were able to visit Erin in California just once. Erin seemed very happy overall and thrilled with the California lifestyle. It made me remember the impact California had on me when I visited it for the first time as a midshipman and then again when I went to Mare Island for Navy nuke school. I could certainly identify with Erin's attitude. Then, after about four years, Erin surprised us with a move to historic Charleston, South Carolina, only a three-hour drive from Aiken. She said she just wanted to be closer to us. Now, it was our turn to be thrilled.

We helped her find an apartment on Chalmers Street in Charleston, and she found a job with the Marine Institute in Beaufort, South Carolina, a semiprivate outfit for helping troubled youth stay out of prison and get their high school diplomas. Her job was about an hour commute from Charleston, but she felt it was worth it. We did get to see her more with visits both ways. We spent one Christmas Day with our friends from Richland, the Johnsons, having breakfast at the Waffle House and serving Christmas dinner to about 12 boys in Erin's program, who didn't have anywhere else to go for the holidays. I was proud of Erin's involvement in this effort. However, after about a year, the Marine Institute offered her a job in St. Petersburg, Florida. She agonized over the decision, but ultimately decided to go.

As it turned out, we helped her with the move, and she ended up living not far from my aunt Grace, my dad's sister. Uncle Walter had died several years earlier, so it was good that Erin could stop by to see her occasionally. More consequentially, Erin met a young man named Mike Fetzer who was also working at the Marine Institute. A year later, he asked her to marry him and, as of the publishing of this book in second edition in 2019, Erin and Mike have been married more than 21 years, both have rewarding careers, and have two great children.

I remember that when we told our friends about Erin's pending wedding, the men pulled me aside and told me to hide my wallet. The women pulled Cindy aside and advised her on how to spend the most money possible. When Mike asked for Erin's hand and we said "yes," he asked for one more thing, which was to have the wedding on Valentine's Day. Cindy thought that was romantic. I thought it was smart: one less date to remember. Erin said she wanted a small wedding and Mike virtually disappeared relative to the preparations. Both things were fine with me, because I thought Cindy would be enough to handle. However, at the first meeting with Erin and Cindy, I brought up the word "budget," at which time I was told my attendance was not necessary at any more meetings. All kidding aside, the wedding celebration was a wonderful three days in Aiken, with friends and relatives coming from near and far. The wedding was at St. Thaddeus, our church in Aiken, and the reception was at a wonderful southern plantation-type hotel in Aiken, the Wilcox Inn.

Erin was beautiful. Mike was calm. I was too serious, and Cindy was at times hyper (and even swore at me the morning of the wedding in a manner that would have embarrassed a sailor). We have one photo I think is really neat, which shows the mother of the bride with her lifelong friends from all the different places we had lived.

By the time of their marriage, Erin and Mike had left the Marine Institute and were enrolled at the University of Southern Mississippi, where Erin was pursuing a master's degree and Mike was working on his doctorate. They found a nice little house in Hattiesburg, and a few years later Camryn, our first grandchild, was born, missing Valentine's Day by one day. Cindy and I were now grandparents.

I had only been the HLW division deputy for about a year when I was contacted by the navigator on my last boat in the Navy who had been hired to lead the recovery of the Millstone Nuclear Power Station, which had been shut down by the NRC. Millstone was in Connecticut, and I was being offered the job of vice president of engineering and services (which included emergency management and training). I viewed it as an opportunity to return to the commercial nuclear arena, enter the executive ranks once again, participate in another nuclear station recovery, and work with some industry leaders. The problem was that Cindy and I liked Aiken and our new home (we had been in it about a year at this time, with the remodeling just completed). I knew I was highly thought of at SRS, and I liked working for Austin and keeping an eye on DWPF. So, once again, Cindy and I got out our decision analysis and ultimately opted for adventure. It was a little easier with both girls now on their own, Erin married and Alyssa enjoying her career and the advantages of being an attractive, single, successful businesswoman in Chicago, where she headed right after graduation from Indiana University and got a job as an Information Technology recruiter, at which she was very good.

As I always advised people facing a career decision, involve your immediate management. So, I went to talk to my boss, Austin. He was very supportive and said it sounded like a deal not to be passed up. (After getting out of the Navy, Austin spent some time at Comanche Peak as an executive before coming to SRS. Therefore, he understood the commercial nuclear business.) When I next went to see Ambrose, he told me the next VP vacancy at SRS would be filled by me. My judgment was that opportunity was still at least two years away. So Cindy and I decided to take the job, break out our winter clothes, buy a four-wheel-drive SUV, and rent our house with the intent of returning to Aiken someday. (This was a pattern that was to repeat itself a few more times.) Once again, I burned no bridges with Westinghouse when I left. Besides being the right thing to do, it turned out to be prescient.

Old Lyme, Connecticut (1997-2000)

Millstone represented another nuclear station recovery after an NRC shutdown of the facility and subsequent revocation of the oper-ating license. Unlike D-B a decade earlier, Millstone had principally had its license pulled due to treatment of employees. As I earlier described D-B, the atmosphere set there by Admiral Williams, my boss at D-B, and tolerated by the NRC to address actual plant issues was pretty rough-and-tumble. However, the continuum of accept-able management behavior in American industry in general, and in the nuclear industry in particular, had evolved from management by authority to more of management by persuasion. At the same time, employee empowerment had increased. There were many things good about this evolution, but it also brought its challenges. When it came to Millstone and other facilities, the NRC was trying to ensure there was an environment where employees felt free to bring up issues without fear of retribution. That was a good thing. But it was also a new thing for older management, especially those of us who had been part of the military. Millstone management found itself under the microscope after a series of incidents culminating in one particular employee — who had brought up a valid nuclear safety issue — and was subsequently mistreated by management (who had their emphasis on the facility becoming more bottom-line focused as they prepared for deregulation and competition, and were apt to rush to those goals, refusing to be slowed down by employees who raised concerns).

The continuum of acceptable management behavior in American industry in general, and in the nuclear industry in particular, had evolved from management by authority to more of management by persuasion.

So a new management team was brought in to address this brave new world of safety conscious work environment (SCWE), even though, at the time, neither the NRC nor the utility management even knew of that phrase (let alone what it might mean). What was clear was that employee confidence in management's willingness to listen and consider their concerns had to be restored or established and demonstrated to the NRC's satisfaction if Millstone was to get its license back. So it seemed I had once again stepped into a very challenging environment. Two things were different. My boss, Buz Carnes, had served with me in the Navy and was a friend, and the move to Connecticut was the first relocation Cindy and I ever made without children.

Because we knew we wanted to go back to Aiken, South Carolina, eventually, we decided to rent out our house in Aiken, and Cindy set about finding a place to rent in Old Lyme. She found a wonderful farmhouse on a back road less than a mile from the ocean. It was built in 1826 and owned by a gentleman from Ireland, Jepson O'Connell, who asked only that he be permitted to come once or twice a week to garden. I didn't have to think about that stipulation for long. We had wild turkeys and deer in our yard all the time, and there were maple syrup distilleries on the same road. Cindy formed a nice friendship with Jepson, and he gave us advice on what to see and do in the area. When Cindy later planned a trip to Ireland with her mother and Alyssa, Jepson helped with the arrangements and the itinerary. Once settled into our new home in Connecticut, it only took me about 30 minutes to drive to work, which was good because, once again, I was working long hours and most weekends.

After about three months on the job, I was aware that the key to getting our license back was the establishment of what became known as the SCWE — the safety conscious work environment. I was also aware that the person in the lead for that effort was Mike Brothers, who was also the vice president for the Unit III, which had become the lead unit to be ready for operations. However, Mike was struggling at both jobs because they were both so daunting. Despite my mother's advice when she dropped me off at the Naval Academy to never volunteer for anything, I volunteered to take the lead for the SCWE effort. After some discussion, my engineering responsibilities were split up between the three Unit VPs while I retained responsibility for training and emergency planning (EP), the thought being that those were people-oriented activities. I was then assigned responsibility for human relations, employee concerns, legal, the ombudsman program, and the special SCWE team. I immediately came under the scrutiny of Little Harbor Associates (LHA), a consultant team the NRC had brought in to determine if we were headed in the right direction and if we had established stakeholder confidence, primarily from the employees. It was truly a learning experience for me, one that was to stand me in good stead for the rest of my career.

It took 10 months to convince LHA we had, however tentatively, established the correct environment at Millstone. I had more than one opportunity to appear before the NRC Commissioners to discuss what we were doing and how it was going. Fortunately, LHA did some valuable coaching (as well as assessments) and Northeast Utilities assigned some very capable people to lead the people-oriented organizations I mentioned above. In the end, I was really glad to return to engineering after those 10 months. At least technical problems, once solved, stayed solved.

An added benefit of the temporary assignment was meeting Billie Garde, one of the members of LHA. Billie was recognized as one of the foremost employee advocate lawyers in the country. Millstone was a learning experience for her as well, as she found that trust and good communication constituted a "people business" requiring effort and honesty on everyone's part, not just management. She gave me good advice and became a friend and confidante for the rest of my career. I brought her in to several of the many challenging situations in which I found myself after Millstone.

As far as engineering goes, when I returned to that exclusive role, the challenge was to reorganize it according to disciplines rather than by units. This realignment had several advantages to the unit alignment, not the least of which was breaking down the cultural barriers between the units. It was not an easy sell. Finally, I told a group of engineers — all of whom were lamenting that they had always been Unit II engineers — that if they would bring me their diplomas and the diplomas said Unit II electrical engineering instead of electrical engineering, we would do it their way. If, on the other hand, it said just electrical engineering (or whatever discipline in which they had earned their degree), we would do it my way. That seemed to get the point across. **I also made it a requirement that the engineers get out of their offices or cubicles and into the plant.** If they had not talked to an operator, a mechanic, or a radiation technician in the field within three days or more, it was too long. That was another adjustment for them, but when I would grab engineers at random and ask them to take me to the last field person to whom they had talked, they began to understand that I was serious.

During this time in Connecticut, Cindy decided to get involved in several activities in the community in which we lived, Old Lyme. One was in archeological exploration. She helped with several digs of early New England artists' workplaces, discovering artifacts that were used at the time. She and I also decided to try kayaking and rollerblading. New England provided many estuaries and trails, respectively, for those activities. Rollerblading was great fun and good exercise. However, it's dangerous enough that we had to give it up in our 60s. We ultimately retired in Ohio, and I still kayak on Lake Erie, because the Lake is right in front of our house. While it is great exercise and I do see some things on the shoreline that I might not otherwise see, New England offered a greater variety of landscape and wildlife.

At work, things continued to be busy and successful. After we had returned Units II and III to service, it was time to turn our attention to preparing for deregulation and competition. Obviously, the number of staff needed for recovery of a troubled project exceeds that of a well-run operating entity. I was informed that the site would be downsizing its staff, including the number of vice presidents (VPs). The number of site VPs would go from six to two, not counting the chief nuclear officer (CNO). I was also informed I would be one of those two and, in preparation for that assignment, which would include much more than engineering and services, I would be sent to receive my executive Business Administration certificate. It was decided I would go to Harvard. I turned engineering and services over to one of my direct reports and headed to Boston for 12 weeks of intense schooling.

Cindy then decided that if I was going to be off to Harvard, she would enroll at Yale. With the help of some friends who graduated from

Yale, she was admitted and enrolled in a course called the American Presidency, for which she attended class three times a week. Because she was taking only one course, she would come visit me in Boston every second weekend. It was a fascinating time. My class had 168 executives in it, only 30 percent of whom were from the United States and only three from the nuclear industry. The diversity led to hearing many different perspectives on a wide range of topics. The professors were interesting, funny, and at the top of their respective fields. I enjoyed it immensely.

A few weeks into my studies at Harvard, I received a call from Ambrose Schwallie, who was president of WSRC while I was there. He had received a promotion to be president of Westinghouse Government Services and asked if I would come back to be his chief operating officer (COO). This was a chance to "go home." I asked Ambrose if I could finish the Harvard course, which had about six weeks to go, and if Westinghouse could reimburse Northeast Utilities for the Harvard education. He agreed to both. I then called my boss at Millstone, the CNO, Lee Olivier, and then Mike Morris, president and CEO of Northeast Utilities, to discuss with them the decision. Both were very gracious and recognized that this move was to the next level of management for me. They also said that no reimbursement was necessary. I finished at Harvard and returned to Millstone to complete a turnover of my responsibilities. I had learned a lot at Millstone that stood me in good stead for the rest of my career. I had also made some good lifelong friends. However, the opportunity provided by Ambrose's offer was not only the next level of management, it was second in command to all of Westinghouse Government Services — the division I had started in as an operator at FFTF almost 30 years earlier. It also allowed Cindy and me to return to our house (which Cindy had named Ballyrose, which means beautiful rose and coordinated with the house on Cliff Road, which she named

Rosecliff) in Aiken, where, at the time, we thought we would eventually retire.

Aiken, South Carolina
(The Second Time: 2000-2002)

Cindy was happy to return to the South, to our home in Aiken, and to her friends there. I was excited about that prospect and about being a COO for the part of Westinghouse I had originally joined as an operator when I left Oregon. I felt like I had come a long way up in that organization, albeit by leaving it, not once but twice. **Each time I left, I had made sure to involve my management in the decision and had burned no bridges, advice I always gave others when presented with an offer from another company**. I also continued to use the decision analysis and involve my family (or at least my wife) in that process.

Once back in Aiken, Cindy quickly devoted herself to decorating the house and buying new furniture and other accessories she felt it needed. Cindy loved to think of each room as a blank canvas and, once decorated to her satisfaction, as a work of art. She also got involved in community activities, such as fundraising for the Red Cross and local politics. I joined a gym near my new office and renewed old acquaintances with Ambrose's staff. However, not long after I returned, Westinghouse Government Services was sold by Westinghouse corporate to Dennis Washington's expanding empire called Washington Group International (WGI). The WGI government contract group was made up primarily of personnel from another purchase Dennis had made, the Cleveland-based Morrison Knudsen (MK) Company. However, Steve Hanks, the president of Washington Group International and a former MK executive, was directed by Dennis to make Ambrose president of the newly formed Washington Government Division (WGD) of WGI. This set the stage for lots of internal intrigue, although Ambrose and Steve eventually overcame their differences. Unfortunately, as usual, **those under the leaders mimic and accentuate what they see and perceive to be acceptable (even desirable) behavior.** However, all these machinations — along with another purchase by Dennis, Raytheon Engineering and Construction (E&C) — set the stage for later developments in my career. In particular, I got to interface with Bob Iotti from Raytheon and got to know him a lot better. Even though he essentially reported to me as the COO, I treated him with the utmost respect because of his technical acumen and tremendous work ethic.

The job of COO had me constantly away from home, flying to visit and assess our far-flung projects. I liked visiting these diverse places and projects but didn't like the travel time or the time apart from Cindy. **One of the things I set about developing was a set of metrics that could allow Ambrose and me to quickly evaluate projects and ascertain where to drill down to find problems that were affecting performance.** The idea came from a visit that the Millstone CNO, Lee Olivier, and I made to Virginia Power. The CNO there, Jim O'Hanlon, a company mate of mine from the Naval Academy, used the Institute of Nuclear Power Operations (INPO) metric format, which was information rich and used by all commercial nuclear plants. However, what Jim then did was to **group similar metrics into subcategories, which eventually rolled up in a weighted fashion to five main areas of focus: safety, quality, schedule, cost, and operations.** The weighted values were then color-coded to indicate how the collected parameters were doing:

- BLUE for world-class, exceeding expectations
- GREEN for meeting expectations
- YELLOW for below expectations and/or heading in an untoward direction
- RED for in the ditch

Included in the metric or rollup parameters were direction arrows that indicated improving or degrading performance. Based on the colors at the top, an executive knew where to direct his or her attention first. He or she could then quickly drill down to the INPO parameters that were causing the area to be less than GREEN. We required the evaluator to always state on the INPO parameter what was being done to address the metric; even if it was GREEN or BLUE, we wanted to know what was being done to sustain that performance.

Selling this approach to the various diverse projects and sites that made up WGD was a daunting task. I learned a lot about how to negotiate with what were usually very type-A personalities and get them to adopt an approach as their own. It took almost a year, but I did get this universal approach to performance measurement and reporting put into effect, and I am proud of that accomplishment.

Another pride-inspiring accomplishment during this period was the assessment and turnaround of the Evolved Expendable Launch Vehicle (EELV) project at Cape Canaveral. This was a project WGD inherited as a result of the acquisition of Raytheon E&C. The EELV was a launch pad being built for Boeing's new Delta IV rocket, and it was badly overrun in cost and behind in schedule. Additionally, as is usually the case with poor project management, safety was suffering. I was sent to assess the project and that assessment led to me replacing Raytheon management personnel with personnel I handpicked. After only three weeks, the new project manager, Charlie Wolf, called me to say that a primary subcontractor was recalcitrant with respect to the changes he felt were necessary to improve safety and overall performance. We had a conference call between Ambrose, Charlie, Steve Hanks, his COO, and me, and I was directed to go to EELV and find a win-win solution with this subcontractor. After a week, I concluded that we needed to terminate their contract, which I felt we could do for cause, but it would be better for all involved if we could convince them to permit termination of the contract for convenience.

When I filed my report with Ambrose, a call was made with WGI headquarters, and they were not pleased that I hadn't found a win-win resolution. I stuck to my guns and asked if they had read my report. They had not, so I asked that they at least do that before jumping to any conclusions. After they did, they agreed with my recommendation but said I was to go to the Cape for the negotiations. I did and that was another learning experience. The subcontractor's executive management was upset, to say the least, and sent a large, gruff VP to intimidate me in the negotiation meetings, which took place in their offices in Orlando.

While these negotiations were underway, other Raytheon projects were discovered to be grossly overrun in costs. It seemed that Dennis Washington was so anxious to acquire Raytheon that due diligence was not done as rigorously as it could have been, a critical mistake that ultimately drove WGI to declare bankruptcy. Declaration of Chapter 11 was to happen at 9:00 p.m. on the last day of negotiations with the EELV subcontractor, and I had a check in my pocket for $2 million to settle with them. Their chief negotiator blustered and yelled and was generally an ass. I calmly asked if he was sure he wanted to reject the check I slid across the table to him. He pushed the check back and fired a long string of obscene adjectives around the words "No deal."

I asked if he was sure and, again, he fumed and swore. With that, I picked up the check, put it in my pocket, stood, and said, "Tonight at nine o'clock, WGI will be declaring bankruptcy and you can get in line with all the other creditors." I left the room. As I was boarding the elevator, the VP came running down the hall, asking me to wait a minute and "could we talk?". I said talking was over and he should have a good day before explaining to his superiors what happened and why zero dollars was a better deal than $2 million. Boy, did that feel good! **Greed is not necessarily good!** As far as I know, the subcontractor never received a penny from WGI, and their contract was terminated successfully.

I also had to negotiate with Boeing on how WGI was going to recover from the poor performance of Raytheon. That kept me at EELV for most of my time for the next six months. Charlie and his leadership team were doing a good job changing performance and completing construction. I learned a lot about rocket launchers and about contract negotiations. I also discovered a major portion of the test program had been overlooked by both Raytheon and Boeing. That saved the project about $20 million and made about the same for WGD's test division, which was hired to recover that test program.

As construction, Charlie's forte, was ending, I decided that we needed a new project manager who was more experienced in startup testing. I was able to talk Harvey Handfinger, who was my chief test engineer at DWPF, into relieving Charlie, who could then return to his family in Denver. Charlie received a significant promotion as a result of his performance at EELV. Four or five months later, Charlie was diagnosed with brain cancer, so it was fortuitous that he was back home. He fought a valiant fight against the cancer and lived for six more years, during which he had lots of surgeries and treatment but also was able to achieve a lot in his altruistic efforts to support treatment and research in childhood cancer. He wrote two books about his fight and made a fortune in the stock market during this time. He was a tremendous individual and a great example of courage and humility as well as engineering acumen.

During this first year at WGD, two significant things happened in our private life. First and most important, our first grandchild was born to Erin and Mike. We thanked God that she was a healthy little girl, who they named Camryn. I remember the first time I held her in

Hattiesburg, Mississippi, where Erin and Mike were both in graduate school and Erin was teaching as well. It was really special that my parents were at Gulf Shores, Alabama, at the time and they drove over to see their first great-grandchild.

The other significant event of this time period was the discovery that my hip pain was due to avascular necrosis, and the only remedy was a hip replacement. We networked all over the country and finally settled on a surgeon in Charlotte, North Carolina. Dr. Bo Mason was recommended by a Harvard classmate of his who did hip replacements at the Cleveland Clinic and was the son of a doctor who graduated two years ahead of me from Sandusky High. I was back at work in two weeks and traveling again within a month. I slowly started to work out. Cindy and I decided to erect a building on our property dedicated to staying in shape. In addition to the weights on one side, where the wall was all mirror, it also had an in-ground endless lap pool, where one swims against the current, and a Jacuzzi on the other side. The building was contiguous in architecture to the main house and, with the shed I added, almost gave the property the feeling of a compound. It was neat getting up in the morning and walking across the driveway to a real gym. Cindy and I got a lot of use out of that investment.

While I was recovering from the first hip replacement, I received a call at home from Harvey Handfinger at the EELV project. He said that he "thought" we had had a fatality on the project. My heart sank. He went on to describe how a young pipefitter, father of two young children, had uncoupled a pipe under pressure and it had hit him in the chest and killed him instantly. Earlier in the shift, that same pipefitter had sought out our construction manager, who I had chosen for the job, and told him he had some safety concerns. The construction manager told him not to do the job, even though his immediate supervisor was pressuring him to get on with things. The pipefitter then went to help some other pipefitters, who had a similar circumstance to the job he had halted, and that's when the incident happened.

Although there were many lessons to be learned, the OSHA investigation exonerated our management team. However, I had many sleepless nights questioning whether I had done enough when I was on site to promote a safety mentality.

I had many sleepless nights questioning whether I had done enough when I was on site to promote a safety mentality.

About six months later, I was getting into my car and dragging my left leg into the car when I felt a familiar pain in that hip and knew immediately what the diagnosis would be. This time, I went to Ambrose to say I needed to get off the road. At the same time, WGI was reorganizing, and it was determined that Ambrose would no longer have WGD but that it would be divided into two divisions. Ambrose would get the one focused on weapons and chemical demilitarization. I would no longer be the COO of anything. I told Ambrose there was only one job I would consider and that would be to replace Joe Buggy, who was retiring, at the SRS as the WSRC president. Ambrose countered with an offer of the executive vice presidency, the number-two position at SRS, as he wanted to reward Bob Pedde with the presidency.

Bob was the current EVP and a good manager (remember he had been my construction manager on RTF), and was well-versed on site matters. Bob and I got along well and this new EVP job for me, with a hefty pay raise and bonus, would allow me to stay in Aiken. I accepted.

It was about this time that Bob Iotti, who had left WGD to become the president of CH2MHILL Nuclear, began to pursue me to join him there. Although I considered the SRS EVP to be the second-best job in the DOE complex, second only to the presidency of WSRC, Bob persisted in making offers over the next year. During this year, Roy Schepens, my DOE counterpart at DWPF and someone I both respected and liked, accepted the job at Hanford, where CH2MHILL was struggling with project management and operations issues at the Tank Farms (where highly radioactive waste was stored).

Roy had the Tank Farm as part of his considerable responsibilities at Hanford and began to suggest that the guy to address CH2MHILL's issues was me. So Bob increased the ante until I told Cindy we couldn't ignore the money being offered. Back to the decision analysis. The position would be as Bob's COO. However, first we would have to go to Hanford (for what I was told would be a year, but turned into two years) and fill in as the deputy general manager of the Tank Farms to address their issues. It was a gut-wrenching decision. Cindy didn't want to return to the Tri-Cities in Washington, and neither of us was crazy about leaving Aiken. However, the money would help with our plans, which included building our investment portfolio to support a comfortable retirement. We accepted even though Steve Hanks himself tried to talk me out of leaving by doubling my salary for a year. So, after just a year at SRS, I handed in my resignation to Westinghouse. Again.

Before we left Aiken, Alyssa brought her boyfriend home to meet us. Dave Pazdan was a banker in Chicago and had lived his whole life in the Chicago area. Cindy and I both liked him. While they were on that visit, Dave asked for Alyssa's hand in marriage, and we were happy to give it. However, a week after they left Aiken, Alyssa called in tears because Dave was insisting the wedding be held in Chicago. His rationale was that his family was all there, as were all their most recent mutual friends. We had planned to have the wedding in Aiken, because that was where Erin was married and where all our friends were. Additionally, we were paying for the wedding and thought that decision was our call. Mike and Erin were happy to have the wedding in Aiken and their friends and families traveled there. Additionally, the wedding in Chicago would be more expensive simply due to the cost-of-living differential between Aiken and Chicago. But Alyssa's tears and distress got to me, so I relented and we agreed to have the wedding in Chicago. It turned out to be a success, with our side of the family and friends considering it a destination trip to Chicago for more than just the wedding. Alyssa and Dave, who both had well-paying jobs (as opposed to Mike and Erin who were in school at the time of their wedding), agreed to pick up some of the costs. It was a grand affair. In fact, we joked that Alyssa didn't have a wedding but rather a coronation.

Richland, Washington (The Second Time: 2002-2004)

The first time Cindy and I moved to Richland, Erin was just about ready for kindergarten and then, less than a year later, Alyssa was born. Therefore, those seven years in Richland the first time were centered around activities typical of young families. Cindy was very busy with the girls, and our life outside of work was with families of our daughters' friends.

This time in Richland, there were no children as the center of our social life. To make matters worse, Bob Iotti just sort of dropped me on Ed Aromi, the general manager of CH2MHILL Hanford, as his deputy general manager. The word had gotten out that part of the reason for my advent was that Roy Schepens wanted me there to address problems with the Tank Farm management. I think Ed handled it better than I might have, but he and his staff didn't go out of their way to welcome either Cindy or me. Ed's second in command was a true adherent to the Machiavellian school of management and took pleasure in workplace intrigue. The relationship with Ed and some of Ed's key staff added to the stress of my arrival at the CH2MHILL organization and to the move back to Richland overall. When we first got there, we settled in a temporary small apartment while we looked for a place to live. Cindy found a condo being built on the Columbia River, but we had to wait until it was finished. At least she had some say in the final touches, and it turned out to be a very pleasant place to live. However, I think due to the stress of the move and being so far away from her girls and her friends in Aiken, Cindy developed some severe back pain issues. I was very worried when she called me at work crying and telling me she was in great pain. I rushed home and took her to the hospital.

To say Cindy was not happy on this tour would be an understatement. But to her credit, she tried to make it work. One day, we were at a casino on the Indian reservation near Umatilla, looking out a picture window at a rather desolate landscape. Cindy, reflecting on her high-society lifestyle in Aiken —where she hosted women's events for the Red Cross, participated on the Heart Board, and attended the Steeplechase horse race in lovely outfits — turned to me and asked, "What the hell happened?" Eventually she got a volunteer job as a docent at the local museum in Richland and began to study Northwest Indian culture and decorated our condo with a taste of what she was learning. We did have some friends from Westinghouse who we saw occasionally and a few of our former neighbors from the earlier time in Richland, but I think overall it was lonely for Cindy and probably one of the roughest moves she experienced.

On the positive side of the ledger, we were making good money. On a trip back to Sandusky to visit my parents, we drove down Cliff Road where we had built the only house out of the 17 we owned over the course of our marriage. Three lots down from that house there was one of the original Cliffs cottages under renovation. Because of the increase in our financial situation, we were able to buy it and it became our summer home. Cindy then had two houses that drew her back east, the Aiken home and the summer home on Cliff Road. I thought the location was perfect, high on a cliff overlooking Lake Erie, and close to my parents who had moved to Milan, Ohio, (my dad's idea of moving south in retirement). It was almost halfway between Erin and Alyssa and their families.

Along came our second grandchild when Alyssa gave birth to a healthy (thank God) little boy they named Carson. She and Dave lived in Chicago; and Erin, Mike, and Camryn had moved to Pittsburgh after Mike completed his doctorate. So the Lake House, as it came to be known, was indeed halfway between the two girls' residences. Additionally, I had hoped that my parents could take advantage of the Lake House as well, but that didn't turn out to be the case. However, Summerose, as Cindy named this house, came to be the focal point for annual family reunions on summer holidays, especially the Fourth of July week.

As far as work was concerned on the Tank Farms, there was no end to the challenges. The most daunting task was working with the unions. Local management had developed an adversarial approach that was not working well. I listened to the union chief stewards and soon developed a good rapport with several of them. I moved my office to the Tank Farms, which didn't make Ed happy, as he preferred I stay near him in the Richland offices. **I toured the worksites each week with a different first-line manager and soon established a First-Line Manager Council. I also established an ombudsman corps patterned after what had been done at Millstone.** All these efforts led to a good relationship with people in the field and further separated me from Ed and his inner circle. I didn't care. The field was where the work was being done.

I did convince Ed to adopt the rollup metrics scheme I had put in place at WGD. He liked the fact that he could easily see where things were not performing up to par. Roy Schepens liked this approach as well. I determined that, like at SRS, reviewing all major projects just once a month was an exercise in futility as well as stamina. **Like at SRS, I changed to a weekly review of no more than four major projects at a time, but at much greater detail and depth.** Roy appreciated this change as well, he and attended most meetings. Meanwhile, Ed stayed in the Richland offices; I never did understand his philosophy with respect to his general aloofness.

Bob Iotti and Ralph Peterson, the CH2MHILL CEO, liked the progress I had made, and after two years, it was decided I could move to Denver to devote myself to the COO activities.

During this time, I had to make trips back to Washington, D.C., on business or took vacation in Ohio at the Lake House. I would always stop to see my parents on these trips. In 2003, I visited my parents alone (Cindy was in Aiken to see to some things there). My mother asked me to take my dad to see his doctor. We had an excruciating wait in the doctor's waiting room, and I could tell my dad was in a lot of discomfort. As usual, he was stoic when it came to admitting he

Dave and Cindy's parents, Ivan, Gertrude, Margaret, and Joseph

was in pain, and he was patient with the doctor — who, once we got to see him, explained that my dad had to get off the steroids he was taking for skin irritation. I didn't realize how frail my dad was, but stayed with him in the car when my mother came to pick us up and stopped at a medical supply store to get a special chair that would help my dad stand up and sit down. He never got to use it.

I went home to the Lake House after that day was over, planning to return the next day. The next morning, I received a call from my sister, Judy, telling me I needed to get there right away because dad had taken a turn for the worse. I stayed in his room with him until my mother sent me on an errand. When I returned, my sister ran out of the house to tell me that dad had passed. I think I may have been in the room when it happened but thought my dad's labored breathing had simply subsided, indicating he was finally able to sleep restfully and that was just when my mother called me for the errand. Regardless, I am very thankful I got to spend that last full day with him. My tribute to him at his memorial service explains what a good man he was and how fortunate I was to have had him for my father.

Denver, Colorado (2004-2005)

Cindy had to stay in Richland to close on the sale of the condo, on which we made a good sum of money. Then she flew back to our home in Aiken. In the meantime, I drove my car from Richland to Denver through Idaho, Montana, Utah, and Wyoming. It was an interesting drive but a long one to make alone, even with an audio book to help pass the time. I found a small apartment in Denver that Cindy moved me out of (on her very first visit) and into a nicer condo in Parker, Colorado. Cindy spent most of her time in Aiken or on Catawba Island, because my job required a lot of travel to various locations where CH2MHILL had contracts, not unlike when I was COO for WGD. She did come out for her birthday week in January, and I treated her to a private ski lesson at Beaver Creek. While she was on the mountain for three hours, I treated myself to a hot rock massage and a steam bath. When I went to the foot of the mountain to wait for Cindy's arrival from her lesson, there was a portable bar where the bartender recommended a hot chocolate with peppermint schnapps. I was on my second one when she skied up, hot and sweaty, out of breath, sunburned, and aching. She said, "What is wrong with this picture?" I took a sip of my drink and said, "Nothin'!"

Besides traveling and assessing how the site managers were doing, I was assigned by Bob to develop the rolling five-year plan, a version of a strategic plan. I had no experience doing this at all. The good news was that Bob then assigned himself to the bid for a major contract and left Denver to work on it in New Mexico. Therefore, I was left to my own designs. I called a colleague in the United Kingdom who I knew from when he worked for Bechtel at SRS and who I knew was a very good strategic thinker. He recommended that I read Larry Bossidy and Ram Charan's book *Confronting Reality: Doing What Matters to Get Things Right*, which is all about strategic planning. I discuss the aspects of this book and how I applied it in the section of this book on management. Fortunately, I had a very hardworking, experienced business development person who was a big help with defining opportunities and assigning probabilities to those opportunities. The key was to get buy-in from the direct reports to Bob. They were all strong type-A personalities and didn't like each other, Bob, or me that much. Again, I was fortunate to have a staff member who had a PhD in psychology, and together we devised a way to gain their support.

What I had noticed in the meetings Bob had with his staff (when they would all come to Denver for a two – or three-day event) was that they loved to shoot the messenger. When one of Bob's staff would present a topic, especially if it impacted the project managers' sites or workload, they delighted in tearing the idea or concept apart.

With my PhD colleague, we decided to break the business areas into segments and look at which of the site/project managers had an expertise or background in that area. My job was then to convince that manager to make the presentation on that area in our strategic plan meeting. I would visit his or her site, flatter him or her on their knowledge in that area, promise to do all the heavy lifting (which allowed me to put my spin on the topic), and then they could present the material as their own. One after another they agreed to do that. What they did not know is that the PhD had advised me that they would be much less likely to be overly critical of their peers, especially when they knew their turn in the barrel was coming. The strategic planning meeting was a huge success, and our strategic plan became a model for the rest of CH2MHILL. You see, Ralph Petersen, who I briefed before the big management meeting with all his divisions (including Bob's), really liked what we had put together. I gave all the credit to my colleagues, but Ralph knew who the driving force was.

In Bob's absence, while working on the preparation of the offer on the project on which he bid himself, there were some planned changes in the CH2MHILL organization. Although I was highly valued by Ralph, who was struggling with cancer (which eventually took his life), I was not a long-time CH2MHILL employee and not part of the upper echelon clique. Coupled with other corporate machinations, this situation led me to activate my feelers for what might be available elsewhere in the industry. One of the project managers with whom I had developed the strategic plan told me he had been approached by Parsons, which was looking to put together a team to bid for the High-Level Waste (HLW) contract at the Savannah Rivers Site (SRS). He knew I had a home in Aiken, and he thought of me because he was not interested for himself. He gave me the contact at Parsons and soon I was involved in that interviewing process. Parsons ultimately made me a very attractive offer to lead their effort to win the contract.

The position allowed Cindy and me to once again "go home" to Aiken. I accepted the Parsons offer.

One important thing that occurred during this time frame was that while Cindy was at the Lake House, Hurricane Katrina struck the southeast United States. After watching the disaster on TV for several days, she decided she needed to help. She went to the Red Cross to see what she could do. She was given a two-day intensive training course in Toledo, her SUV was packed with supplies, and she was on her way to Mississippi and Louisiana. Her good friend, Diana Southard, accompanied her. I am very proud of her courage and generous heart for providing that service. As it turned out, it was the beginning of an ongoing relationship with the Red Cross in South Carolina and Ohio, which was eventually to involve me when I retired some years later. When she returned to Aiken, she went to the Aiken Red Cross office to volunteer her services. Eventually she started a women's club event dedicated to raising money for the Red Cross called "Sherry and Chocolates." She started a similar women's effort in Ottawa County, Ohio, called "Club Red." Over the years, these events have raised a significant amount of money — and their organizers and attendees had fun doing it. The annual Red Cross gala in Ottawa County is a growing and ongoing event to which people look forward.

Aiken, South Carolina (The Third Time: 2006-2009)

Different from the Hanford CH2MHill experience, Cindy and I were warmly welcomed to the Parsons contingent in Aiken by Chuck Terhune, the program manager of the Salt Waste Processing Facility (SWPF), Parsons's only nuclear project in the DOE Complex. SWPF was being designed and built by Parsons for the SRS. Its mission was to process the supernate in the million-gallon tanks, removing and concentrating the cesium it contained. Cesium is the highly radioactive isotope contained in this aqueous liquid, which sits on top of the sludge as the tank material has stratified over the years. The low-level radioactive constituents of the supernate would be sent to the Saltstone facility to be captured in cement, which would remain on site forever. The concentrated cesium solution would be sent to the DWPF, where it would be combined with the sludge that was already being processed at the DWPF. It was economical to combine the concentrated cesium with the sludge because there would be fewer cans of glass due to the concentration and because the cesium only had a half-life of 30 years while the sludge constituents had isotopes with a much longer half-life. It made no sense to produce cesium-only cans to be sent to long-term storage like the sludge-only cans.

Chuck Terhune, the SWPF program manager, was a long-time Parsons employee who had a successful career managing large construction projects in the Middle East for Parsons. However, SWPF was his first nuclear project and his first time working in the DOE Nuclear Complex with DOE as his client. There were a lot of additional, different demands and stresses of this job, which he had not faced before. My group did not report to him and was in a different building, but he was a great help to me in getting established and learning how to accomplish things in the Parsons bureaucratic structure. My main challenge was to educate my chain of command on what it would take to win the contract at SRS. The first priority was to put together a management team that no one could deny was first-class. So I began the task of hiring people who had impressed me over the course of my career and who would trust me that this was a real opportunity — even though not a sure thing, by any stretch, due to the vagaries of the DOE contract acquisition system. **My mantra was to always surround myself with people who were smarter than me and then support them to do their jobs in any**

way I could. I felt good about being able to convince a number of outstanding people to take a chance and join me on the effort to win the contract at SRS. A few had to move their families to Aiken and others were already in the area. We formed an outstanding team with people like Roy Schepens, Charlie Hansen, Tom Burns, Heatherly Dukes, Theresa McMullen, and Bill Pettigrew.

While I was settling in with Parsons, which included going to Pasadena, CA, for several training sessions, Cindy was continuing her involvement with the Aiken Red Cross and the Aiken County Republican Party. She also was spending her summers up on Lake Erie where I would join her whenever I could. Usually I planned business trips around stopping in Ohio for long weekends. Of course, I would spend the summer holidays up at the Lake House — usually with one or both of the girls and their growing families. To be able to better accommodate both girls' families at the same time, we decided to add a garage with a loft, which had a bedroom, full bath, and a playroom. The back entrance became a hallway between the garage and the kitchen. We made the area directly above it into a dorm room with two bunk beds to accommodate four grandchildren. During this time period, Erin and Alyssa each had a second child, Cade and Lucciana, respectively. Cindy had to manage the garage project and we chose the same contractor who had remodeled the house. Eventually, we had him add a front porch as well, to protect the front door from those cold winter storms.

The team I had assembled at work was busy writing the proposal for the contract with SRS and each were beginning to think about orals (a DOE board review where several DOE managers would challenge the team with questions and situations), when Chuck Terhune abruptly stood up in a meeting at SWPF offices, insulted the DOE client from D.C., and stormed out of the meeting. He resigned from Parsons later that day. I happened to be up at the Lake House at the time and received a call from the Parsons division president, saying I had to return to Aiken immediately to take over the SWPF project. Once again, I found myself being brought in as the leader of a troubled facility in duress. I had to win over the client (the DOE), but also convince the Parsons team of my leadership. Suffice it to say that the intensity of my workdays increased dramatically. I was on the SWPF project for 15 months, during which time I brought over some of my SRS HLW bid team to help. The DOE acquisition process was lumbering along, so taking a few of those stellar folks did not hurt the bid process and SWPF needed them more. In fact, if Parsons was not able to turn things around on the SWPF project in the DOE's mind, we could kiss the SRS HLW bid goodbye anyhow. The project was in transition from preliminary design to final design and just starting construction as well. I made some changes in the existing staff after convincing Parsons upper management of the need to do so. We ended up with a solid team and stakeholder confidence was increasing as we moved things along. It was actually fun.

Once again, I found myself being brought in as the leader of a troubled facility in duress.

During the time away from the bid team, a very successful retired Navy captain was hired. He had a sterling record in the Navy and was to be part of our team when we won the contract. He accepted this role as a transition into civilian life, and I thought it was commendable of him to realize that there are differences between civilian business and how things are done in the services. I had seen too many Navy captains and admirals brought into positions of high visibility and significant responsibility in the civilian world who subsequently didn't make successful transitions under the microscopic examination to which those positions were usually subject. As I said earlier, it's usually much easier to make the transition from the military world to civilian world when you come out as a low-ranking officer and go into a lower-level management position where mistakes are not as visible and there is time to learn the ropes. With the SWPF project on an even keel and orals looming, along with a Red Team review of our proposal, I recommended that this retired Navy officer take my place. I was desperate to get back to the bid effort and should have taken more time evaluating his capabilities in the civilian world. But the transition was made.

I had seen too many Navy captains and admirals brought into positions of high visibility and significant responsibility in the civilian world who subsequently didn't make successful transitions under the microscopic examination to which those positions were usually subject.

Soon after returning to the team, we were all to go out to Pasadena for the Red Team review of our project. On the way out, I stopped in Ohio to spend time at the Lake House with Cindy, who was already there. She picked me up at the Cleveland Airport, and we had a nice dinner on the way back to Catawba Island and a nice night once we got "home." However, I woke up the next morning with a tremendous pain across my lower abdomen. After some self-diagnosis and attempts at relieving what I thought to be constipation, I had Cindy take me to the emergency room (ER). It was a hot Saturday morning in July and the ER was full of drunks, bar fight casualties, and the victims of the types of accidents that occur in a summer vacation area. I looked fine by comparison, but my body temperature was dropping while I waited to be seen in accordance with the ER triage methodology. When I was finally examined and the X-ray was reviewed, the doctor told me that I needed to be scheduled for surgery. I said fine, I would have my wife go to the car to get my planner. The doctor said, "You are going to surgery right now." I had a perforated lower intestine, which resulted in me going septic. Fortunately, the surgeon and his team were available on a beautiful Saturday morning, when they could have been out sailing. I was in the hospital a week and then home another four weeks recovering. The recovery from that surgery was much more difficult than the recovery from the orthopedic operations.

I tried to keep up with my team as they went through the Red Team review and began to accommodate the team's recommendations. Three-hour conference calls absolutely exhausted me. At first, reading for more than an hour at a time was difficult. Naps were easy to do. Cindy was an angel, taking care of me and patiently waiting on me. I slowly recovered my strength, but it was a close call, and I thank God that the local hospital in Port Clinton had such good surgeons and nurses. I eventually returned to Aiken, where the team was preparing for orals and fine-tuning the proposal. I felt the finished product was excellent, and I know we did a great job at orals.

What we were not able to do was convince our senior corporate executive management of the need for them to "press the flesh" of the DOE leadership and do it often. The trip from California was "just too difficult for them to make," and the one person they did send was both inept and not of significant stature. In the meantime, our competition, who was home based in Aiken, was up in D.C. every week wining and dining the leader of the DOE division who was responsible for the contract. Even though we know that the Source Evaluation Board decided in our favor, that manager in D.C. over-turned our selection in favor of people she felt she knew.

During this timeframe, my mother's condition started a downhill slide. She had been staying home with assisted care individuals who had been arranged by me and my siblings and with the help of former nurses who worked for Mom. I would visit her every time I came to the Lake House. She was taking more than 22 different medications, which just seemed to be disrupting her bodily functions. I went to the doctor with her and got the meds reduced by two or three. One time, I received a call from the day care person who had found my mother had fallen and could not get up and was having other difficulties. When I arrived, I had no choice but to call an ambulance to come get her. She was in the hospital for approximately three weeks, and at times she seemed to be getting better. Cindy spent a lot of time with her (as I still had to make a living and couldn't be there continually), but I saw her every time I came home. It was not easy to see this once vibrant and extremely intelligent woman, who had raised me and passed on to me many of her qualities and philosophies, struggling. Finally, she was moved to hospice in the hospital, and we began making arrangements for assisted care living. Mom was 89 and had lived on her own until this critical time. It was hard. Before we could make the move, she passed away while I was in D.C. Cindy was by her side, for which I will be eternally grateful.

It was a season of loss, in many ways. Losing the contract bid set the stage for yet another move in my career. It quickly became apparent that Parsons not only didn't have much influence in the DOE Complex, they also had sold most of their nuclear engineering exper-tise and didn't have much to offer either commercial or DOE nuclear projects. I began to look around. I contacted an old friend who recommended I contact Babcock and Wilcox (B&W). As it turned out, Bob Cochran, the president of the Technical Support Group (TSG), was a colleague from the Energy Facility Contractors Group (EFCOG). I had served on EFCOG for several years and eventually became the chairman, a collateral duty, which I had to give up when I assumed the program manager slot for SWPF. Bob Cochran had a driving need for someone to replace the startup manager on a project TSG was bidding. The person they had on the bid had quit just when the bid was to be submitted, with only five weeks to prepare for orals. Although I was not anxious to go through the bid and orals process again after the SRS HLW experience, B&W's desperate need put me in a strong bargaining position. Cindy and I knew retirement was not far off, and we also knew we would not be wise to have two homes in retirement. We had decided to make our summer house on Cliff Road our permanent home. I negotiated for B&W to buy our Aiken house at market prices to help solve that problem. Fortunately, that deal was consummated just before the bottom fell out of the real estate market.

Lexington, KY, and Erwin, TN (2009-2011)

The project on which B&W was bidding, DUF6, would have its corporate offices in Lexington, KY. Therefore, I could rationalize moving into a condo in Lexington in anticipation of winning the contract. At first, my work was in Cincinnati and then it shifted to Oak Ridge, Tennessee. In either case, I would leave Lexington early Monday morning and generally return Friday evening. This allowed Cindy to spend time with her mother, who was in a nursing home in Lexington, where she and Cindy's father retired and where Donna, Cindy's older sister, was a long-time resident. Colonel Brigandi had passed away in 2003, a few months after my dad. Eventually, Mrs. Brigandi needed to move out of their house into an assisted living facility. As it turned out, Cindy was able to spend quality time with her mother during the final six months of her mother's life. I feel really good that I was able to arrange that, especially because Cindy was at my mother's side when she passed away in 2007. There was no better person with whom my mother could have spent her last hours than Cindy. I am very thankful it worked out that she was also there for her own mother's final days.

Once we completed orals, I did move my office to Oak Ridge, where I had a variety of assignments from Bob Cochran and was also working on proposal follow-up items and contract assumption preparations. Even though the DOE can take many months to decide to whom to award a contract, they expect the awardee to hit the ground running. I had been working in that capacity, which included visiting other sites, when it became obvious to B&W leadership that the Nuclear Fuel Services (NFS) president had to be replaced. B&W had acquired NFS, the sole supplier for the Navy's nuclear fuel for submarines and aircraft carriers, and within a year the NRC shut down the plant for operational and management concerns after several in-plant incidents. NFS also had responsibility for down blending DOE enriched nuclear fuel received from all over the world in a variety of forms and conditions. It was, in fact, in that part of the facility where most of the problems occurred. Bob threw my name in the hat as a candidate for the NFS president job, and I was selected to assume that position. I considered it a real honor and a tremendous responsibility, even though I hated to leave the DUF6 team with whom I had bonded in pretty short order.

NFS is in Erwin, Tennessee. At first, I lived in a hotel in Johnson City, Tennessee, and once again began to put in tremendous hours to assume control of the plant and restore stakeholder confidence. The first thing I had to do was gain the confidence of the leadership team and the workforce as I assessed what was wrong and how to fix it. It took a lot of in-plant time as well as extra time to learn yet another technology. It was an opportunity to deploy all that I had learned over the course of my career that might apply to the NFS situation. I set forth the strategy I deployed at NFS.

As keys to those efforts, I:

- Began a concentrated effort to learn the NFS technology as quickly as possible
- Hired Bill Pettigrew to help develop a resource-loaded schedule
- Had Bill lead the POD as an accountability to the schedule meeting
- Developed a set of metrics and posted them for all to see
- Met with the union president and chief stewards to build rapport

- Met with the NRC Region and changed the licensing restoration to a segmented approach, which they much appreciated
- Met with Naval Reactors to explain the approach
- Made some organization realignments to support the above and made a few management changes accordingly
- Established a People Team, including an ombudsman program and a strengthened Employee Concerns Program; hired Ed Morgan who had developed expertise in these endeavors at Millstone Station
- Established a Senior Review Board
- Spent one backshift per week with a first-line manager (FLM) to understand their challenges and build rapport with the rank and file; established an FLM Council
- Spent at least two or three hours each day touring the plant, talking to employees.

When I told Cindy that our nuclear Navy only had a six-month backlog supply of fuel for our submarines and aircraft carriers, she saw the importance of my new job. She got chills at the prospect that this job was related to our country's national defense, which could be put in jeopardy if the plant's issues were not successfully resolved in a timely manner. She felt it was our duty and honor to facilitate the restart of NFS.

Cindy came to Tennessee after she had closed out our condo in Lexington, which was near her sister's condo. She ultimately found a cabin in an exclusive and unique development in North Carolina. The cabin was back in the woods and could only see one other cabin nearby, which was unoccupied. The cabin was only a short drive from the Appalachian Trail and about 20 miles from Ashville, North Carolina. Even though it was a hard drive of about 45 minutes from work, which on those steep mountain highways could become treacherous in foul weather, we did enjoy the time there. It was unique.

I had been consulting with my orthopedic surgeon, Dr. Bo Mason, who had performed both of my hip replacements and whose colleague, Dr. Thomas McCoy, had replaced my shoulder joints, because it seemed my left hip was becoming more and more unstable. X-rays revealed I was experiencing a phenomenon called osteolysis, which meant the debris from the hip-replacement pros-thesis was causing the body's own enzymes to attack the bone behind the prosthesis and basically turn it to mush. The only option was to do a hip revision, which entailed taking out the prosthesis, vacu-uming out the affected bone, replacing the missing pelvis bone with a bone graft, and putting the joint back together. Once I knew my left hip joint would have to be "revised," we decided to move to Johnson City for an easier drive to work, more shopping amenities for Cindy, and closeness to a hospital fitness gym for recovery from the hip revision surgery.

When I took the job with B&W, I had to have a physical. The phys-ical indicated that my prostate-specific antigen (PSA) had risen to 4.1 so it was decided to do a biopsy on the prostate gland. The results came back negative, and I thought I had dodged a bullet. However, six months later, when I was selected as the president of NFS, I had to have another physical. Now the PSA had risen to 4.7, so another biopsy was ordered. This time, it showed cancer in some of the pros-tate samples. I discussed the situation with the orthopedic surgeon, and he recommended that I see an oncologist colleague of his in Charlotte where he also was located. This doctor studied the biop-sies, consulted with a colleague at Johns Hopkins, and applied a logic diagram to my situation using all the various parameters. The result was that I would undergo Brachytherapy (radioactive seed inser-tion in the prostate gland) after the hip revision. Of course, during this time I was continuing with the recovery of NFS, which was a pressure-packed endeavor, especially considering the governance I was receiving from B&W corporate. Despite all the great progress that was being made at NFS, due to my medical issues and the job pressures, the stress was mounting for Cindy more than I could appreciate.

I informed my B&W management of the need to have the two surgeries and then informed the NFS workforce. I turned the leadership over to the most qualified of my staff and left for the hip surgery in Charlotte. I felt good about the timing, as the plant had been returned to service and the various stakeholders (Naval Reactors, NRC, and the DOE) seemed satisfied with the progress being made. I felt good about the hip surgery because I had been through it twice before. Although I had once quipped that I was glad I didn't have three hips, as I told Cindy, "The good news is I know there is a light at the end of the tunnel. The bad news is I know I have no choice but to go through the tunnel." I was back to work in two weeks, and off crutches and cane in another two. I also returned to swimming and lifting.

The good news is I know there is a light at the end of the tunnel.

When I returned from the hip surgery, I still had the cancer with which to deal. It became obvious to me that all these medical challenges, along with the stress of the job, were taking their toll on Cindy. So, in early December 2010, I told her that I would tell B&W management that I would work until July of the next year and then retire. I felt my ultimatum would give them enough time to find my relief. Although I would have originally probably have worked another six or even 12 months to assure the approaches and practices I had put in place to regain NFS's license were firmly taking hold, the main mission had been accomplished and it was a fitting capstone to my career.

I then went for my Brachytherapy treatment back in Charlotte. The procedure was completely successful, inserting palladium seeds in my prostate to kill the cancer. My PSA has been dropping ever since, and Dr. Tiegland, the oncologist, assured Cindy after the procedure that he was "confident they got all the cancer." I consider that God works in mysterious ways. Although ultimately the osteolysis was the result of debris from the rubbing of the stem of the prosthesis against the cup of the prosthesis, I still had confidence in my orthopedic doctor, Bo Mason, and he had referred me to one of the best oncologists on the east coast for the treatment of the prostate cancer. I retired from NFS and B&W on April 1, 2011, and Cindy and I headed for our Lake House on Catawba Island and the next phase of our life together — retirement. The lessons I learned over my career, and the application of those insights to the situation at NFS, are outlined in detail in Section III of this book.

I need to mention that during this timeframe, Alyssa called to tell us "one slipped by the goalie," which was her humorous way of telling us she was pregnant with their third child. Francesca Rose was born in 2010. Lis's statement that it was "wonderful to fall in love all over again" may be more appreciative of Francesca than the "goalie" statement. One thing we know for sure is that this child is the spitting image of her mother in both looks and temperament. We may need to get another plaque that says, "I guess I will keep my shoes on" and give it to Francesca because she has the same undaunted determination her mother exhibited at the same age.

Before I close the literal and figure chapter on my career, I should mention That two times I was interviewed for the chief executive officer (CEO) of a company and both times it came down to me and one other person. Both times, the other person was chosen, but I feel honored to have made it to the "championship round" in the selection process. The first time was for the CEO of Oak Ridge Association of Universities (ORAU), a consortium of universities doing research at or for the Oak Ridge National Laboratory. A member of the board told me they decided to go with an incumbent professor because "he was less of a change agent."

The other job was at the Nuclear Decommissioning Agency (NDA) in the United Kingdom. They decided to go with a British national already on staff. The right decision was probably made in both cases, and I do believe all things happen for the best. Had I been chosen for either job, I would probably have taken the offer and then would have never been president of NFS, which served as a better finish to my career than either of those jobs would have.

RETIREMENT

Catawba Island, Ohio
(The Second Time: 2011–present)

We had always thought we would sell the Lake House on Catawba Island and retire to Aiken, South Carolina, which is the direction most people head in retirement, south. However, about three years before I retired, we arrived at the Lake House on a glorious spring day and asked ourselves "how could we sell this beautiful home overlooking this tremendous body of water?" Also, we knew our grandkids loved to come to the Lake House and, at that time, both girls lived about five hours from Catawba Island. So we reversed course and found a way, thanks to B&W, to easily give up the house in Aiken.

The transition from 80-hour work weeks with significant responsibility to taking it easy was not as difficult as I had heard it could be. Cindy and I quickly established a workout routine, and she immersed herself in Red Cross activities and political activities in Ottawa County. I found myself invited to be on the Ottawa County Red Cross Board of Directors (BOD) as well as invited to meet with Republican movers and shakers in Ottawa County. The Red Cross BOD involvement led eventually to heading up the Speakers Bureau, which proved to be a time-consuming and rewarding endeavor. Then I was asked to participate on the Lake Erie Improvement Association (LEIA) and the Catawba Cliffs Association (CCA) Board. Cindy was elected to the Ottawa County Republican Central Committee in 2013.

Through Cindy's contacts with some Erie County Tea Party folks, I was also asked to participate in the Energy from Thorium Foundation (EFTF). This group is promoting using thorium, one of the most prevalent substances in the Earth's crust, to be used in a Liquid Core Molten Salt Reactor (LCMSR) to breed uranium-233, which would fission to produce power. There are many advantages to this type of reactor, which I will cover later, so I enthusiastically joined that effort. I was already on the Ohio State University (OSU) Nuclear Engineering Program (NEP) Advisory Board (AB). I also tried to spend a couple of hours each week at the Ohio Veterans Home (OVH) in Sandusky, talking to the residents there. I am sure I got more out of it than they did. I now understand the statement I heard many retirees make, "**How did I ever find time to work?**"

I tried to get involved in substitute teaching in that first year of retirement but that proved to be a very unsatisfactory experience. That experience with the local high school, as well as my experiences the Ohio State NEP advisory board, opened my eyes to the state of education in this country and left very unfavorable impressions. I eventually told the outfit contracted to hire substitute teachers and provide them to the schools to take my name off the list. It was apparent that what they really wanted were babysitters on a moment's notice, not real educators. Nonetheless, I was asked to serve on the Sandusky Education Foundation, and I agreed to do that. So, my dance card was filling up with volunteer activities when my priority in retirement was to be with Cindy. After dragging her all over the country in support of my career, now it was time to do what she wanted to do. She had priority over any of the volunteer activities and any consulting assignments as well as the criteria below indicate.

Bruce Noordoff, the program manager at FFTF, once remarked to me "how soon they forget you when you retire." He was referring to the amount of contracting he was doing where his considerable experience was tapped to advise people he used to work with or who worked for him. I signed up with a friend's consulting company to do occasional consulting. But I had clear guidelines for what I would say "yes" to. For me to be interested:

- I had to feel I would add value to the endeavor.
- The job had to be interesting.
- I would only be away from home a week at a time.

Those criteria significantly limited candidate assignments, but that was the intent. In 2011, I had three significant consulting activities, none of which came through the consulting company but rather through former colleagues and friends. In 2012, I had no assignments and only one in 2013. I had one assignment in January 2014, which meant leaving our winter vacation spot (that year Alpharetta, Georgia) for a frigid week in Tennessee. In the spring of 2015, I was on a team that the DOE hired to review the Mixed Oxide Fuel Fabrication Facility (MFFF) on the SRS. That assignment afforded me the opportunity to get together with old friends and colleagues.

It's nice to keep my hand in the industry in which I spent my career, but there are plenty of other things in which to involve myself. One nice thing I have discovered is that I finally have the time to read books of my choosing, rather than always having a mountain of work-related reading to do.

One significant event on which I worked in 2011 and 2012 was my high school class reunion. Although I was the class president all those years ago, I had never before been part of the planning and organizing of reunions, because I was always living somewhere else. Now that I was living only 30 miles from my hometown, I could be involved and the 50th reunion seemed like a real milestone to me. We had had reunions every five years since graduating, and I (usually with Cindy) attended all but two. One missed reunion occurred when I was out to sea in the Navy, and the other missed one was due to a hard work commitment. It was great to work with my class-mates to arrange a very full three days of activities, which everyone seemed to enjoy.

I called my old friend Wayne King, who was best man in my wedding, co-captain of both football and wrestling with me, and, in high school, my best friend. I convinced him to come and to stay at my house the whole three days. Wayne's wife, a Huron, Ohio, girl, Diane, had passed away a year earlier. I also called our high school wres-tling coach and convinced him to come. He stayed with us as well, and we even hooked him up with his old flame, Jackie Mayer, who was a former Miss America and grew up across the street from me. It was a great three days, even though the list of deceased class-mates continues to grow and is a sobering reminder of our mortality. I could not know that I would lose the love of my life not long after the next reunion following a four-year struggle with the progressive disease, ALS.

After the 2012 U.S. presidential election, I founded the Ottawa County Conservatives Club (OCCC). I called a few of the people I had met since retirement and we formed a core group to determine a vision, mission, and values and then set about attracting other members. Suffice it to say, we are a group of conservatives who are seriously worried about the direction in which our country is moving. We will focus first on Ottawa County, but also hope to have an influence beyond our county. I'll share more about politics later in Section IV of this book. Although I had to stop participating in this activity, as well as most others after the November 2014 diagnosis of Cindy's disease and my increasing caregiving responsibilities, the OCCC has continued and grown in number and stature.

Suddenly in control of our schedules and our whereabouts since my retirement, Cindy and I had decided that we would always spend the winter months somewhere else, because they can be brutal living right on the Lake. The first two winters were spent in Charleston, South Carolina. A very significant event during our second winter (2013) in Charleston has driven home to me two very important aspects of life. The first is that things can change in an instant, frequently due to circumstances beyond our control. Second is how much Cindy has always been part of my life and how much I have always loved her. Starting in Charleston, Cindy began having difficulty working out and then even with swallowing. At first, we thought her muscle cramps and loss of control of certain movements, like swallowing, might be due to some sort of vitamin deficiency, especially since we had switched our diet to essentially a vegan approach as the result of reading two books, *Younger Next Year* and *The China Study*. Her situation seemed to be deteriorating such that she started working out less and less, and had trouble with our walks around Charleston.

When we returned to Catawba, we contacted our doctor friend, Bill Bauer. He is a neurosurgeon, and he recommended we see a doctor in his office, a practice he set up for his son who is also a neurosurgeon. That led to a series of tests, including MRIs, blood work-ups, EMGs, and some other tests. The initial diagnosis could not rule out the possibility of amyotrophic lateral sclerosis (ALS) or multiple sclerosis (MS), both of which can essentially be death sentences. I told Cindy that we should not worry until we knew for sure what the diagnosis was, which may have seemed easy for me to say but I was trying to put on a brave face for her. I was worried for sure. The local doctor strongly recommended we get a second opinion and equally strongly recommended a doctor at the Cleveland Clinic under whom he had studied. We followed his advice, which led to more and more tests. The good news was that the Cleveland Clinic doctor immediately ruled out ALS and eventually ruled out MS. The Cleveland Clinic diagnosis was that Cindy had suffered a "minor" stroke due to something called a venous angioma. I use the word minor, but no stroke is minor. However, who would have thought that the diagnosis of a stroke would be viewed as a blessing (when compared with ALS or MS)?

However, a year later, Cindy's condition was slowly degrading, which is unusual for stroke victims, who typically get stronger over time. We returned to the original neurologist, who once again sent us to the Cleveland Clinic after running a series of tests. We also consulted a doctor at the University Hospital in Cleveland to whom a friend referred us. Ultimately it was determined that Cindy did indeed have ALS. All the doctors agreed it was a variant that 10-20 percent of the ALS patient population gets, and which proceeds at a slower rate than is experienced by the other 80 percent. We had to learn to deal with this new challenge.

Throughout this year-long ordeal, Cindy showed great strength and courage. I realized more and more how much I love her. We had to learn to cope with the challenge of increasing interruption of the neuro pathways from the brain to the affected muscles. At first, the primary impact was to the right side of her body and to her overall stamina. In the first two years, she was helped out by water aerobics and weekly massages that Cindy started in our 2014 winter spent in Naples, Florida.

At the Ohio State football game for Dave's 70th birthday, 2014 – Erin, Dave, Cindy, and Alyssa

For about two years after her diagnosis, we could still enjoy a game of cribbage after dinner, especially when it is too cold to go outside.

We inherited my parents' cribbage board on which they had kept count of who had won. Now we are doing the same thing on the same board, and somehow it brings me a little closer to my parents.

When I published the first edition of this book, it was not quite two years after Cindy's diagnosis with ALS. During that time, many adjustments had to be made and many more were to come as the disease progressed. I was Cindy's primary caregiver for the duration of the disease, although we had two wonderful nurses who came in Monday through Friday during the day shift, alternating weeks. I had all the back shifts and the weekends in their entirety. I do not regret one second. On the night Cindy died, she asked me to hold her hand, which I did until I just had to lie down with exhaustion because I had been up most of the night before. I wish I had known it was her last night alive. I would have held her hand all night.

Shortly after Cindy was diagnosed with ALS, we made the trip from Ohio to Naples, Florida. Obviously, there was a lot to contemplate on that trip. As was Cindy's nature, demonstrated by her reaction to Katrina, she wanted to do something to help inspire other ALS victims, their families, their caregivers, and even researchers. She wrote the lyrics and enlisted the help of the talented O'Regans, Michael and Mary Jo, to turn her vision into a song — the "ALS Odyssey Anthem" — which has gone viral all over the world via YouTube. The ALS Association has adopted it as their unofficial anthem and awarded Cindy posthumously for the attention her song has brought to the disease, the Association, and the need for research.

ALS Odyssey Anthem
written by Cindy Amerine

The garden path that I once chose, became I place I could not stroll,
But flowers still will grow, Alleluia.
The ballroom floor that we explored, we'd twirl, and swirl, and dance and soar
But we can stand embraced, Alleluia.
Raise us up on angels' wings; Soothe us with the choirs that sing,
Guide us through this odyssey, we implore Thee.
All is well, Trust in Me; The storm will change to calming sea;
In morning's light there will be beauty.
The altar steps, too much to bear, so seated I begin my prayer,
And still my lips proclaim, Alleluia.
"Be still and know that I am God," The Psalm assumes I'll beat the odds;
I'll trust there'll be a cure, Alleluia.
We now anticipate the day when ALS will go away
And all will sing His praises, Alleluia.
The joy as we accept his plan, Health and Peace to every man
With lifted hearts we sing our Alleluias.
Raise us up on angels' wings; Soothe us with the choirs that sing
Guide us through this odyssey, we implore Thee.
All is well, trust in Me; The storm will change to calming sea;
In the morning's light there will be beauty.
Alleluia, Alleluia!
Alleluia Alleluia Alleluia Alleluia Alleluia Alleluia
Seek and ye shall find
The elegance of His design.
The riddle will unfold
The answer in God's time.

Cynthia Brigandi Amerine
January 10, 1947 – August 11, 2018

LIFE AFTER CINDY

As I prepare to release this book in its second edition, Cindy has been gone just over a year. Here is her last letter to me, which I found going through her files. I think the nurses must have helped her write it.

David, my beloved,

The last words I will ever speak will be to you, and the words will be "I have always and will always love you completely and eternally." When I say I love you it is with my whole being. I am hoping you understand, with no words needed, from this moment forward that you are my everything. Thank you for being my husband, rock, mentor, best friend, teacher, coach, our children's wonderful father, incredible provider, risk taker, adventurer, listener, fixer, defender, Greek God, lover, and hero.

In our beautiful marriage, with our beautiful daughters, "we took the road less traveled … and that made all the difference!"

I knew just how much you meant to me when I realized I received the death sentence of ALS. My heart was torn out the moment the thought of being without you entered my mind. It was too much to bear. I got a glimpse of what it would be like in an abyss void of love, void of God.

I turned to God to guide me through our separation on earth. He will bring us together for eternity! I will never really leave you. I will be watching over you and I will keep my smile knowing we will be in heaven side by side, and with all those we love.

I wish for you a beautiful, purposeful, healthy life. I want you to be loved again. You are too sweet to not share your wonderfulness with another woman. I trust you will choose carefully!

Don't stop contributing!!! You have so much to offer! Go for it!

Lastly, love our little jewel box! Take care of our chalet on Cliff Road. Know how I felt so blessed finally have a place to call home! Cherish our mementos of our life together. Summerose allowed us to see the beauty out the window. Keep looking for beauty and bask in God's graces.

I'll be seeing you!

Love,
Cindy

Here is my response, of which somehow I think Cindy is aware:

Cindy,

I just read your last letter to me for the umpteenth time. I miss you so much, some days or at some times, more than others, but you are always there. I try to visit your gravesite every day and make sure the headstone is clean. It is a time to talk to you, but I reflect on our life together throughout the day. It is mostly a very happy reflection. We did so much and did "take the road less traveled." And finally we ended up at this beautiful spot on the shores of Lake Erie. The house you made possible by agreeing to the second move to Richland reflects your taste and your love. I do believe you "finally felt at home" and that made me immeasurably happy. After your support over the years, I just wanted to make you happy.

Retirement was to be Cindy time, and it was for a few years. How I wanted it to be your reward for all that you put up with and all the encouragement you gave me when I needed it. We were really,

really happy I thought until ALS entered the scene. Even then your courage, your dignity, your selflessness helped us both deal with the overwhelming ordeal. I tell people you never once complained or felt sorry for yourself. Yes, we cried and you may have cried more than I know, but your strength gave me, and others, the ability to cope with your disease.

I could not bear to think of losing you. I always shoved that thought away and busied myself with the tasks at hand. My greatest regret is not realizing our last night was our last night. You asked me to hold your hand and I did for a while, but then exhaustion made me go lie down. Had I known, I would have not only held your hand all night, I would have told you over and over how much I loved you and thanked you for the life you gave us. I hope I do get to see you again and am able to hold you once more.

I am trying to find my way. I do want to contribute with the productive time I have left, as you encouraged me to do in your last letter. I don't think I can actually love anyone again as you suggest, at least not the way I loved you. As I told you many, many times, you were always the very best part of my day. Coming home to your smile, your hug, and your kiss made the troubles and challenges of the day just melt away. Thank you! Thank you!

Forever.
Dave

Her friends and Club Red members (a group Cindy founded within the American Red Cross of NW Ohio) honored Cindy with a marble bench across the street, which looks out over the Lake. It has an inscription engraved in it, which is a line from her song. I like to think someone walking down our beautiful street will stop to contemplate all that is going on in their life. I like to think they will find solace in

Three generations on the porch of Cliff Road house, 2015

Cindy's words and wonder about the person who wrote them. Her legacy of helping others will continue far into the future.

I will stay in her Summerose until I cannot. As I explained, we could afford this house because she agreed to go to Richland for a second tour there. She directed the finishing of the house remodeling and, of course, decorated it in her inevitable style. It remains that way today.

I have tried to date and try not to compare those women to Cindy. I also try to avoid discussing my life with Cindy. Neither would be fair. Whether I will love again, as she directs above, remains to be seen. If I do, it will be different and in no way will detract from our 51-year love affair and the memories associated with it.

Our children and grandchildren are well, and I am blessed to be surrounded by family and friends as I adjust to life after Cindy.

I have started to consult again although my criteria remain the same, which limits the opportunities, which is fine with me. I am slowly re-engaging in volunteer activities as well. I support nuclear power any way I can, writing editorials, talking to politicians, and providing testimony wherever appropriate. I volunteer to talk to young people about careers in engineering and project management, which usually offers me an opportunity to correct wrong impressions about nuclear energy. My highest priority is to continue my studies of religion and God, followed by staying in good shape with daily swimming, weight lifting, and diet. So far, my annual physicals indicate I am doing just fine.

SECTION III

WHAT DOES IT ALL MEAN?

Time has a way of moving quickly and catching you unaware of the passing years. It seems just yesterday that I was young, just married, and embarking upon my new life with Cindy. Yet in a way, it seems like eons ago, and I can't help but wonder where all the years went. I know that I lived them all. In the previous sections of this book, I have provided glimpses of how it was back then and of all my hopes and dreams in those early years.

But here it is, the winter of my life, and it catches me by surprise. How did I get here so fast? Where did the years go and where did my youth go? I remember seeing older people through the years and thinking that those older people were years away from the life I was living. My own personal winter was so far off that I couldn't imagine fully what it would be like.

Here it is, the winter of my life, and it catches me by surprise. How did I get here so fast? Where did the years go and where did my youth go?

Today, my friends are retired and getting grey, and they move slower. Now I see an older person where once there was a younger one, including when I look in the mirror. I enter this new season of my life unprepared for all the aches and pains and the loss of strength and the ability to go and do things that I wish I had done but never did! But at least I know, that though the winter has come, and I'm not sure how long it will last, that when it's over on this earth, it's over. A new adventure will begin!

So, if you are not in your winter yet, let me remind you that it will be here faster than you think. Whatever you would like to accomplish in your life, please do it quickly! Don't put things off too long. Life goes by at an accelerated pace. Do what you can today, as you can never be sure what tomorrow will bring. You have no promise that you will see all the seasons of your life. Plan for tomorrow but live for today, say all the things that you want your loved ones to remember, and hope that they appreciate and love you for all the things that you have done for them in years past.

Yes, I have regrets. There are things I wish I had not done and things I should have done, and things I could have done differently. But indeed, there are many things I am happy to have done. It is all in a lifetime. At the end of the movie *Saving Private Ryan*, Private Ryan — who was saved at the sacrifice of many soldiers and is visiting Normandy Beach many decades later, in the winter of *his* life, asks his family, "Have I been a good man?" It is a good question to keep in mind your whole life. Within your sphere of influence, which may be larger than you know, and includes your inner self, known only to you, do the pluses exceed the minuses? Have you been a good man or a good woman? In my case, I think so. I hope so. God knows, and he will tell me.

Life is a gift to you. The way you live your life is your gift to God, to those you love, and who love you, and to those who come after.

WHAT HAVE I LEARNED FROM THESE EXPERIENCES?

Work

In reading my book to this point (and I humbly thank you for doing so), you have seen where I have been and much of what I have experienced as a son, husband, father, officer in the Navy, friend, neighbor, and leader in the nuclear industry. I have no doubt you have inferred many lessons from my story that apply to your own life and work. It's time for me now to formalize my own life lessons — for your benefit and mine. In the following pages, I will attempt to translate the life experiences from Sections I and II of this book into the lessons I have learned and how those lessons helped shape the way I worked, related to people, and handled situations. Capturing those lessons learned helps me put my life in perspective. I hope that they may be of value to you as well.

I start with the industry in which I spent almost all my productive adult hours: the nuclear industry. I think the lessons learned and the approaches taken by me in that industry can, for the most part, apply to any industry and any management or leadership position. I think you'll agree.

Hopefully my recounting of my career experiences — in the chapters that preceded this one — will serve as more than just an interesting memoir. I believe it will provide insight and even lend credence to the philosophies, lessons learned, and resultant advice that follows.

Confucius once said, "The man who loves what he does for a living will never have to work." However, for most of us, we never determine what it is that we really want to do other than make a living for ourselves and for our family. I believe that my father was one of the lucky ones, who really loved his job. My life's work did not happen by design. I liked math and physics in high school and at the Naval Academy. Taking those kinds of courses and doing well in them led me to the nuclear submarine force, which in turn led me to the nuclear industry. My career in that industry was the result of luck, determination, taking control of my destiny from time to time, and, most importantly, hard work. I was lucky to have a wife who believed in me enough to take the career path chances we chose.

Admiral Rickover, a brilliant and driven man, once said, "Success is 10 percent IQ, and 90 percent I will." It became apparent to me my first year at the Naval Academy that I had chosen to swim in the big pool, and the pool was full of talented sharks, many of whom were a lot smarter than I am. The only way I could keep up was to work hard, usually harder than everyone else.

I believe hard work is sometimes its own reward. I am sure that I got the hard work ethic from my parents. Nothing was overtly said but the example was surely there. It would have helped if I really loved my job, but usually I didn't love it with the passion that drives some people in their careers. However, I almost always looked forward to going to work each day. For the most part, the jobs that I have had in my "chosen" industry have been important jobs and rewarding in the doing as well as in the final accomplishment. There was no question that each was challenging. There were a few times, usually associated with knowing that I had led a successful team effort, when I felt a sense of true fulfillment. In the scheme of things, in our industrial-ized society, not much more can be asked.

I believe hard work is sometimes its own reward.

The most intriguing, frustrating, and rewarding part of being a manager is dealing with people. I will elaborate on this paradox by including some papers and talks on project management and leadership in the Leadership and Management section that follows this one.

The most intriguing, frustrating, and rewarding part of being a manager is dealing with people.

With all aspects of work, **it is healthy and useful to have a sense of humor**. It helps us to keep things in perspective, especially when it seems like the sky is caving in. As I told one group I took over at a very dark time in their project, "If you do not have a sense of humor, GET ONE!"

My career has been one of challenges, diversity, failures, and successes. I have worked for 11 different companies, if I count Westinghouse all three times I was employed there. Almost all the moves I made from one job or company to another were the result of being pursued to take over an endeavor, many times an endeavor that was in some distress. I bellied up to the bar 16 times, and five times chose to stay where I was. I followed a few hard and fast rules when making these decisions. They are:

- Use the Decision Analysis tool to categorize thoughts and desires (see Appendix A).
- Involve the immediate family in the discussion.

- Before you make a decision or an emotional and financial commitment, consult with present management. In so doing, I never experienced any retribution and frequently learned things I might not have otherwise known.
- Get the best deal possible (regarding salary, work conditions, etc.) going in, because after that point in time, negotiations are typically out of the question.
- Don't be afraid to take a calculated risk.
- Don't burn any bridges.

The most important truth in my rather exhaustive, 18-page resume is the last line, which reads, "None of this would have been possible without the support of my wife and life partner, Cindy." She was practical but also up for adventure. Most important, she had faith in me.

Leadership and Management

My experience in the nuclear industry for more than 45 years ranges from being an operator and a test engineer, to managing engineering at a multiple-reactor site to being the program manager for several multi-billion dollar projects. Half my career was in commercial nuclear, half in the Department of Energy (DOE) nuclear complex. I have been in top leadership positions on two nuclear reactor site startups, two nuclear power station recoveries, three major DOE project turnarounds, and one rocket launcher startup recovery. I was the COO for two major nuclear contracting companies and president of the company that is the sole producer of the Navy's nuclear fuel.

My acknowledged expertise was in project management, conduct of operations (CONOPS), and safety culture. I have been at ground zero for instituting matrix management at several endeavors. I was responsible for the first installation of mandatory drug testing in the commercial nuclear industry, which set many of the precedents still in effect today. I led the effort to institute — for the first time in the commercial nuclear industry — the safety conscious work environment (SCWE). I had a leadership role in the development of the DOE Project Management Order, the document that sets project management expectations in the DOE Nuclear Complex, and the joint effort between DOE and the Energy Facility Contractors Group (EFCOG) in defining a safety culture and how to assess it and how to nurture it.

The main virtue of excellent leadership is the unerring ability to separate the essential from the trivial. Leadership is having a vision and being able to convince others it's in their best interest to buy into that vision. Management is creating the structure that allows the team to achieve that vision. In politics, it is very difficult to find someone who is both a good campaigner and an effective manager once in office. It is the same in the work environment with respect to finding someone who is inspiring and who has the intellectual capacity to channel that inspiration. I can count those individuals who fit that mold, over the course of my career, on one hand.

My approach to leadership has been to realize that I must first serve those I wish to lead. One way to do this is by example; actions speak much louder than words. Mean what you say and ask no more of your team than what you are willing yourself to do. Set the right environment by showing that you care about the team as individuals, care about the workplace as the location where people will spend more than half of their waking life, and care about the value of your collective mission and/or product. **Be present and be accessible.** Be ready to help them get the right resources, the right support, the right environment, and the right attitude.

My management philosophy is simple. Surround yourself with people who are smarter than you, listen to them, support them, and trust them, but verify what you are told. My overall career experience has taught me one thing more than anything else, and that is humility. **None of us are as smart as all of us working together**, which includes contractor, client, and regulator. I had an abiding sense of my inadequacies, which kept me from ever becoming arrogant and experiencing the accompanying downfalls that being too full of oneself can lead to.

My management philosophy is simple. Surround yourself with people who are smarter than you, listen to them, support them, and trust them, but verify what you are told.

My passion is teamwork and care for the worker. I have instilled in organizations a sense of team and a confidence in participative management (which I will define in detail later) at all levels. I believe these are the attributes that support accomplishment of mission more than anything else. This aspiration will benefit the job and the community in which one lives.

I highly recommend for any manager not to have meetings in their office. Meet with your employees in their workspace, which is their comfort zone. Besides the obvious courtesy you extend in doing so, you will meet people and see things — going from and returning to your office — that you would not otherwise see if you are holed up in there, behind a desk. Reserve meetings in your office for special situations, like discipline or when absolute privacy is required. **And when someone comes to your office, get up from behind your desk and sit with them without that barrier.** Another bit of advice concerns e-mails, texting, and social media. I believe in the workplace they are the poorest form of communication. Go see someone or call him or her on the phone. The assumptions that someone instantly sees your electronic communication and understands it may both be incorrect. Also, anything you put out electronically should be something you would be comfortable reading on the front page of the local paper. Never send an e-mail while you are angry;

wait at least 24 hours, and then remember once you send it, you have lost complete control of it.

In any organization where I was brought in to address issues and restore stakeholder confidence, I wanted my legacy to be the following:

- Enhanced safety by establishing a Safety Conscious Work Environment (SCWE)
- United the workforce under a new vision of project management
- Established an inclusive approach to problem solving and decision making
- Inculcated new technologies and ideas from across the nuclear industry to accomplish the mission
- Imbued the organization with a new sense of energy and pride through accomplishment.

As mentioned above, **the first thing a leader must understand is that to be able to lead, he or she must first learn to serve**. The leader must provide their employees with the tools they need to do their job and then trust them to do it. **While the leader needs to check on how things are going, that should be done with the attitude of finding people doing things right, not wrong.** The leader should seek to see if there are impediments that can be removed or resources that can be provided to make the work go better. This can only be done through communication, and **the most important part of communication is sincere, active listening**.

Fortunately, over my career I have had extremely talented and experienced employees. They have been driven to succeed but also to maintain a balanced life perspective. My job was to serve them and to listen to them.

What are the most powerful statements a leader can make? They are:

- "Thank you!"
- "I was wrong."
- "I am sorry."

Of course, if you are saying the second two statements too frequently, you need to examine how you are leading and managing. However, you can never say "Thank you" enough.

I have seen leadership shift over the years in the United States from "leadership by authority" to "leadership by persuasion." At the same time, I have witnessed employee empowerment go from a little to a lot. Both changes are in the direction of goodness, but the overall change may not be all good, especially when taken to an extreme.

For example, in the case of leadership and management, the continuum from authority to persuasion includes participative management, which I think is the most beneficial approach for any organization. In this style of management or leadership, the leader genuinely solicits input and sincerely considers it. However, he or she, having dialed in that information to the extent he/she thinks appropriate, ultimately makes the decision on what the organization should do and then the group moves forward. If there is success, it is shared all around. If there is failure, the leader takes full responsibility without any finger pointing. The organization then regroups around lessons learned.

At the extreme on the "management by authority" end of the continuum, the approach moves from a military-type style (there is no vote to be taken when it is time to leave the foxhole), to dictatorship, and finally slavery. From my vantage point, those who espouse total equality in the workplace or in society as a whole, in their efforts to ensure that everyone receives the same benefits regardless of their contribution, also require central control of decision making, which results in an eventual move in the direction of slavery instead of freedom. At that other end of the management continuum, the style moves from persuasion to a form of leaderlessness I call group grope to finally anarchy. Employee empowerment can have the same detrimental results when taken to either extreme, a little or a lot, and cannot exist for long in either state (although unions, perhaps the ultimate workplace dictatorship, would have us think differently).

The following is an explanation of the extraordinary business challenges every leader of a complex technical organization faces when coming into a new organization:

The top person in an organization's hierarchy has, as their first responsibility, the leadership of the leadership team as well as of the organization as a whole. They need to **set the priorities in the workplace. My priorities for the workforce were always safety, quality, schedule, and cost, in that order.** The leader should acknowledge that any successful endeavor must be schedule-driven, but that there must be an allegiance to the first two priorities (safety and quality) on both a principled and a pragmatic basis or the schedule will eventually suffer. He or she needs to ensure that the workers know that a SCWE will be established, focusing on high performance initiatives, and on including the individual workers in problem solving and decision making. The workers need to know that the leadership team sincerely believes that they, the individual contributors, are the best source of problem identification and ideas for solutions. The workforce needs to know that the manager or management team will build on their already fine safety record and not let safety suffer as new approaches, new thoughts, and new energy are instituted.

The workers need to know that the leadership team sincerely believes that they, the individual contributors, are the best source of problem identification and ideas for solutions.

Leadership needs to establish a project management mentality toward the business approach and a sense of urgency. That sense of mission and purpose needs to be balanced with a dedication to the first priority, safety, and the second priority, quality. A new leadership team is responsible to ensure that it quickly assimilates the inherited management team and then energizes those leaders to inculcate any new values with their values. A new leadership team is also responsible to ensure that all workers know they are valued. The employees must understand that any new approaches also need incorporation of their ideas to improve upon those innovations. This team approach is fundamental to the group's success.

The major challenges, problems, and issues in managing a transition to a new management team or a new approach include:

- Ensuring focus on safety
- Maintaining continuity of ongoing work
- Building trust and fostering morale
- Engaging all stakeholders.

Additionally, there are other potential concerns that are dependent upon the mission:

- Addressing technical innovation
- Understanding budget and funding issues
- Ensuring adherence to existing regulations and requirements
- Learning about the workforce and the client (and/or regulator) at all levels requires leadership to do the following:

- Assure them of the commitment to integrated safety management core functions and principles
- Convince them that the overarching philosophy is all the cards on the table, face up, all the time
- Demonstrate that listening to them is paramount (as Stephen Covey would say, seek first to understand before seeking to be understood)
- State the intention to meet or exceed all contract end states
- Foster an approach that looks for the technical solution first, then the cost/benefit, and finally where it fits within the contract scope.

Embracing the existing organization tactfully and converting it to new management approaches takes time, patience, and care. Work to understand what has inhibited the success of the existing organization and explain how the new plans will eliminate those barriers. In the process, ask workers for suggestions that might improve upon approaches that did not have the benefit of the experience of the day-to-day struggles in the trenches.

Embracing the existing organization tactfully and converting it to new management approaches takes time, patience, and care.

In parallel with assimilating the workforce, new leadership needs to learn and understand the other stakeholders, from regulators to citizen groups, to the other oversight groups, to the Congressional delegations, to stockholders and governing boards as applicable. **A new leadership team will need to listen to their concerns and see where there is commonality and where there is opposition and then figure out how to find common ground.** This is much harder work than tackling the technical issues, in my opinion.

There are assumptions, both implicit and explicit, that need to be considered in any new leadership situation (even though assumptions are dangerous and must be considered carefully). The first set of assumptions will be tied to inevitable reservations about the new leader (or management team). The new leader (or team) must convince the existing workforce that they are bringing to the endeavor the benefit of external experiences to help the organization as a whole accomplish the task ahead.

The new leader (or team) must create a vision that makes a difference. The intent is to ultimately leave the endeavor a better place to work and in better shape to accomplish its mission. The assembled leadership team, consisting of new and old members, can do that. The team is a blend of talent and experience that ensures beneficial changes will endure.

The leadership team needs to believe their clients (and their regulators) are hardworking, dedicated, and smart. They can and will make good teammates, but they are first and foremost clients (regulators). The leadership team needs to realize it exists to serve the workforce to accomplish the client's mission within the regulator's boundaries. Understanding these things can best be done by walking in their shoes and understanding their drivers.

The leader must create strategic goals/objectives for the organizational unit in line with the things I mentioned I wanted my legacy to be. Namely he or she must:

- Establish a Safety Conscious Work Environment (SCWE)
- Meet and beat the schedule and associated goals
- Develop contingency plans for the vicissitudes of projects, as determined by the projects' risk profiles
- Gain the confidence of the regulators by understanding their role in protecting the worker, the environment, and/ or the industry

- Create and nurture a nimble, responsive workforce.

The leader and his team must develop a plan of action, which starts with the transition from the old leadership, and is based on good and frequent communication. To facilitate implementation of plans and meet commitments:

- Publish targets and explain them
- Be flexible without relaxing the conviction when it comes to these goals
- Practice participative management at all levels
- Use metrics to manage the effort and publish those metrics monthly
- Deploy mature technology, leveraging what others have learned
- If your endeavor is part of a larger organization, use any corporate reach back (the larger organization's resources) to tackle problems and to self-assess.

There are little tidbits I picked up over the course of my career that helped me, especially when I was encountering a new situation and wanted to ensure people knew what was important to me. One thing was that I wanted everyone to know that surprises were totally unwanted. I had signs that had a circle and a line through the circle imposed upon that word: *surprises*. **In staff meetings and planning meetings, I made sure everyone knew to bring up problems early and ask for help with commitments that were in jeopardy.** It was a bad day at the office when someone reported day in and day out that an activity was on track only to ask for more time on the day of delivery. In short, **NO SURPRISES!**

People are energized by a common focus. Having that common goal can help set aside many other issues. Also, every opportunity a leader can take to explain a direction or a decision will help in those situations where there is just not enough time to provide that explanation.

Explaining also helps get buy-in and/or compliance. It helps if the leader has practiced and taught active listening skills and insisted upon common courtesy from all participants in meetings. I explained to everyone that sidebars during meetings were not only discourteous to whomever was speaking but prevented the participants from truly hearing what the speaker had to say, as well as denying everyone else the benefit of what they were sharing on the side. In short, **NO SIDEBARS**!

Accountability is essential! Accountability cannot occur if everyone is said to be responsible. Every activity must have a single person responsible for the outcome, no matter how many are involved. As I've always said, "there are no statues of committees." A person must always be assigned responsibility, as responsibility can't ultimately be borne by a group of people. With accountability comes commitment. I expected people to meet their commitments and ask for help when a commitment was in jeopardy. People who did not behave that way did not last long in organizations I led.

I always told my direct reports that I respected the person who could disagree with me without needing to get personal. I expected my reports to tell me if I was making a bad decision or an error of any type. I told them those discussions are best done behind closed doors. In that environment, we could discuss, we could debate, we could argue, we could fight, we could even do takedowns (just joking). However, once the decision was made and the door was opened, it was *our* decision. I also told them that while I encouraged and even enjoyed this robust relationship, the one thing I could not tolerate was to be ignored. **Do what I have directed or confront me, but do not ignore me.**

In any organization, the first line managers (FLMs) are the most important members of the management team. They are the proverbial "rubber meeting the road." They need to uphold policy and administer discipline and then turn right back around and ask for 110 percent from their work force. They need to be good listeners and good explainers. When promoted from the ranks, as difficult as it may be, they need to put some distance between themselves and their former comrades. FLMs are not born; they are made. They need training and support to back up their natural ability to lead. I always had an FLM council, where I could meet with the FLMs to find out what they needed and how policy was perceived. Whenever I could, I trial-ran big decisions and changes through them first. And never forget those people working on the backshifts if you have them. There needs to be a special effort to communicate with them.

Communication is the toughest part of any job (or any relationship, for that matter). Being a good listener is essential.
It's important to set up as many venues for communication as possible. I always used roundtables with a spectrum of employees and then published the results of those meetings for everyone to understand what was said. "I do not know" was a perfectly good answer, as long as I immediately found the correct response and relayed it back to the group and included it in the meeting summary. In all settings, I liked to use brief stories to make my point; most people remember stories or anecdotes more than just abstract words.

Another tool I used was quarterly all-hands meetings. Even though that can be difficult to plan and achieve, sometimes taking as many as four or more meetings to cover everyone, especially if backshifts are involved, employees always seemed to appreciate these meetings. It is a good way for everyone to hear the same thing. Finally, there is "management by walking around" (MBWA). This tool is essential but is only worthwhile if the leader takes time to talk to the employees and takes a genuine interest in what they have to say. If there is a commitment or directive that comes out of those discussions, the circle must immediately be closed with the management chain. Care must be exercised in that regard.

Metrics are key to communicating progress. The Institute of Nuclear Power Operations (INPO) format is information rich, but as far as the number of metrics, this is a case where less is more. The metrics need to be meaningful and relate to the mission to be accomplished. Another thing to remember is that most people are conceptual, especially technical people. Drawings, diagrams, frag-nets (mini-schedules), and even cartoons should be used liberally to get the point across. With respect to reports, always have an executive summary and always spell out *every* acronym on first use.

A few other things to remember. **First, people are neither lazy nor stupid.** They usually have the best ideas on how things could be done better or at least where the problem(s) truly lie. Their input needs to be valued and, whenever possible, they should be included in problem solving and decision making. The greater their involvement, the more ownership they will take in the outcome. However, remember success can breed complacency. Operators in nuclear plants are trained to be skeptics and to never relax, always asking themselves what could go wrong. It is this mental exertion, as opposed to physical exertion, that tires them. Another thing to remember is that any change, large or small, is a distraction. Again, communication before the fact and as much involvement as possible in the change decision can ease the transition.

Operators in nuclear plants are trained to be skeptics and to never relax, always asking themselves what could go wrong. It is this mental exertion, as opposed to physical exertion, that tires them.

I have mentioned the workplace priorities of safety, quality, schedule, and cost. It is important to be able to explain these priorities to the workforce, so they understand why you want them to be adopted and ultimately for them to be able to explain in their own words why the priorities are important. I also let people know that my life priorities are God, family, health, and work … in that order. That lets them know where work falls and most can relate. Again, I also let them know that a sense of humor is important to keep things in perspective.

When I would first come into an organization, I let them know what I was looking for in a teammate. The qualities I sought in my teammates, in order of importance, were:

- Hard Worker
- Aggressive
- Thorough
- Possessive of Perspective.

Being a hard worker means not wasting time. Everything worth doing is worth doing well and frequently that means being willing to go above and beyond. Double checking, putting in the hours when required, helping others when your assigned task is done, always thinking about how things could be done better, and so on. Aggressiveness is an extension of that approach. It means stepping up when something needs to be done and volunteering for the tough tasks.

Being thorough means double and even triple checking. It means understanding the task … not only in its full breadth but also in detail. It means educating yourself beyond the boundary of the assigned task, so you know you are providing a good product and a good handoff. And having perspective means not taking yourself too seriously. It means being fun to be around and realizing that, as important as work is, there are other things in life even more important (for me, those things are faith, family, and health). In a word, perspective means having balance in your life. **It also requires a sense of humor; innate or acquired, it is essential.**

All the above is hard work but can also be fun, especially as you see things come together. I will never forget walking across the DWPF project the day I could detect a spring in people's steps and a new sense of purpose and team. It felt good! As I have said, there is a fine line between leadership and management. Both are needed for success.

Culture and Safety Culture

In any organization, there is an all-encompassing environment called the culture. It is most easily described as "it's the way things are done around here." A subset of the culture is the safety culture, that is the organization's approach to safety. Safety usually starts with personal safety or what is sometimes called industrial safety. This applies to the office environment just as much as it does on the shop floor or in operating spaces. (I recall that one year during my career, 30 percent of the injuries that occurred in the nuclear industry occurred in office spaces.) In almost all businesses, there is a need to protect the environment as work is accomplished. This is called environmental safety. In handling radioactive material, there are radiation and contamination control considerations. This is called radiation control (radcon) safety. In the nuclear industry, we have an obligation to protect the plant workers and the public from the impact of a nuclear disaster of any dimension. This is called nuclear safety. Regardless of the business, safety should be paramount and ultimately is good business. The top 25 commercial nuclear plants in efficient operation are invariably the same top 25 in safety, as measured by any of the above parameters.

There are several approaches to supporting the safety culture of any business. One is a systematic way to define the job, its hazards, the protection measures to address those hazards, and feedback on how the work went so that there can be continuous improvement. The next aspect is a SCWE, which is fundamentally the ability for any employee to bring up any issue without fear of retaliation, or the questioning of his or her motive for doing so. Finally, there is conduct of operations or conduct of business (CONOPS). I will expand on these three topics a little later.

I have mentioned SCWE many times in this book. It is a vital ingredient for a well-managed endeavor of any complexity and hazard. It engages employees at all levels to bring up issues and concerns so those issues can be appropriately addressed and rectified for the benefit of the endeavor. What I have not mentioned — and which is important to acknowledge — is that no matter how well management establishes that there will be no retribution for bringing up an issue, even if it turns out not to be valid, it still takes courage on the part of the employee to bring up the concern. They must be convinced that their motive will not be questioned and that there will be no embarrassment for having brought up the issue, even from their peers. This is difficult both to establish and to convince people it is in place.

Billie Garde, mentioned earlier in this book, tells the story of the actions taken by several nations after Chernobyl to establish SCWEs in their nuclear industries. At a conference in St. Petersburg, she asked for a report from each representative on the progress in his or her country. When she got to the Russian representative, his response was "Nyet." When Billie pursued an explanation, he said that Hitler and then Stalin had killed all the courageous people in Russia. Their children and their children's children developed a mentality of obsequiousness in their relationship to any position of authority. They did not have courage in general to question orders or approaches that seemed wrong or dangerous. Therefore, in Russia this inbred attitude was difficult to overcome. To a lesser extent perhaps, this attitude has to be overcome in all cultures. After all, people must bring up potentially unwelcomed issues created in many cases by the same people upon which their employment, promotions, pay increases, and benefits depend. Creating an environment where people are convinced that those things are not in jeopardy is challenging work. One misstep by management, however unintended, can eliminate a lot of progress.

The facilities in the nuclear industry range greatly in size, complexity, and regulation. These differences also set the stage for widely varying approaches to, and even understanding of, the importance of safety culture. While the commercial nuclear power facilities began to collaborate in fundamental ways relating to safety, security, and reliability in the 1980s, and then on the related area of safety culture in the 1990s, the DOE nuclear complex lagged in this activity. The importance of safety culture is frankly the same to the nuclear industry as a whole, both in the commercial industry and in the DOE Complex. This perspective has two parts:

- The success of the business relies on a strong safety culture. No long-term success is possible without it.
- We are all in this together. A major problem at any nuclear facility (fuel cycle operation, power plant, or DOE nuclear endeavor) could literally change the future for all nuclear facilities, including bringing about a premature end to the hope for any nuclear renaissance.

The facilities in the nuclear industry range greatly in size, complexity, and regulation. These differences also set the stage for widely varying approaches to, and even understanding of, the importance of safety culture.

The key to a strong safety culture is a safety conscious work environment. It is the pedestal upon which all other attributes rely. A SCWE, in turn, requires as many venues as possible for employees to express a concern or bring up an issue. Those venues include management, a robust Corrective Action Program (CAP), an Employee Concerns Program (ECP), viable Human Relations (HR) and Legal departments, and, perhaps, some sort of an ombudsman program. However, regardless of the efficacy of those vehicles for registering a concern, a true SCWE relies on the respect of all employees for other employees regardless of their position in the organization. I will touch on that attribute by using the closing remarks at my last all-employees meeting (AEM) at NFS provided below. (As I mentioned before, I held those meetings once per quarter with all organizations for which I was responsible.)

The key to a strong safety culture is a safety conscious work environment. It is the pedestal upon which all other attributes rely.

As I said above and it is worth repeating, an organization's culture is like an opinion — everyone has one. It takes years to establish a culture, and it's always slowly evolving. It takes years, as well, to actively change a culture. A safety culture is an organization's values and behaviors, modeled by its leaders and internalized by its members, which serve to make safe performance of work the overriding priority to protect the workers, the public, and the environment.

The acronym ISMS, which stands for Integrated Safety Management System, is an approach to accomplishing work adopted in the Department of Energy (DOE) Complex. It is based on the following five core functions, which I have mentioned earlier:

- Defining the scope of the work
- Analyzing the hazards associated with that work
- Developing the protective measures to be taken to address those hazards

- Obtaining proper authority to do the work and then executing the work observing those hazards controls.
- Providing feedback on how the job ultimately turned out, to be used in future similar work, promoting continuous improvement.

These attributes apply to all work, not just physical work in the plant facility. By applying these attributes and the associated guiding principles, the DOE has achieved unprecedented safety records. Other parts of the nuclear industry have similar approaches.

As I indicated above, the SCWE is based on the principle that any employee can bring up *any* issue, not just a safety problem, without fear of retribution and with full confidence the issue will be addressed on its own merit without ascribing motive.

The bridge between these two precepts is CONOPS or, as I like to call it, Conduct of Business because the attributes below apply to all aspects of any endeavor, not just the operations of the facility.

Those attributes are:

- Personal accountability
- Procedure compliance
- Technical inquisitiveness
- A willingness to stop in the face of uncertainty.

Let me describe briefly what each of these attributes is and is not:

Personal accountability is taking seriously what you are tasked to accomplish and doing it to the best of your ability. Said differently, like a painter, you must be willing to sign your name to the end of the day indicating you did your very best.

Procedure compliance is thoughtful adherence to the documents developed by experts, which, when combined with your training and experience, offer the best chance to achieve the desired outcome. It is neither blind nor malicious compliance. If the procedure does not make sense, stop and get help. Then either proceed with understanding or change the procedure and proceed.

Like a painter, you must be willing to sign your name to the end of the day indicating you did your very best.

Technical inquisitiveness is that sense of wonderment that drives you to understand as completely as possible all aspects of the activity in which you are involved.

A willingness to stop means never proceeding in the face of uncertainty but obtaining the help to gain confidence in the outcome of your actions.

An important aspect of good CONOPS is what is called three-way communication. When direction is given, it is important that the person receiving the direction responds by repeating what they have been instructed to do. This "repeat back" assures the sender that their message or direction has been understood, which is a good indication that the person will do what is desired. This is called two-way communication and, while good, is not enough. The original sender must then acknowledge that the receiver did indeed understand what is required of them by saying, "That is correct" or "Correct." This three-way communication sounds a little stifling, but it goes a long way to ensuring that the correct action will occur.

I will take this opportunity to mention one other thing regarding complex project management, and that is trouble shooting. Things will go wrong and the challenge is to determine why and what the corrective action should be. When looking for the cause of problems or accidents or untoward events, the first thing I always assess is what has changed from when things were going well. Sometimes the change is subtle and sometimes the change is simply time itself, but it is a good place to start with the apparent cause analysis. Of course, there are tools for formal root cause analysis, but implementation of those formal techniques may not always be warranted or a necessary use of precious resources. The first step in any case is to simply ask what has changed.

The application of the above aspects of a safety culture is not easy. During my 45-year career in the nuclear industry, as mentioned earlier, I have seen the acceptable management style move from management by authority to management by persuasion. This is mostly good but not completely good. Too far in the new direction and the result is weak leadership. I have learned a great deal starting with the Millstone epiphany relative to the acceptable management style aided by guidance (not always gentle) from my mentor in this arena, Billie Garde. For instance, at Hanford, when dealing with the impact of vapors emanating from the tanks, we learned that the technical evaluation can pale in comparison to the emotional reality. At D-B, we witnessed a form of discouragement for bringing up issues (different from overt retaliation but just as damaging). I call it "hierarchical suffocation" when the processes for bringing up an issue are so laborious that they discourage one from doing so. At a whistle blower conference that I attended, where I represented the management perspective during a panel discussion, I made the point that if a viable SCWE exists, it obviates the need for whistleblowers.

There is a wonderful book entitled *The Five Thousand Year Leap* (by W. Cleon Skousen), about the creation of our Constitution by our Founding Fathers and the 28 principles upon which that work is based. The work of the framers of the U.S. Constitution was based, in large part, on the philosophy of Adam Smith, who wrote *The Inquiry into the Nature and Causes of the Wealth of Nations*, and on the perspectives of John Locke, and the teachings of Marcus Tullius

Cicero, a member of the Roman senate. Without delving into the many aspects of Natural Law, upon which our Constitution is based as described in Skousen's book, one of the basic tenets is that human beings are really seeking individual happiness and self-realization. One of the aspects of those two tenets is meaningful work of one's own choosing, done in an environment of mutual respect.

I believe I can take pride in the fact that the work of my career was very important to national security and the protection of the Constitution and all that it stands for. To some extent, my work was also in support of world stability, to which the United States has always been a singular shining light. As I would tell my employees, each of us chose our employment of our own volition, so we owe our work our very best effort. This approach to work requires each employee to show respect and consideration to his or her workmates who also chose to be there. These statements apply to any work well done anywhere.

With that in mind, let me repeat excerpts from my closing message at my last NFS All-employee Meeting (AEM):

"All that has preceded has been positive. [What preceded was a review of the considerable accomplishments over the past three months, including restoring most of the plant to operation from an extended shutdown mandated by the NRC and following an exhaustive review by the NRC.] As a workforce, you have much of which to be proud. Although many challenges remain, you have essentially weathered the storm, emerged a better and wiser workforce, reflecting the new paradigm of the nuclear industry in more recent years, and you have returned much of the plant to service. Equipment reliability, plant material condition, and assimilation into a new corporate structure remain as preeminent challenges. None of these challenges will be successfully met without the right attitude. I would be remiss if I did not take this opportunity to talk about attitude. We are all in this together. An attitude of "we vs. they" or "us vs. them" will not succeed.

"I discussed briefly our Strategic Plan. There are significant possibilities for expanded business. However, as I have said before, **the first rule of business development is to do well with the business you have**. Our principal present clients, the Navy and the DOE, want several things: reliability, a quality product, and the least cost possible. The first two items are essentially the same thing.

"The principal component of reliability is how we work together. In any organization, you do not have to like the people with whom you work or for whom you work. But as a professional, and we are all professionals until proven otherwise, you must respect the jobs your coworkers do or respect the positions those people are filling. Over my career, I have had bosses I did not like. I have met peers who I thought were jerks, but in the nuclear industry I have met very, very few evil people. I have been able to treat the positions of all those people with respect and, looking back, I am not ashamed of how I have behaved as a professional.

"Now let me switch gears to help me get to the bottom-line point by telling a few stories, which, as you know, I like to do. My paternal grandfather was an itinerant farmer, tilling other people's land and tending to other people's livestock. His son, my dad, put himself through college and veterinarian school at The Ohio State University by working two jobs. Upon graduation, he went to into the Army and served in the Pacific theater during World War II. I have a lot of stories about growing up as a veterinarian's son but here is just one.

"A man in my hometown of Sandusky, Ohio, lived in a trailer, which contained all his worldly belongings. He also had a little dog of which he was very fond. One day, his trailer burned to the ground and, as he sifted through the ashes, thinking his dog was dead, he heard the animal whimpering under some debris. The dog was badly burned, and the man brought the dog into my dad's clinic to be euthanized and left my dad's office in tears. My dad examined the animal, cleaned him off, treated his burns and his pain, and bandaged him. He and my sister, who worked for him at the time and from whom I learned of this event, then changed those bandages three times a day for a month, tenderly replacing the ointment each time. After a month, my dad called the man, who immediately responded that he was sorry he had not paid my dad for putting the dog down. My dad said, "Well, you better come in here to make things right" and the man agreed he would. When he came in, my dad told him to wait just a minute as the man was pulling out his wallet and Dad went into the kennel and brought out the dog. Everyone was in tears, maybe even the dog. The man asked how much he owed and my dad, knowing the man had little, said he owed nothing and refused any payment. Dad put the bill on a spike where he kept all the bills for which he never charged people.

"The week before my dad died, he asked to speak to my wife and me. He told my wife to never let me retire, a task she took very seriously. He told us there was not a day he did not look forward to going to work. How many of us can say that? Should that not be our goal? It can be. Most of the problems and issues at work are created by lack of good communication and lack of respect. Lack of respect for the importance of the task with which each of us is charged, lack of respect for the job our workmates have, lack of respect for each other, and lack of respect for our time on this earth. Our time, which is all too short, is a precious commodity that should not be wasted involved in things of which we cannot be proud. We need to see our lives in the retrospective my dad had in his final week.

"We are teammates and we are in this thing together. Since we have recently witnessed the World Cup of soccer, I am reminded of the great Brazilian team a few decades ago that had two of the greatest soccer players the game has ever seen, Pelé and Casemiro. They hated each other and off the field quarreled and even had fistfights. But on the field, they put all that aside and were like magicians together, each anticipating where the other was with uncanny brilliance.

"I am also reminded of Carl Rove's account of witnessing President Bush talking to two parents and their younger son who was a Marine headed for Iraq. They had lost their older son, who was also a Marine, in Iraq. The mother did all the talking and the father sat there in silence. Rove's experience in these situations was that the silent parent was angry and sometimes erupted in a scene that was uncomfortable for all. Finally, the father spoke, and he told the President he was 61, in good shape, and a surgeon. He asked the president for dispensation so he could serve in Iraq as a military doctor in honor of his first son and alongside his second son, a request with which his wife concurred. He was eventually commissioned as a Marine medical officer and did serve in Iraq. Isn't that what this is all about? Americans willing to sacrifice to take the war to the enemy whether it is, as the press likes to label them, Bush's Iraq or Obama's Afghanistan, doing what your country asks of you? And we can be proud we are doing our part by fueling the nuclear Navy.

"The men and women of our armed services, and I know many of you have served as did I, protect our right to live under the rule of law. Those laws include the right to form bargaining units and to go out on strike if it is felt necessary to do so. However, our laws, which so many have died to protect, also include the right to come to work during a strike, motivated by whatever drives one to cross the picket line, such as the need for income to support a child with special needs or indigent parents or whatever. The laws give us all both rights. We must honor those laws or get them changed. So, treat each other with respect that allows us all to do our very best. Do this regardless of what happened during the strike that took place almost four years ago. Whether you like the person or not is unimportant. The job is. The job or task, done to our very best ability, is important because of our role in national security. Performance of your task is also important to our job security. In this regard, I am aware of unacceptable actions between fellow employees. I have zero tolerance of harassment, intimidation, retaliation, discrimination, and other misbehaviors, which negatively impact fellow employees and potentially affect our work. There will be no second chances. It is wrong, and I will deal with it.

"Like my dad, some day you will look back on your work experience here. You will know that it was an opportunity to do something well that was important, more important than just a job, more important than just you as an individual. Your heart will tell you whether you did the right thing, made the best use of your time here, treated others with respect, did your job to the best of your ability, and upheld the law people have died to protect.

"Thank you for what you have achieved. Thank you for what you will achieve. Thank you for letting me be part of it. Let's go forward with renewed dedication for our work and respect for each other."

————————————

I believe this speech, which I delivered to NFS employees some years ago, could have just as easily been stated in most endeavors, at any time — perhaps at your own organizations. Leaders and managers should consider what their message should be to promote behavior that exemplifies a safety conscious work environment and, thereby, a true safety culture.

Culture Change

What follows below is a discussion of several situations where one of the primary challenges was to accomplish what was, at the time, determined to be or referred to as "culture change." The first of these occurred at Davis-Besse Nuclear Station between 1986 and 1988. The next two occurred at the Replacement Tritium Facility (RTF) and the Defense Waste Processing Facility (DWPF). Both of these facilities are located at the SRS, are unique facilities in both purpose and technology, and were both at about 80 percent construction complete when it was determined that significant changes in the approach to work were necessary, which were June 1990, and October 1991, respectively. Both were struggling to make progress. The next culture changes to be considered occurred at Millstone Nuclear Station from 1997 to 2000 and then the Hanford Tank Farm from August 2002 until September 2004. Finally, the last organization in which I was brought in as a member of the leadership team or as the chief leader was NFS, which is mentioned above. I was selected as president of NFS in March 2010, after NFS had been shut down by the NRC for management and operational difficulties.

From these experiences, I have ascertained that the following basic elements are necessary to affect a long-lasting and successful change in the general attitude of any group regarding their approach to the work environment:

Inclusion: To the extent possible, all levels of the workforce must be involved in developing the new culture.

Focus: It is useful, if not mandatory, that the desired change in collective attitude be associated with a tangible focus, target, or goal. Frequently the work schedule is used for that focus, but it could be something else. The point is to have a common purpose around which the group can rally. Such a goal helps the culture change, even though it may complicate the workload to affect two significant tasks (i.e., the tangible goal and the culture change) at the same time.

Transition: It is important to recognize there are three parts to change:

- Letting go of the present (collective attitude or mindset)
- Transition toward the new approach
- Embracing the new culture.

None of these phases is without its own pain for those going through it.

Communication: The reason for the change and its associated anticipated benefits must be communicated over and over, using every possible venue.

Involvement: Top management must be involved from the outset. This is one activity that cannot be delegated and requires a constant presence of top management.

Feedback: Input must be actively sought from all levels of the organization; something done with that feedback; then that "something" communicated.

Tenacity: The key is to stay the course, believe that the view will be worth the climb, and, at the same time, have a certain flexibility to accommodate those changes in strategy and execution that make sense and are responsive to the needs of the group without seeming to be spineless. Not an easy task.

Celebration: Throughout the transition, time must be taken to celebrate the successes, whether they involve something to do with the culture or the tangible goal.

What follows are some observations regarding the working environment today that must be considered in any attempt to change the overall attitude:

Any discussion of culture change needs to be set in the context of the change in the past two to three decades in what is acceptable behavior of both management and employees. Over the above period, from 1974 to 2011, an evolution in acceptable management styles occurred. As I noted earlier, and it is worth stating again, this evolution moved from management by authority to management by persuasion. This evolution was not always for the better and was very situation dependent. **The theory is that the more involvement that staff have in the decision making that goes on in any given situation, the more buy-in there will be by that same staff who must make things work.** What I believe works best is what I call participative management, which I defined earlier but is worth repeating.

Participative management is defined by the leader taking charge of the situation and setting an environment where everyone's input and opinion is solicited and genuinely considered. Establishing and maintaining this environment is not easy and requires sensitivity on the part of the leader, which is not usually innate. Some people can be easily discouraged by the leader's words or actions, even when the leader genuinely had the best of intentions. However, ultimately the leader makes the decision on whatever is being considered and that is the path on which the group embarks. If the endeavor is successful, then the success is shared. If it is not successful, the leader accepts full responsibility and regroups around the lessons learned.

As mentioned before, **there has been a dramatic increase in the empowerment of employees**. There is a lot of goodness involved in this transformation also, but it's not all good. **The erosion of the goodness, a modicum of control and buy-in, begins when the**

empowerment starts to turn into entitlement. It is exacerbated by management not being educated with the new skillsets required to be effective in management by persuasion and by them dealing inappropriately with employees who feel more empowered than they have in the past. In order to maintain the open environment, sometimes action or reaction taken by management must be revised or even overturned. As a result, management can feel impotent and can experience a lot of frustration in trying to accomplish their work objectives.

Without an appreciation of the above work environment, any discussion of culture revision can result in short sighted conclusions on how one goes about changing a culture. What was experienced at D-B was brute force management by intimidation and even fear. As mentioned earlier, the nuclear vice president there practiced what I characterized as the Pol Pot theory of culture change. As a reminder, Pol Pot, the leader of the Khmer Rouge in Cambodia, is credited in changing a culture that was 700 years old, in a year. He did that by changing the language. Only Khmer could be spoken instead of French or other languages and dialects. The old icons, churches and mosques were destroyed and replaced by symbols of the Khmer Rouge. People were moved from familiar settings to unfamiliar settings, as characterized in the film The Killing Fields, as city people were moved to the country, and country people were made to live in the cities. Finally, all the intellectuals were killed. The Pol Pot comparison is a harsh and less than equitable comparison, but one that comes to mind for me when I think about how one leader at D-B shook up the entire organization, accomplishing much at the expense of creating an environment of inclusion. The nuclear VP did all these things, in a manner of speaking (no one was killed). He restored D-B to initial successful operation on the sheer strength of his will and expertise.

A gentler form of this culture change approach was practiced at the RTF and DWPF. At these two facilities, there were many factions of employees not working together and focused on their own parochial agendas. As a result, not much was being accomplished. After over a month of walking and listening, the new management team, which I headed, began to change the language from one of "finger pointing" to one of accountability. The icons of individualism were replaced by a common schedule and milestones that everyone could recognize. The religion of common failure and blame was replaced by shared successes and accomplishment. The warring factions had their leaders moved to the group they were opposed to so that they could see what it was like in "the other guy's shoes." And, unfortunately, a few people had to go. However, experience shows that someone usually volunteers to "be killed" (i.e., to leave the department). Initially there was some metaphorical bloodletting and hard language, but as those who could accept accountability rose to the challenge, the toughness was replaced by esprit de corps, and humor was woven into the fabric of striving to meet objectives.

D-B, RTF, and DWPF all needed their tangible progress turned around in a hurry for different reasons. They needed their cultures changed as part of being able to make sustained progress. However, the participative approach taken at RTF and DWPF, as opposed to the authoritative approach at Davis-Besse, resulted in the changes being more lasting. One could speculate that the problems D-B experienced in the late 1990s had their seeds sown in the middle 1980s. DWPF and RTF, on the other hand, have continued to perform in a stellar manner and the inevitable management changes that subsequently occurred had its leaders come from within the middle and first line managers who were there during the culture change. They got to participate in the decisions and problem solving that resulted in the startup turnaround. They felt ownership for that turnaround and the mode of operation established by the culture change they witnessed and in which they participated. By contrast, the managers under the D-B vice president had some of their decisions dictated to them and, worse, they tried to emulate the VP's style with much less success.

Millstone was an altogether different learning experience. The approaches to culture change used at D-B and even at RTF and DWPF would not work in that environment. What had changed is that employees felt considerably more empowered, and there was empathy in the press and in the legislature for any alleged mistreatment of employees. The regulators reacted to the pressure from those sources, even though in the beginning they did not know what they wanted or how to go about getting it. In fact, no one did. **However, eventually it was realized that a true safety culture required every employee to believe that they could bring up any concern, and it would be fairly and appropriately addressed by management without any question of motive and certainly without any retaliation.**

While, in principle, this mode of operation is appropriate and ultimately the only one that takes true advantage of collective knowledge to obtain the safest facility and safest approach to its operation, it has proven to be a difficult adjustment for management and employees alike. Management at Millstone, in general, was comfortable with the "management by authority" model and felt that productivity suffered when too much time was spent on touchy-feely issues. The employees fell into several camps. Some wanted the days when they came to work, were told what to do, did it to the best of their ability, and went home, hopefully with a feeling of accomplishment, whether they really liked their jobs or not. Then there was the group of employees who were genuinely concerned with safety and wanted to have their concerns heard and addressed.

Finally, there was a very small set of employees who took advantage of the new situation for their own purposes, which had little to do with safety or productivity, but more to do with their own agendas, whatever those happened to be. What all these groups have in common in both establishing a safety conscious work environment as well as changing a culture is that they need to be heard. There needs to be a venue set, training for all employees provided, and the administrative processes available that do indeed encourage employees to bring up issues and concerns, along with ideas and suggestions. **In this situation, the safety conscious work environment and the participative management culture are in harmony. Productivity will go up and safety will become a way of life.**

Awareness of the above must be folded into any attempt to change a culture and that's why it is mentioned first. With that in mind, how then does one go about changing the culture? What has been found to work best, as briefly mentioned before, is to have a common goal or purpose, which is well understood by all levels of the organization. This requires effective communication and much repetition of what the tangible goal is and why it is of value. It is also mandatory to have some visualization of what that common focus is. On all the above projects, it was the schedule and its attendant milestones. They were posted and kept current wherever employees gathered or frequently passed by. We could *see* where we were headed.

This approach can work, although there is a trap that needs to be addressed from the beginning, which is the accusation of production (i.e., schedule) over safety. The logic, as well as the principle behind the workplace priorities — safety, quality, schedule, and cost — is used to explain the relationship of successful schedule execution relative to putting safety first. Safety, in this case, includes both industrial safety and nuclear safety. The principle is that no one wants to get hurt or put someone else in harm's way. All employees want to return to their families in the condition in which they reported to work. When that principle is extended to the general public, it covers nuclear safety as well as industrial safety. The practical matter is that if safety (or, for that matter, quality) ever suffers, the schedule will soon follow.

The practical matter is that if safety (or, for that matter, quality) ever suffers, the schedule will soon follow.

The best performing nuclear plants with regard to cost per MW and short outage duration also have the best industrial safety statistics. In other words, **good safety is good business**. So once again, in a safety conscious work environment, it is understood that issues that affect safety (and quality) will eventually affect schedule or production, if not addressed. That is the concept that management and employees alike need to embrace.

It has been shown that the schedule and its attendant milestones are an excellent way to achieve a common focus. At RTF, DWPF, and NFS, the schedule was built from the top down and the bottom up. It was resource-loaded, and milestones were developed with input from throughout the organization. The effort was publicized, and schedule contingency was incorporated. The first milestones admittedly were low-hanging fruit so the team could start to build a sense of accomplishment where there was none before. **The "schedule over safety" issues were addressed by empowering all employees to stop work whenever they considered conditions to be imminently unsafe. That action was rewarded whether the concern turned out to be real or not.** A Safety Pause was also instituted, which was essentially a "Stop Work" but without the same formality. Employees were successfully taught to differentiate between jurisdictional issues and personal preferences versus genuine potential safety problems.

Changing the safety culture requires a very frequent presence of upper management in the facility. At RTF, DWPF, and NFS, program management walked the facility daily and upper executive levels were encouraged to visit frequently. Time spent in the facility needs to be productive, with maximum interface with the employees. First line and middle management must not fear this presence of upper management or the discussions that take place with employees so that they are aware of upper management's presence. Rather, those FLMs and middle managers should welcome it as an opportunity to show upper management that they are fostering a safety conscious work environment. This change in approach also requires training and communication.

Everyone must realize that this gaining of trust and buy-in takes time. The strong sense of team and the weaving of humor into the day-to-day work environment can take as much as three years to become endemic. The key is to realize that all employees want to feel good about their workday. The more control they have with respect to the workday, the better they will feel. Management must learn to trust that this is so and involve the employees in decisions that affect them — to the maximum extent possible. Employees must learn that they are involved in a business and it must be successful ... or they will not have a job. A third-generation union employee once told me that the advice he received from his uncle (a long-time union steward) when he joined the union was not to forget that a successful union requires strong management, just as successful management requires a strong union. That sentiment is true whether there is a union involved or not, and it ultimately involves two-way **trust, which is hard won and easily lost**.

What has preceded is a personal observation of the history of the evolution of acceptable management styles, the establishment of the goal to have a safety culture, and the emergence of the concept of a SCWE. This is but one person's perspective, but I hope you deem it a valuable one, as it was gained by living through the aforementioned management evolution in some watershed events in the nuclear industry.

What is important to note is that safety culture and SCWE are two distinct but related concepts:

- "Safety culture" refers to the necessary attention, personal dedication, and accountability of all individuals engaged in any activity that has a bearing on safety.
- SCWE refers to the willingness of employees to identify safety concerns (really any concern) without fear of reprisal or apathy.
- SCWE is an attribute of safety culture.

The safety culture of an organization is the product of individual and group values, attitudes, competencies, and patterns of behaviors that determine the commitment to, and the style and proficiency of, an organization's health and safety programs.

The safety culture of an organization is the product of individual and group values, attitudes, competencies, and patterns of behaviors that determine the commitment to, and the style and proficiency of, an organization's health and safety programs.

What the NRC did about safety culture after Chernobyl was:

- Benchmark good safety cultures
- Establish expectations for licensees
- Strengthen internal regulations against retaliation for raising concerns (10 CFR 50.7)
- Issue SCWE policy statements identifying SCWE attributes (May 1996 and October 2004)

- Aggressively investigate retaliation allegations
- Monitor licensee SCWE performance indicators
- Take enforcement action when appropriate.

The DOE followed some years later after the Cold War was won, and the veil of secrecy about the nuclear activities at its sites was lifted. Eventually, the DOE established what it calls the Integrated Safety Management System (ISMS) approach to nuclear and other aspects of safety, as previously discussed.

It is the DOE's belief that robust implementation of ISMS could lead the DOE and its contractors to a stronger safety culture. However, without robust and active support by DOE management and contractor senior management, ISMS will not lead to an enduring safety culture. Furthermore, ISMS was not specifically designed to improve an organization's safety culture.

ISMS is a good foundation for a safety culture, but more is needed. This is where the active establishment of the SCWE applies.

Behavioral attributes expected in the workplace must be articulated and a plan to develop, measure, and monitor progress toward building a safety culture put into place with continual, visible involvement of senior management. The following aspects of this endeavor must be remembered:

- Safety culture is not the soft side of management issues — it is the hardest!
- Safety culture can be built, or rebuilt, using proven organizational development methodologies, but a bad culture will not simply evolve into a good one by declaration.
- Safety culture behaviors are often counterintuitive and must be learned and reinforced.

- Driving fear and apathy out of a workplace by implementing a SCWE takes consistent performance management and mitigation strategies.

Furthermore, leaders must *make the case* for change. The organization must collectively identify the desired end state for the new work environment (i.e., behavioral attributes):

- The management team must understand the baseline issues and challenges facing the organization under each attribute.
- There must be a single, clear set of behavioral expectations for everyone, and additional expectations for leadership.
- There must be measurable performance indicators.

In fact, there must be a dedicated infrastructure to guide culture change and establish new norms. The organization needs to receive training on new skillsets and new expectations. Work plans to address problem areas and behaviors should be developed and implemented. Progress should be measured regularly through self-assessments and external reviews.

There are certain essential steps to be taken to address or establish a SCWE. First, there must be some sort of an assessment of the current state of the safety culture. This is most often done by a survey or several surveys. However, this must be done carefully. The results *must* be published and an action plan in response to the results must be articulated. Both steps are difficult to do and take courage, lots of courage. The action plan may necessitate some painful change and will test the sincerity of the management team.

Behavioral expectations must be articulated for everyone, particularly the management chain. There will have to be actual training to reinforce these behavioral expectations and the attitude they portend. Key SCWE performance measures must be established, tracked, and published. These key performance indicators (KPIs) must have owners and must be frequently reviewed and acted upon. As with the assessment and action plan, this is important and difficult to do. Ultimately, the KPIs are part of the commitment to the free flow of information fundamental to a SCWE.

There may be additional support required to assist an organization in establishing and nurturing a SCWE, such as:

- Executive involvement in personnel decisions that may impact safety culture
- SCWE mentors to ensure consistency and fairness
- Alternative avenues for minority opinions or employee concerns.

There also needs to be an awareness of the spectrum of communication deterrents. It is not enough to prevent the overt retaliation for bringing up issues or concerns. At the other end of the continuum is an equally damaging attribute to the free flow of information, which I mentioned earlier and labeled "hierarchical suffocation." If there is not established protocol for bringing up issues with the expectation that they will be welcomed and addressed (expeditiously), an overly cumbersome administrative system for registering concerns can eventually discourage the concern from surfacing, even though no one did anything overt to discourage it. Management and organizations must guard against this almost natural aspect of large endeavors.

I have described the culture evolution in the nuclear industry. In doing so, some fundamental steps were provided in the establishment of the desired safety culture and supporting SCWE. **The most essential element is the resolve of the leadership to do the right thing.** All these attributes are necessary in the complex and dangerous endeavors of an industrial society to prevent the unacceptable consequences of not having a SCWE. This is especially true of those industries I call "high-consequence, low-probability endeavors," where the probability of an untoward event is very small but if it occurs the impact can be devastating. Avoiding such an occurrence makes the investment in the safety culture essential.

Diversity

Not long after returning to the SRS site as the executive vice president, the number two position in management at the site, I gave a speech to the SRS Diversity Council. Interestingly, when I left the site four years earlier, I wasn't even an executive. This fact says something about two management philosophies I will briefly mention here. **"Sometimes you have to move on to move up"** and **"Never burn bridges you may need later."** Given the present-day emphasis on diversity in the workplace and in society in general, I suspect that readers of this book might enjoy knowing what I said to our diversity council back then.

"It is an honor and a pleasure to be standing before you tonight. Actually, it would be a pleasure to be standing anywhere tonight because, after my recent hip replacement operations, I no longer take that capability for granted. I had my right hip replaced last August and my left hip replaced June 18th. I am sure both operations are a result of my years of wrestling, followed by years of marathon running. I have enough metal in me now that I could probably qualify for the heavyweight class. Recently, during a severe lightning storm, my wife got up out of bed and was heading out of the room when I asked her where she was going. She said that she was not going to stay in bed with me because she was sure that I would attract the lightning.

"In thinking about this evening and how to tell you something about me, I thought about a book Jennifer Large gave me for my convalescence titled, *The Learning Journey.* The book explained that one of the best ways to communicate and to teach is by the telling of stories. I thought that I would use that approach tonight to convey my feelings about diversity and how it has affected my approach to management and to life in general. My approach to these subjects and management in general has been an evolution and is a work in progress. And it begins, as most adult perceptions do, in my childhood. I have been told that this is a group that appreciates candor and openness, so here goes.

"When I was a young boy about 12 years old, a group of friends of mine and I had just finished playing baseball on a hot summer day. My father was a veterinarian and he had his hospital behind our house, which had a long driveway running along the side of it to a parking area between the house and the hospital. I knew that in that hospital my dad had a meat freezer where he kept the dog food, but he also kept a stash of Popsicles. I asked my buddies if they would like some Popsicles and they said 'sure.' So about five of us — all of us white — headed down the driveway for the hospital but two of our friends, who were black, said that they were not thirsty and sat down on the curb in front of the house. I didn't think anything about it; I was just thinking about the Popsicles.

"However, my dad had been watching everything from his office window, which had a straight line of vision to the street. As he was dolling out the Popsicles to my other friends, he asked me why the other two boys were sitting on the curb. I said they said they were not interested in the Popsicles. My dad said, 'You go out and tell those two that I said for them to come back here and get their Popsicles and that I said it was all right.' Through the Army and college, Bee and Bobby never came home without stopping to say hi to my dad. It took me years to understand that subtle situation and my dad's sensitivity to those youngsters. Those boys had exempted themselves from the Popsicle break because they were questioning whether the adults would welcome them because of the color of their skin.

"When I went to junior high and the seventh grade, I met Dean Earl who was in the eighth grade and 6 feet 5 inches tall and about 220 pounds. I came home and told my parents there was a giant in the eighth grade who was 7 feet tall. Dean, who is black, and I became friends through junior high and high school. Everyone in the sports-minded city of Sandusky, Ohio, expected Dean — by virtue of his physical size and strength — to be the next three-sport, all-state athlete to lead the teams to state titles. Dean was a good athlete, but his heart was in playing the piano. He never reached everyone's athletic expectations, but he sure could play the piano. Anyhow, in high school, Dean asked my mother, the ex-Army nurse who was the city golf champ, to teach him to play golf. She said she would. My mother was the original women's lib person, and she did not care what anyone thought about her. She spoke her mind and all the doctors at the hospital were afraid of her. From a distance, she and Dean made quite the pair, and she taught Dean how to golf. That lesson did not take as long to register on me.

"When I first went to work for Westinghouse, it was as an operator on the FFTF. I was chosen as one of the first shift managers and soon found myself leading a crew that had women engineers and technicians on it. I had gone to the Naval Academy, which was at that time an all-male institution. I had been in the submarine service, which still is an all-male endeavor.* I had coached wrestling and that was an all-male sport. I was surrounded by men, everywhere but at home. I am blessed with two daughters, and they have taught me a lot about life and what it means to be a woman in this world.

---

* The Navy began accepting women into the submarine service in 2017.

"While I was experiencing women in the workplace for the first time and very unsure of how to handle that situation, I was also asked to coach a girls' soccer team on which my older daughter was a member. These girls were nine and 10 years. It took a while, but what I discovered in both situations was that the key was to treat the girls as athletes and the women as professionals. Once I did that, both situations settled down.

"I went from FFTF to Palo Verde Nuclear Station to D-B Nuclear Station for the recovery and restart of that nuclear plant. I was the assistant vice president nuclear and the VP, an ex-Navy admiral, was determined to change a very relaxed culture that had resulted in the NRC shutting the plant down and to change it in a hurry. He did so by changing all the icons, changing the language, moving the people to new environments, and replacing people who were reluctant to support these changes.

"The Admiral also had a penchant for chewing people out in public. I asked him one time why he did that and what happened to *praising in public, chastising in private*. He replied that he never attacked the person, only what the person did or did not do. The public forum left a lasting impression on the person and the people who were witnessing it, and it was a quick way to calibrate everyone as to what his expectations were. I never quite got comfortable with his approach, but I did exercise a modified version of it at RTF and DWPF. By the way, you have another retired admiral on your board for whom I worked and from whom I learned considerably more about the long-term approach to people than I did from the first admiral.

"I was hired at SRS to address the RTF startup and then the DWPF startup, both of which were in the ditch and needed to be resurrected in a hurry. I needed to establish a culture of accountability and achievement. This had to be done quickly so, as I said, I used a modified version of the Admiral's approach. I found people clinging to DuPont Cold War philosophies rather than adopting the post-Three Mile Island (TMI) methodologies for operating nuclear facilities, organizations fighting with each other, and things not being accomplished with any sense of urgency or commitment. These weren't bad people; they just weren't galvanized around a clear mission. After three or four weeks of walking and talking and watching and listening, I set about to revise the schedule, set milestones, and commissioned a Plan of the Day (POD) where people would report on their commitments, which supported the schedule. The language of accountability replaced the lingo of complacency. Our new icons became the posted milestone charts and metrics by which we would measure ourselves. I rotated many of the managers to now oversee the organizations with which they had been warring. In the beginning, it was rough and even bloody. A few people fell by the wayside, but most responded to the challenge. Usually, those who fell by the wayside volunteered in one way or another to do so.

"Not long after I had arrived at DWPF, a young black female supervisor came to see me. Her concern was that there was not much opportunity afforded to minorities and females to advance at DWPF. I told her that there was only one thing that mattered to me and that was productivity. I would surround myself with those who were productive, and I didn't care what color or gender they were. I committed to her that I would treat all people the same and I told her to wait three months and come back to see me to tell me if I was good to my word. After three months, she returned and said, 'Mr. Amerine, you certainly do treat us all the same. You treat us all like caca.'

"I said to her, 'Okay but do I have your collective attention?' She said, 'Yes, Sir, you really do.' To which I replied, 'Well, as we learn to be accountable and as we learn that as a focused team we can accomplish things on the schedule we set for ourselves, I will back off on the intensity. If I have to provide that focus, I will, but eventually we will replace toughness with esprit de corps, and we will weave the humor into our daily activities.' And we did just that."

"Now, at that time, I felt that the situation at Millstone needed to be galvanized in the manner described. When I arrived there, I had another experience that increased my understanding of how different situations require different approaches. But first, let me tell you another SRS story to flesh out where I am coming from. At DWPF, we were preparing to close out the melter cell. Once we exited the cell, no human would ever again enter that place, as the eventual radioactivity levels would prohibit entry. Managers, engineers, and technicians were intently inspecting the cell in these final preparations. We also had the cleaning crew in the cell trying to make sure it was spotless, because any foreign material would surely become radioactive and further contaminate the canyon. The head of the laborers, a young lady named Shirley Cartledge, came to me and said, "Mr. Amerine, would you look at something for me?" She showed me two large holes in the frame that held the melter, which should have had bolts in them. They were in an out-of-the-way place in the cell and none of the managers, engineers, or technicians had noticed or thought to question their absence. But this laborer had.

"Later, I learned that Shirley had also pointed out to Jim Wilson, the plant manager, that the routing of personnel in and out of the Radiological Buffer Area (RBA) would create a potential spread of contamination and create more waste than if it was done another way. Again, operators and radcon personnel had overlooked this approach, but the questioning attitude of a laborer led to significant improvement. Shirley and I have since become good friends. She and her husband, Steve, have been to my house, and Cindy and I have been to their house. She has prayed for me and I have prayed for her as we both suffered through some infirmities. We wrote to each other while I was in New England.

"What could these two people possibly have in common? She is black. I am white. She is female. I am male. I am Naval Academy and Harvard educated. She began working after graduating from high school. At SRS, I was at the top of the management chain. She was at the bottom. What attracts me to Shirley is that she works hard, she thinks about what she is doing, and she takes care of her people. In short, she cares. She gives no quarter, as they say, and she asks for none. She does her job to the best of her ability with integrity and purpose. In short, she is a professional and so am I. It does not hurt that she has a sense of humor. I am proud to call her my friend and I have learned a lot from her.

"I tell you this story because I believe it illustrates that when we focus on a person's character (not their job title, their academic credentials, their gender, the color of their skin), only then may we gain the full benefit of what that person has to offer. I believe that approach, person by person, is the answer to generalisms or stereotypes that impede our collective ability to reach our full potential. I know I was a better manager and DWPF was a better facility because of Shirley. As an individual, I have benefited from our friendship. By the way, when I went to ITP, I took from DWPF the Cost and Scheduling Manager, the Startup Manager, the Engineering Manager, and Shirley. I would want her on any project team that I manage. I believe every person on the team is just as important as every other person on the team, regardless of their position or rank, as long as they do their job and do it well.

"I believe we in management need to look for opportunities for women and ethnic and social minorities. However, management also needs to ensure that these underrepresented groups have the chance to become qualified so that they are prepared when those opportunities come along. I believe this extra attention is appropriate because of the decades of limitations these groups have endured, which has made their membership in the ranks of management disproportionate, and this will not be corrected without overt action. This is not, however, Affirmative Action because preparation and qualification are prerequisites for placement.

"Let me share one last story on the topic of diversity, which concerns Millstone Nuclear Station. In trying to help a friend who got caught up in a reduction in force (RIF) at SRS, I called Millstone because I knew they were shut down by the NRC and looking for people to help them recover. After telling me to send the friend's resume along, the CNO asked me if I would like to throw my hat in the ring for the VP of Engineering. Long story short, I ended up at Millstone. After three months, I could see that the establishment of the Safety Conscious Work Environment (SCWE) — although we didn't know to call it by that name at that time — was the main impediment to startup, and the VP of Unit Three Operations, who had the SCWE as a collateral duty, was struggling with both of these individually daunting tasks. I had achieved some credibility with the SCWE oversight organization on how I had handled a significant personnel problem in the Training organization, so I volunteered to relieve him of that responsibility. After much discussion, my engineering responsibilities were parceled out to the other VPs and I became the VP of Human Services.

"In addition to the Employee Concerns Program (ECP), I had responsibility for Human Relations (HR), Legal, Emergency Preparedness (EP), Training, and an organization called the SCWE Group. I learned more in the 10 months in that job than I could have learned in 10 years as a line manager. One of the main things I learned was that when an employee has a concern, the one thing that must not be done is to question the possible motivation behind that concern. Instead, the concern must be addressed on its own merits. I also learned that there are many ways to build collaborative efforts. The longest-lasting approach is the one where employees are empowered, and, as such, plans, policies, and problem resolutions are created and managed from the bottom up. Employee ideas are solicited and genuinely considered. **When it comes to communication, you never get to cross the goal line and spike the ball; it is an ongoing, never-ending process**. Personally, I discovered pools of patience that I did not know existed. I have folded these new philosophies and approaches into the drive for team accomplishment mentioned above and have found them to be mutually compatible.

When an employee has a concern, the one thing that must not be done is to question the possible motivation behind that concern.

"I will close this my talk with some of the words I used at my last all-personnel meeting at DWPF. I told those employees that we represented the best of what America is all about. We were Jews and Muslims; we were Protestants and Catholics; we were white and black; male and female; we were even Democrat and Republican. But together we had created a fabric woven from those diversities, which was stronger than any cloth that could be made from a single strand alone. We had become a microcosm of what it means to be American. When we diverted our differences to a focus on a common goal, there was nothing we couldn't accomplish. I plan to expand on that same philosophy now to all of SRS. The strength of such a collective effort is the source of continued accomplishment. Not only does it make good business sense, it is something everyone will be able to look back on with pride. Their effort in that retrospective view will not be just a job. It will have been the opportunity to be part of a mission of excellence and importance."

Experience with Unions

Relative to the topics of work and diversity, I want to comment on what I consider to be one of the biggest detriments to America's success in a global market: labor unions. There was a time and place when this country needed unions to stand up for workers who were underpaid and whose work conditions were unsafe and unhealthy. The creation of the need for unions at that time is a good example of one of my sayings, which is "**The price of expediency is often inconvenience.**" Because management and business owners took advantage of the workers (expediency), we are now being "inconvenienced" by the unnecessary and detrimental existence of unions, not to mention many crippling laws and regulations stemming from the same era.

Unions are unnecessary now because there are a plethora of laws protecting workers and a legion of lawyers all too ready to see that those laws are enforced to the maximum extent possible (and then some). Instead, unions today have become an avenue for corruption and organized crime. Worse, they drag performance down to the lowest common denominator and, thereby, negatively affect American productivity and global competitiveness.

This opinion is an informed one, as I have seen unions have this effect on worker performance time and again. When I tried to institute reward for performance at NFS on top of already existing wage structure, the unions adamantly resisted, insisting that all workers were the same in their contribution. That is not true in the executive or salaried ranks; it is not true of hourly workers either. Unions also resist what is known as creative destruction as technology evolves, and old jobs should be replaced or eliminated. Not doing so impacts the ability of that business to remain competitive.

However, if your workplace has a union or unions, you will have to learn to deal with them. The first thing to hope for and influence (to the extent you can) is to have strong union leadership. As an experienced union official once told an underling, we need strong management just as management needs strong union leadership. In both cases, this does not mean antagonistic or quarrelsome leaders. It means that leaders in both the union and management know that ultimately the business must be well run and clients/customers must have confidence that the endeavor will reliably produce a quality product on the committed time schedule. It also means those leaders are good for their word and act with full integrity. Management must work hard to establish that kind of trust and understanding. It is not easy. Some union leaders and some management are win-lose personalities, and this must be overcome. Win-win situations need to be the goal.

I believe in the right to work, which is the situation where workers can decide freely if they want to join the union or not. It is not union busting but really a question of liberty. No worker should be forced to join a union and pay those dues if he or she doesn't want to do so. The union needs to compete for the workers' dollars by explaining what benefits are provided for that money. Contracts between management and unions to require workers to join the union represent a loss of freedom. Interestingly, union membership actually increases in right-to-work states, not only because businesses move to those states but also because the unions have to actually perform to attract and retain workers.

The worst example of the impact of unions, in my opinion, is when it comes to teachers' unions. Coupled with the intrusion of federal government into education, the teachers' unions have made sure the student is the last consideration in public education. The United States spends more money per student than any other industrial country, and yet its students continue to rank at or near the bottom in almost every category. I don't think it's a coincidence that America has been on this decline ever since President Carter put the Department of Education in place in 1979.

Teachers' unions have made sure the student is the last consideration in public education.

Another anathema is federal employee unions. Even Franklin Roosevelt, who, following in the footsteps of his cousin Teddy and of Woodrow Wilson, set this country on a road to socialism, advised against the evils of unionizing federal employees. Yet federal employees were, in fact, unionized and we have witnessed the impact of that mistake as the civil servants have become anything but.

Politicians have aligned themselves with unions to capture a block of votes. Unions have supported those politicians, in ways both legal and illegal. The politicians then pass legislation favoring unions even if detrimental to the country overall. I will say more about politicians later.

PRESIDENT OF NUCLEAR FUEL SERVICES: IT ALL COMES TOGETHER

In March 2010, I was selected to take over as President of NFS in Erwin, Tennessee. NFS was acquired by Babcock and Wilcox (B&W) about a year earlier and had experienced several mishaps that resulted in B&W agreeing with the NRC to the shutdown of the facility to address safety culture and conduct of operations issues. NFS is the sole supplier of nuclear fuel to the Navy for its propulsion reactors. NFS's additional functionality is for the DOE, turning weapons-grade material into fuel for reactor plants.

It was decided that NFS needed a new leader, experienced in recoveries of struggling or shut-down facilities. I was chosen to be that new leader. This assignment was an opportunity, in a very important and challenging venue, to put into practice all that I had learned. Because NFS was the capstone to a 45-year career in the nuclear industry, much of it spent in startup or recovery of nuclear facilities, I will break down what was done to recover NFS. It represents an accumulation of experiences, techniques, and philosophies developed over those 45 years — lessons I hope will be meaningful to you.

Coming into this pinnacle leadership experience, I had experience being a member of the leadership team or the head of such a team brought in to recover seven other nuclear facilities in a condition of forced shutdown or under serious disappointment of the regulator or client in the facility performance. I used that experience to evaluate the situation at NFS for several months before invoking any organizational realignments or introducing any new programs or approaches.

After a month of evaluation of the effort to regain the facility's total license, I suggested to the NRC they grant permission to restart in a segmented manner. Even though this meant more work for everyone, it gave the NRC some relief to focus on the most important aspect of the plant, Navy nuclear fuel production. The return to full operation was accomplished over the next six months after nuclear fuel operation recommenced. This accomplishment restored confidence from many stakeholders including the NRC, NR, the DOE, and, most importantly, the employees themselves. It also meant that NFS was back in the business of providing nuclear fuel to the Navy.

To accomplish the required safety culture and conduct of operations improvements to the satisfaction of ourselves, our B&W corporate parent, our clients (the NR and the DOE), and the NRC, many actions had to be completed to improve NFS's safety culture and conduct of operations or, as I call it, conduct of business — because the attributes that define good conduct apply to all disciplines in an organization, not just production or operations.

First, there was a lot of walking around and meeting with employees, one-on-one or in small groups, in all parts of the organization. (As suggested earlier, **I never required employees to come to my office. I always went to their workspace because that's their comfort zone**. Additionally, on the way to the employee's space, I was apt to see things or meet people I would not have encountered if I stayed sequestered in my office.) Using collective brainstorming of various groups, we then defined eight cultural safety traits. The point was to identify **desired organizational traits** that could anchor us. Our team concluded they were:

- Leadership values
- Problem identification and resolution system
- Personal accountability
- Efficient work processes
- Continuous learning
- Environment conducive to raising concerns
- Effective communications
- Respectful work environment.

Then we established a new NFS vision: *"NFS is one team, respected as a safe and reliable supplier of innovative nuclear products and services — for our nation and the world — today and into the future."*

After those stakes were put in the ground, the leadership team developed a new safety culture definition:

Safety Culture at NFS is defined as the core values and behaviors resulting from a collective commitment by each of us to emphasize safety over competing priorities to ensure protection of people and the environment.

We then itemized and defined the Core Values for NFS, which were:

- Integrity
- People
- Formality and discipline
- Respect for health and environment
- Technical excellence
- Accountability
- Cost consciousness

So, how do these exercises integrate? One can think of the "desired organizational traits" as *what* an organization does as part of its daily functions. The "core values" are *how* it goes about doing those things. These things are important to form a basis for communication that supports a bias for action. However, they each have a definition and are a lot to remember as one goes about their day. They basically serve as a foundation and a reference to be used in training and discussions. To make things easier, I established the following two items (obviously based on the experiences explained earlier):

Established Workplace Priorities (in order of importance)

- Safety
- Quality
- Schedule
- Cost

Conduct of Business Attributes

- Personal accountability
- Procedure compliance
- Technical inquisitiveness
- A willingness to stop in the face of uncertainty

These priorities and attributes were then discussed and explained in every possible venue, repeatedly. In fact, these priorities and attributes were put on a small card every employee was encouraged to attach to their badge lanyard. All managers and supervisors were encouraged to be able to discuss them in their own words as often as possible. They were welcomed to use my words if they understood and believed in them. These priorities and attributes, which are easy to remember, formed the foundation for all our actions and communications at NFS. And they resonated with other stakeholders, such as the NRC and NR and DOE.

After being at NFS for approximately six months, I also worked with my team to publish the **Expectations Policy**.

It is summarized in the following:

Expectations of All Employees

- Practice safety in all endeavors.
- Treat all others with respect.
- Support our workplace priorities, a SCWE, and good conduct of business.
- Display a questioning attitude in a professional and courteous manner.
- Seek to understand management's direction and to follow the direction as it was intended.
- After providing input, do what management directs.
  - Unless the direction is unsafe, illegal, or immoral.
  - If you believe the above is the case, elevate your concern to the next level of management or other avenues (e.g., the Employee Concerns Problem [ECP], ombudsman, regulators, etc.).
  - If you are a union employee and you feel the instruction is in violation of the contract, follow the grievance process.
- Do what you say you will do; take responsibility for your actions.
- Report to work areas at the scheduled time in appropriate work dress; union employees are to adhere to the provisions of the contract in this regard.
- Communicate; keep your management informed and ask for help from others.

Management Team Additional Expectations

- As much as possible, explain "why" when you give direction.

- Listen to feedback from employees and understand their concerns.

- Clearly set expectations for employees.

- Manage all employees in accordance with company rules; additionally, interface with the union employees in accordance with the contract.

- Document and advise your management and HR of problems and shortcomings.

- Manage performance: recognize positive behavior and apply discipline within company guidelines.

- Support the management chain, especially first line leadership, so that work rules and contract provisions can be consistently applied.

- Communicate; keep the workforce informed and call on resources when needed for advice and assistance.

We established a **Nuclear Safety Review Board (NSRB)** to address an ongoing need for high-level expert oversight. The NSRB reports directly to the board of directors (BOD), as well as to me, the company president. It was charged with advising NFS senior management and the BOD on opportunities and methods to improve the strength of NFS's safety culture and programs that have a material effect on safe operations (e.g., support and production operations, safety, engineering, maintenance, decommissioning). It was also charged with being an advocate for issues requiring attention or action of the BOD. They visited NFS on a regular basis (usually quarterly) to conduct reviews and work with the NFS management team.

An **Executive Review Board (ERB) was established**, which was designed to provide a centralized forum for management personnel to be aware of and review employee and contractor issues. The ERB was an oversight and advisory body, rather than an investigative body. The intent of the ERB was to detect organizational challenges and to take prompt, consistent, and appropriate action.

I also put in place, as I had done at several other recoveries that needed to establish a SCWE, a **People Team and an Ombudsman Program**. The purpose of the People Team was to work through issues or concerns brought up by employees in a way that best addressed the problem. The People Team also served as a support group for the Ombudsman representatives. All issues and concerns brought to the People Team were kept strictly confidential, consistent with HR and security requirements. People Team members included a representative from the Legal, Human Resources, Communications, Industrial Safety, and Training departments, the Ombudsmen personnel, and the Employee Concerns Program (ECP) manager.

To provide as many venues as possible for employees to bring up issues, the Ombudsman Program was put in place. The mission of the Ombudsmen was to provide informal and, if requested, confidential conflict resolution assistance to NFS managers, employees, and contractors in a manner that was separate from the normal formalized options, such as the Employee Assistance Program, the ECP, human resources, and other avenues. The ombudsmen had access to anyone in the organization, including the NFS president, to resolve issues. The Ombudsman Program functioned outside of the line management structure with no management decision-making power; it was independent in structure, function, and appearance.

The ombudsmen held all communications with those seeking assistance in strict confidence unless, with the individual's permission, additional resources were required. Selection and training of the ombudsmen personnel is critical. They must be personnel who the employees trust with a capability to listen empathetically. Frequently, when folks have an issue but are not comfortable talking to management about it or are not ready to go the ECP route, all they want is someone to listen to them. I saw the ombudsman function defuse a great many situations during my career.

For similar reasons, the **Differing Professional Opinion (DPO) was put in place**. The DPO program provides an avenue to register an opinion different from a prevailing NFS technical position. It is administered as part of the corrective action program and adjudicated by the Corrective Action Review Board (CARB), which I'll cover later.

We also established a **Management Advisory Council (MAC)**. The purpose of the MAC was to advise the senior management team on policy changes, employee issues, employee of the month selection, and other items as determined by its members or senior management. Members of the council were selected by the president from the first line managers' ranks. Members were periodically rotated out in a staggered fashion to make room for new members.

Communications among employees was enhanced by several initiatives, including:

- The existing NFS intranet was completely overhauled to provide a better communications interface between employees and management.
- Executive management communicated a top-down, face-to-face message to all managers to set clear behavioral standards (e.g., do not proceed in the face of uncertainty, require personal accountability, and marshal appropriate resources to address priority problems).
- A series of All-Employee Meetings (AEM) were conducted to discuss recent incidents, core values, and expectations, and to point out progress on milestones.
- Clear expectations regarding management and staff behavior and performance established and communicated in writing.

- An enhanced all-employee newsletter was instituted.
- Round tables with the president and a cross-section of employees were established; questions and answers (Q&As) from these sessions were published on the NFS intranet.

After several months of assessing the NFS structure and functions, I decided to make organizational changes, which I explained in detail to the workforce and other stakeholders. The NFS organizational structure was changed to provide increased checks and balances through direct access to the board of directors by the assurance director and the quality, safety, and safeguards director. In addition, the engineering and training departments were moved to report directly to the president. A program management group and a work management department were created, which contained among other entities, the Work Control Group. The Work Management Department reported to the operations vice president.

The organization's evolved structure is shown on the following page.

Organization Restructured to Provide Checks and Balances

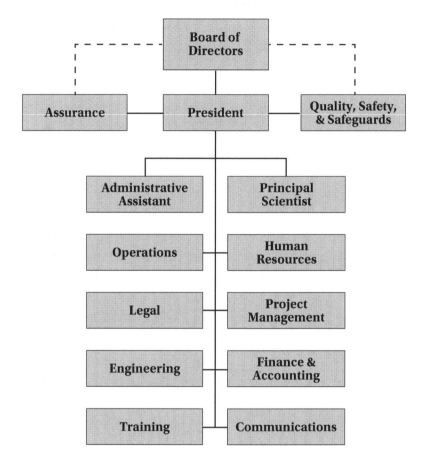

To improve communication of our goals and to more efficiently allocate our resources, the existing schedule was expanded, far beyond its previous boundary of only capital projects, to include all the work planned in each department across the company. Each department loaded their resource requirements into the schedule. Then, based on comparing the resource requirements with the personnel available, adjustments to planned completion dates and personnel assignments were made. The result was **a fully integrated, resource-loaded schedule, which charted the path ahead and provided guidance to achieve our goals. It was a top-down,**

bottom-up effort like that mentioned for RTF and DWPF. We implemented those project management tools, such as WBS, RAMP, and Critical Path Analysis. However, the most important change was our collective goal to gain commitment and a sense of accountability.

Accountability meetings (the Plan of the Day and the Plan of the Week) were implemented that enabled the management team to review progress, resolve issues, and reinforce core values of safety, quality, schedule, and cost — in that order. Milestones were established to measure, advertise, and celebrate accomplishments. The fully integrated, resource-loaded schedule was the basis for those meetings. Creating the schedule and teaching people how to behave in the POD/POW took several months of concentrated effort and was iterative in nature. The creation of an integrated schedule, in any organization, is a tremendous task, but it is essential that it be done as a top priority and that **ALL** activities are included in it. I had NFS **develop a corporate metrics system using a common presentation format based on INPO formats**. The system contained more than 100 key performance indicators (KPIs) with color coding and trend indicators. There were rollups at multiple levels in a variety of performance areas, culminating with top-tier rollups in the areas of safety, quality, schedule, cost, and conduct of business. This system was a duplicate of the one I created at WGD.

To capture all facets of the new safety culture paradigm, a **Safety Culture Improvement Plan (SCIP) was developed**. The purpose of the SCIP was to provide employees and other stakeholders with information about NFS's actions, both underway and envisioned, to improve the company's safety culture. This document captured what had been accomplished, described actions presently underway, listed future potential actions under consideration, and served as NFS's overarching safety culture guidance. It was a living document and intended to be updated periodically.

Employee surveys were used to determine NFS's safety culture status. Follow-up surveys would be conducted at appropriate intervals to measure longer-term progress in improving safety culture. Because survey interval lengths do not provide necessary short-term information about the effectiveness of newly initiated programs and processes, less lengthy and more focused surveys were conducted at about six-month intervals.

NFS's previous employee evaluation system had fallen into disuse about two years earlier. Actions were put in place to reinstitute **a new employee evaluation system** based on B&W's program. Essential elements of the system included individual performance goals and competencies, and required informal quarterly feedback sessions, training and learning goals, safety culture performance, and an annual written evaluation. Promotions and pay raises were to be based, in large measure, on performance evaluations.

By the end of the first year, we developed and shared a strategic plan that provided a vision for the future. The plan was intended to be a living document that would be adjusted to reflect the changes in the business environment, and also would be able to provide a sense of continuity. It started with the principles we wanted the organization to embody and then used those principles to determine how to sustain and grow the business. The basic first principle of business development is that an organization must do well with the business it has if it is to obtain new business. To do that, it must have a strong safety culture, which, in turn, rests on the pedestal of a viable SCWE.

The NFS training department partnered with Development Dimensions International (DDI) and The Ken Blanchard Companies to **provide world-class training courses to develop leadership skills for all employees.** Working with B&W Talent Management, Development Progression Guidelines for NFS employees were established for emerging leaders, frontline supervisors, unit managers, and section managers. Additionally, frontline supervisors received training, and a Supervisor Coaching and Positive Reinforcement Observation program was implemented. This training provided supervisors with the knowledge and tools to reinforce the desired behaviors of their workers and coaching to address any issues. The approach included a focus on selected topics on a quarterly basis for continuing training of the first line managers to maintain and enhance their leadership knowledge and skills.

On the technical side, I also drew upon my previous experience within organizations that had faced operating systems challenges. In addition to the other programs established to increase conduct of business and support the safety culture, the Joint Test Group (JTG) Program was put in place. **The purpose of the JTG was to establish a body of stakeholders, selected from key parent organizations, with the function to formally review and approve proposed test plans, test procedures, and test results for plant component and system testing.** Such stakeholder groups included Safety, Engineering, QA, and Operations. In addition, the JTG also reviewed and had to concur with any equipment changes as a result of the tests or make recommendations for further testing to achieve test objectives.

A **Senior Engineering Watch (SEW) was implemented**. The SEW was established to provide additional coverage on the process floor by NFS personnel with technical knowledge of the operations. The SEW spent 80 percent or more of their time on the floor, observing and engaging with management, supervisors, and employees and were readily accessible for communications on tour. This effort may be targeted based on operations or as directed by the engineering director. The SEW's primary responsibility was providing technical oversight to operations. The SEW can actively engage in trouble-shooting and other technical support of operations when needed, or can call on an appropriate resource to provide specific technical support as needed.

An **Operating Experience Program (OEP) was created** under the assurance director to provide a formal, systematic process for the collection, documentation, distribution, review, and retention of internal and external operating experience. I also assigned the assurance director the responsibility for **Root Cause Analysis (RCA).** This capability to analyze an event after the problem has occurred is essential to understanding why the issue happened and how similar events can be prevented in the future. RCA is a formal dissection of what happened and why. The technique is formal and well known in the nuclear industry, as is its related short form, **Apparent Cause Analysis (ACA).** Not every event requires an RCA or an ACA, but there are criteria for making that determination. The key is to have a small group that has received that training and is assigned to tackle that analysis. The size and membership of that group is critical. The size must not be so large that the individuals don't have an opportunity to practice their skillset frequently enough to keep sharp. However, it cannot be so small that the members get burned out or are taken away from their primary assignments too frequently. The membership should cover several skillsets and experiences.

Part of the RCA process is to examine the **Extent of Condition (EOC).** The EOC is the process of examining similar activities, procedures, processes, and so forth to see if they may be subject to the same failure or problem. **One thing I added to this standard practice in the nuclear industry was the instruction to ask the holistic question, "Is this event telling us we have an endemic management or workforce issue?"** Hopefully the answer is no, but the question must be asked and the facts examined with this concern in mind. I also insisted that we track an **Effectiveness of the Corrective Actions (ECA).** This requirement involves formally coming back three or six months later to assess if the corrective actions taken as a result of the incident have, in fact, been effective in correcting or improving the situation.

Numerous actions were taken to **strengthen the Corrective Action Program (CAP)** because it is an essential component of a vibrant SCWE. Examples include:

- Revised CAP procedures to include a Safety Culture Implications Review (SCIR) as a part of a full team root cause analysis.
- Revised programmatic guidance to provide specific criteria to invoke Corrective Action Review Board (CARB) review of investigations, corrective actions, and effectiveness reviews to help ensure appropriately broad investigations and effective corrective actions. One of the CARB responsibilities is to determine the need for an RCA and then review the results of that endeavor if it is executed.
- Conducted an independent review of investigation processes to ensure the tools in that suite were being properly applied and executed.
- Developed and implemented a standard operating guide and flowchart for evaluation of unusual incidents.
- Established single point accountability of CARB and Change Control Board (CCB) chairmen by changing the Board from consensus to advisory.

The organization's most senior executive, in this case me, would be the CARB and CCB chairman.

We initiated a Documentation and Procedural Improvements Program. Examples of improvements include:

- Conducted a review of procedures, policies, etc., for instances of institutionalized production priorities over safety (or production pressure).

- Added a requirement to the Training and Qualification (T&Q) form originator to route the form with associated documents as part of the formal review and approval process to ensure accurate assignment of training.

- Developed a comprehensive Conduct of Operations document based on guidance from INPO and industry best practices, which included rules for proper communication of information with safety implications.

- Included a requirement for the Safety and Safeguards Review Council (SSRC) members to be on guard for the issue of having production priorities over safety during their routine reviews of change documents to prevent that from happening.

- Added restrictions on changes to procedures via Letter of Authorization (LOA) to require approvals by the Director of Safety and Security, VP Operations, and/or the Principal Scientist.

- Improved the Quality Assurance Oversight of Technical Documents and Programs that included a technical basis review of Configuration Management, Corrective Action, and NRC Response documents.

- Reviewed Training and Qualification (T&Q) document to eliminate "orphan" procedures — where the procedure is approved and in T&Q, but has not been assigned to any individual or job to execute.

- Implemented an Engineering Work Request Record of Review to ensure appropriate engineering disciplines are engaged and work package quality was maintained.

- Established Independent Design Reviews to ensure technical accuracy and comprehensiveness.

Activities at NFS require a high level of alertness from employees and contractors to ensure safe and compliant operations and security for everyone at NFS and the community. Excellence in safety, security, and compliance was fundamental to achieving its business objectives and could only be maintained by employees and contractors that are not suffering from excessive fatigue. Therefore, we **implemented a Fatigue Management Policy**. The fatigue management policy limited the number of hours an employee could work in certain circumstances. **A senior management oversight program was established to increase senior manager presence in the operating areas**. The program required that a senior manager be present in the field about six times a week to observe plant operations. The observations were spread over all shifts and senior managers attended turnover shift briefings, approximately two hours of observation of plant operations, interaction with safety personnel, and with the SEW. A report was filed by each senior manager after each observation period. The reports were reviewed weekly by the Operations VP and were trended.

An Equipment Reliability Program was developed, and a Reliability-Centered Maintenance program was instituted. The equipment reliability program and reliability-centered maintenance included the following attributes:

- Preventive Maintenance administration
- Common cause failure analysis (looking for common component failures across multiple pieces of equipment)
- Risk-based failure analysis (thoroughly analyzing one piece of equipment for likely failure modes to prevent or mitigate risks).

The processes for preparation, revision, review, approval, training, and execution for Letters of Authorization (LOA), Standard Operating Procedures (SOP), and Procedures were refined to eliminate duplication, improve quality, and to adjust the extent of administrative requirements to match the level of risk to safety and quality. I stressed the importance of good housekeeping. It is essential because:

- Good safety cannot be achieved without good housekeeping
- Housekeeping and material condition of the facility say something about the workforce
- Housekeeping and material condition are the first impressions made upon visitors.

To improve the cleanliness of interior and exterior spaces, the entire plant site was divided among the president's staff into areas of responsibility for the purpose of housekeeping inspection and improvement. Each staff member conducted a weekly inspection and corrections were generated, with the entire plant being covered every quarter. Additionally, a schedule of area organization activities was developed and executed to improve and sustain material organization and storage, and to reduce clutter. Finally, additional painting resources were funded, and a schedule was developed to improve plant preservation.

The techniques employed at NFS represent a culmination of lessons learned and trials-and-errors over my career. Not all of them may apply to every situation. So, as you read this book, you're likely selecting a few key ideas that could make a meaningful difference in your organization. It may be appropriate to use some variant of the above approaches or develop your own. One way to make that decision is by deploying Decision Analysis, which is explained in Appendix A. Regardless, the different approaches are to address the human and organizational side of project management, especially for endeavors that find themselves in extremis. These are in addition to the fundamental organic tools of project management, which, of necessity, must be used and used well for success. However, without addressing things like the SCWE, the organic nuts and bolts project management tools will not guarantee success and, I believe, eventually the project or endeavor will suffer and backslide into poor performance. **Again, to be a leader, one must first serve those they want to lead.**

Due to some health issues, I decided to retire about six months earlier than originally planned. Many of the above programs were in their infancy when I left, so I didn't get to ensure they took hold. However, I have been subsequently advised that many of them survived and even thrived under the management of my relief. And I am told people still refer to my sayings and instructions from time to time. I find that quite gratifying. NFS truly represented a capstone on my career, and I am blessed to have had that opportunity and to have worked once again with some truly dedicated and talented people at all levels of the organization.

SECTION IV

PHILOSOPHY

When I began writing this book, it was an exercise in creating what is sometimes called an "Ethic Will" — an accounting of what one believes and how those guideposts came to be; it would be primarily for the benefit of my family, friends, and close colleagues. And while I am pleased that the project ultimately took shape as a published book (now in its second edition) for the wider public, the initial aims of my writing challenged me to think at length about what I believe … about my philosophies on the various facets of life and work. Due to the nature of this book, I am only going to share two of those Ethic Will survivors, Energy and Nuclear Power. However, the Ethic Will concept and the impact that endeavor has had on me encourages me to provide more insight below.

I came upon the idea of writing an Ethic Will when reading an article on aging. Even though I was in good health and had begun lifting weights again after my second shoulder replacement surgery, I had just turned 61. I was still working and had recently changed companies for what I hoped was the last time (it wasn't), and I was engaged in work that was stimulating for me. My portfolio seemed to be in good shape to allow retirement even then and sustain the lifestyle Cindy and I wanted for the rest of our lives. I worried that we needed more margin for the unexpected, but that alone is not what kept me working at an age when many of my peers had long since retired.

In fact, I planned to shift vocations in a few more years, out of the nuclear industry that had been very good to me and provided me with a challenging and fulfilling career. I thought I wanted to teach as a way of giving back to my community. I had enjoyed working with and being around young people in the past when I coached wrestling at the high school level.

Life was good at that moment. So why did I feel motivated to start this rumination about what life means to me and how my life unfolded to that point? Well, for one thing, the article suggested that looking at what your values are and how they came to be and writing that down is good for the person doing it. It causes them to pause and ask, "What is it that I have lived for and what does that say about what is important with the time I have left? Are there things I really want to do with whatever time I have left? Are there things I should do that I have not done?"

Additionally, the previous few years at that time had shown me that things can change in an instant and not always for the better. We had seen the rise of terrorism and witnessed the impact of natural disasters that impacted millions of people, changing their lives forever. Cindy's father and my father passed away within months of each other in 2003. Then, almost five years later, both of our mothers died. All had lived robust and full lives. However, their departure not only left a hole in our lives, but their passing drove home a sense of mortality that was not there when they were alive. The bottom line is that it is never too soon or too late to do some serious reflection.

It is never too soon or too late to do some serious reflection.

In addition to the article mentioned above, I have read several books that stimulate my thinking in this direction. Some of those books are listed here because I think anyone reading these words would be well served to read them too. They are:

- *Man's Search for Meaning*, Victor Franklin
- *A Brief History of Time* and *The Grand Design*, Stephen Hawking
- *A Purpose Driven Life*, Rick Warren
- *The Leadership Wisdom of Jesus*, Charles Manz
- *The Year of Magical Thinking*, Joan Didion
- *The Shack*, William Young
- *My 90 Minutes in Heaven*, Don Piper
- *The Reason for God* and *King's Cross*, Timothy Keller
- *The History of God*, Karen Armstrong
- *Politics*, Aristotle
- *Atlas Shrugged*, Ayn Rand
- *The Prince*, Nicolo Machiavelli
- *Rules for Radicals*, Saul Alinsky
- *Things That Matter*, Charles Krauthammer
- *Liberty Amendments*, Mark Levin

Some of the thoughts and wisdom of these books have undoubtedly woven their way into the words I have written and will write. Obviously and hopefully those thoughts will be bent to my own vision. However, reading books like those above is one of the things of which I have not done enough. **Maybe this is a valuable piece of wisdom I can provide, which is to make time to read books that are stimulating to your thought process**, as it may be one of the most important and beneficial things a person can do with their spare time. Thank you for reading *my* book. I am honored and humbled.

ENERGY

As of the release of this book in its second edition in 2019, this country has gone nearly 45 years since the first energy crisis without developing a comprehensive energy policy. This is due to failed leadership and lack of resolve. As evidenced by other policies that haven't received the attention they need, most career politicians are driven by political expediency rather than commitment to doing the right thing for this county. The result is that our country is often at the mercy of foreign governments that share a collective disdain for us and would like to see us fail. Importing oil from unstable and hostile countries puts both our economy and our security in jeopardy. We are, in effect, financing Islamic terrorism. Long, complicated story short, even though we have become an oil exporter, we are still heavily dependent on imported petroleum for a variety of technical and political reasons.

We need a balanced portfolio of domestic energy as well as reliable and inexpensive broad-based electrical power generation. We have the oil and natural gas reserves. We have the potential nuclear capability in generation III and IV reactors, as well as life extension of the presently operating nuclear plants. We have the technology to reprocess spent nuclear fuel to recover approximately 95 percent of the unused nuclear fuel in those "spent" subassemblies. We have the capability to build small modular reactors (SMR) using either light water reactor (LWR) technology or molten salt technology fueled by plentiful thorium. We have clean coal technology as well as plenty of natural gas.

Yet, politicians invariably allow themselves to be held hostage by lobbyists, environmental extremists, and the press rather than taking a leadership position. They espouse the benefits of solar, wind, biomass, and some unknown technology that is just over the hill. The first three, while having a role in a mixed energy portfolio, will never be the source of the broad-based, reliable electrical power our economy requires to support an ever-increasing standard of living. As a source of broad-based electrical power, these types of energy could not exist in a free market without tremendous government subsidies, which come from our tax dollars. Solar and wind farms require huge amounts of land and require long new transmissions lines. As a result, local communities and conservationists trying to preserve wildlife, particularly birds and their landscape, usually oppose these "farms" unless placated with large sums of money whose source is also invariably tax dollars.

When the sun stops shining and the wind stops blowing, you must quickly be able to ramp up another source of energy. Renewables are generally backed up by rapid responding but less efficient fossil-fueled plants, which use twice the natural gas and spew twice the pollutants into our air compared to more efficient but slower-responding Combined Cycle Natural Gas Plants. That is twice the pollution being created 70% of the time that wind and solar cannot provide power when it is called for. It's no wonder the natural gas industry partners with wind and solar against nuclear. Additionally, both solar and wind generation are dependent on rare earth metals for key components. We must import those metals from China, where they are mined without regard for the environment. Both wind and solar, if implemented to provide broad-based electrical power, are environmental disasters.

Dealing with energy sources that are inherently unreliable, and which require large amounts of land, comes at a high economic cost. Germany, for example, has been forced by the Green movement to shut down its nuclear plants and become the world leader in solar and wind energy. As a result, its electricity prices increased 50 percent between 2006 and 2017, as it scaled up renewables. Meanwhile, France produces one-tenth the carbon emissions per unit of electricity as Germany and pays little more than half for its electricity. France gets almost 85% of its electricity by nuclear generation. By the way, "renewable energy" is a misnomer. Wind and solar machines are built from nonrenewable materials. And they wear out. Old equipment must be decommissioned, generating millions of tons of waste. The International Renewable Energy Agency calculates that solar goals for 2050 consistent with the Paris Agreement would result in old-panel disposal constituting more than double the tonnage of all today's global plastic waste.

In the meantime, the Environmental Protection Agency (EPA) has taken it upon itself to rewrite American energy policy without so much as a "by your leave" from Congress. It has been shutting down coal-fired plants, our main source of broad-based electrical power. At the same time, green energy proponents are resisting any nuclear renaissance, any offshore or public lands drilling, and any pipelines that could bring oil from Canada. Any discussion about environmental concerns with the generation of electricity that does not include nuclear power as a viable environmentally benign source is disingenuous. I am worried that when the energy crisis is fully realized, it may be too difficult a situation from which to completely recover. This lack of leadership, perspective, and knowledge promises a dark (literally) future for my grandchildren.

Any discussion about environmental concerns with the generation of electricity that does not include nuclear power as a viable environmentally benign source is disingenuous.

NUCLEAR POWER

I have dedicated my life to nuclear endeavors and, of course, believe very strongly that it should be an important part of our national energy portfolio going forward for the following reasons:

1. Nuclear plants in the U.S. are fundamentally safe

2. Nuclear plants are environmentally benign

3. Nuclear power plants are extremely reliable

4. Over the life of the plant, nuclear plants are economically sound

5. Being a world leader in nuclear technology is strategically vital to the U.S.

6. Nuclear power is the foundation for other nuclear applications, like medical isotopes

7. The next generation of reactors are passively safe and more economical

8. Nuclear waste is the good news with respect to electrical generation.

First, we need to start from a broad perspective, which begins with our standard of living. What I am about to say applies to the United States but can also be applied, for the most part, to the rest of the world.

We have achieved the highest standard of living in the history of mankind, and our technological advancements are increasing at an exponential rate. That would seem to hold a promising future for mankind if we can keep from destroying ourselves in the meantime. However, our standard of living is tied to our economy, sometimes expressed as our Gross National Product (GNP). The GNP is in turn tied to the availability of (relatively) inexpensive and reliable electrical energy. Broad-based electricity is measured in megawatts (MW) and is the supply of electrical power to cities, factories, government facilities, and other users of electricity. It must be available on demand and in large quantities (thousands of MWs).

Just as the technological advancements are increasing exponentially, so too is the demand for electrical energy. The forecast for increase in electrical power in the next 25 years is approximately 25 percent just to power things we know about in our expanding economy and increasing population. But what about things we cannot foresee? For example, approximately 20 years ago, the use of personal computers and the Internet was in its infancy. Today, that usage of electrical energy has increased from almost nothing to 10 percent of the electrical power demand used in the United States. If we convert, at least wherever it makes sense, to electrical cars, the electricity to power those cars will require another significant increase in the demand for electrical energy. Who knows what other requirements for electricity will emerge?

Where will all that electrical energy come from? Let me say right now that I believe in a mixed portfolio of sources of energy, including conservation. But conservation — the elimination of energy waste and the increase in energy efficiency — is a one-time act. It can only help once; its contribution will not increase supply, only decrease demand. With the known technology today, solar and wind power generation can only help on the fringes and will not be a source for broad-based electrical energy in this generation or the next.* Additionally, solar, wind, and biomass, besides being tremendously expensive, relatively unreliable, and doomed to fail without significant federal government subsidies, actually increase the carbon footprint, as I will explain later on. That leaves oil and gas, coal, and nuclear. Each has its own challenges and its own benefits. However, a smart, safe, ecological deployment of all would permit the United States to become completely energy independent in a decade, if we have the resolve to do it. (In my opinion, it is important that this goal be established and intently pursued for national security and international political flexibility.)

Of the above sources, only nuclear has no impact on the environment and is fundamentally safe and is undeniably reliable. The safety record of nuclear energy in the United States is unmatched by any other industry. No civilian in this country has ever been harmed by the nuclear generation of electrical power. The workers at nuclear facilities are the best trained, most tightly screened, highest monitored of any workforce anywhere. Their exposure to radioactivity is limited to well under what is considered acceptable to protect health and prevent short-term or long-term biological effects.

No civilian in this country has ever been harmed by the nuclear generation of electrical power.

Scientists have studied the health and safety of different energy sources since the 1960s. Every major study finds the same thing: nuclear is the safest way to make reliable electricity. Strange as it sounds, nuclear power plants are so safe for the same reason nuclear

---

* One 900 MW nuclear power plant = approximately 8,100 acres of solar panels. Two 1,000 MW nuclear power plants = a windmill farm two miles deep, covering the coast of South Carolina, assuming they could operate every day.

weapons are so dangerous. The uranium used as fuel in power plants and as material for bombs can create one million times more heat per its mass than its fossil fuel and gunpowder equivalents. It is not so much about the fuel as the process. Breaking atoms releases more energy than breaking chemical bonds. Because nuclear plants produce heat without fire, they emit no air pollution in the form of smoke. By contrast, the smoke from burning fossil fuels and biomass results in the premature deaths of seven million people per year, according to the World Health Organization. As a result, climate scientists have determined that nuclear plants save nearly two million lives to date that would have been lost to air pollution.

Strange as it sounds, nuclear power plants are so safe for the same reason nuclear weapons are so dangerous.

Thanks to its energy density, nuclear plants require far less land than renewables. Even in sunny California, a solar farm requires 450 times more land to produce the same amount of energy as a nuclear plant. Energy-dense nuclear requires far less in the way of materials, and produces far less in the way of waste compared to energy-dilute solar and wind. A single Coke can's worth of uranium provides all the energy that the most gluttonous American's lifestyle requires for the average lifespan. At the end of that lifetime, the high-level radioactive waste that nuclear plants produce is the very same Coke can of (used) uranium fuel. The reason nuclear is the best energy from an environmental perspective is because it produces so little waste, and none enters the environment as pollution. All the waste fuel from 45 years of the Swiss nuclear program can fit, in canisters, on a basketball court-like warehouse, where like all spent nuclear fuel, it has never hurt a fly. By contrast, solar panels require 17 times more materials in the form of cement, glass, concrete, and steel than do nuclear plants, and create more than 200 times more waste.

But what about Three Mile Island (TMI)? Not one member of the public received any exposure due to the contamination created by that accident, most of which was contained inside the reactor and the containment building. The other plants at TMI were eventually restored to operation and have operated without incident ever since. More importantly, after TMI the nuclear industry created an instrument for self-monitoring and improvement called the Institute of Nuclear Power Operations (INPO). As a result of information sharing, increased training, increased oversight, using lessons learned at one plant to benefit all other facilities, the safety and efficiency statistics have steadily improved ever since TMI. World organizations have been established patterned after the American regulator, the NRC, and INPO. The former is called the International Atomic Energy Agency (IAEA) and the latter is called the World Association of Nuclear Operators (WANO).

But what about the nuclear waste? In my opinion, that is the good news. Coal, oil, and even natural gas generate waste, much of which is dumped into the atmosphere unless expensive filtration is applied to plant stacks. I don't believe that fossil fuel burning causes global warming (global warming and cooling, or climate change as the advocates of this nonsense have adopted, has been going on long before man even existed, let alone generated significant energy), but it does affect air and water quality, which impacts human health here and now. Each coal-fired plant generates acres of slag each year (slag is the waste left after the coal is burned). In all cases, there is research underway to address these issues, but only nuclear operation generates just energy and heat, and the heat can be dissipated in a variety of ways to minimize, if not eliminate, the impact to the environment.

However, nuclear power plants generate two types of radioactive nuclear waste, low-level and high-level. Low-level waste — from sampling, maintenance, cleaning, and other activities — must be carefully monitored and handled; but it is not the issue because hospitals, universities, and other endeavors also generate low-level radioactive waste. This waste can be and has been safely packaged and transported to several waste sites that have been in operation for years without incident.

High-level waste comes directly from the fuel rods themselves. Some relatively small amounts of high-level waste come from maintenance on what is called the primary system, which is the cooling system that comes in contact with the fuel. The fuel rods that have been used to their calculated material limit, generally before no more than 5 percent consumption of the nuclear fuel in the fuel rod pellets, are presently considered high-level nuclear waste. The rods are removed before the neutrons and other nuclear particles generated in the reactor can structurally weaken through embrittlement of the fuel pin metal or the fuel pellets. The fuel pins contain the fuel pellets. The fuel pellets are stressed due to expansion caused by the fission product generation, particularly gaseous fission products like xenon and krypton.

All these forces could cause fuel pin cladding (the stainless steel rods that house the fuel pellets), cracking, or failure, and subsequent release of fission products into the primary coolant, thereby allowing radioactive particles to get out of the fuel rod into the coolant that passes over the rods. This situation would remove one of the barriers between the highly radioactive fuel and the environment. Today, these spent fuel rods reside in spent fuel pools at our commercial reactor sites or, after sufficient decay, in dry cask (large shielded containers kept on concrete pads) storage at those same reactor sites. As Fukushima demonstrated, this on-site storage of spent fuel has safety, as well as security, implications.

Why then do I say nuclear waste is the good news? Those spent fuel rods are supposed to go to a national disposal repository for storage in very stable basalt formations approximately three thousand feet underground. The designated site is called Yucca Mountain, but political concerns have kept this facility from opening, and it possibly never will. However, what should happen to those spent fuel rods is called reprocessing to recover the 95 percent of unused nuclear fuel so it can be used in new fuel assemblies. The reprocessing of spent fuel has been shut down in this country for what I consider very specious reasons but when it is allowed again, the actual waste generated from this process would be very small in volume (reprocessing all the spent fuel generated in one year in the United States would create enough [highly radioactive] waste to cover a football field ten feet high). We have already demonstrated that we can immobilize that nuclear waste in borosilicate glass poured into large (10 feet tall, two feet in diameter) stainless steel canisters and then safely store those cans of glass. I was the program manager for starting up the vitrification (glass making) plant at the Savannah River Site. To date, that plant (DWPF) has safely generated over four thousand cans of glass as it stabilizes the nuclear waste from our nuclear weapons program. Having the highly radioactive waste immobilized in glass contained in those stainless-steel cans, hanging in concrete vaults, is much safer than having it in liquid form in those aging and corroding carbon steel tanks.

What about Fukushima, Chernobyl, and Codolet? First, none of these plant accidents were as the result of a nuclear explosion. All of them were distorted in the press, as usual, impacting the general public opinion. The most recent accident was an *industrial* explosion in an incinerator near Codolet, France, which is near the nuclear research center at Marcoule. France, which has had the resolve to generate most of its electrical energy from nuclear. The incident (which unfortunately killed one worker and injured three others) was quickly explained, and local authorities declared the event over. Within days, it was off the front page, but our press never rectified its initial announcement of a "nuclear explosion." Chernobyl was careless operation of a nuclear plant whose design would never have been approved in the United States or any country abiding by the regulations and oversight of the IAEA and WANO. Additionally, the steam explosion occurred in a part of the plant that would be inside a containment building in this country and most other countries, which would have limited, if not prevented, the spread of contamination experienced.

At Fukushima, the plants did shut down automatically when they detected the earthquake, and everything initially proceeded as it should have. However, the tsunami was far greater than the restraining wall was designed to handle. The design of the emergency diesel generators and their supply tanks was faulty and not what we have in the United States, so the plants lost necessary emergency power. Both design flaws are a result of groupthink and in opposition to concerns expressed years ago.

Similarly, the cultural impact on the ability to react to the situation once it occurred exacerbated the situation beyond what should have happened. Had the reactor buildings been vented to release the hydrogen being generated due to the zirconium-water reaction when the fuel "melted," there probably would never have been an explosion resulting in the release of radioactive debris. Advice from America to vent and do other mitigating acts was ignored until it was too late. These risks may be unique to the Japanese nuclear industry (based on conversations I have had with experts who have been consulted by the NRC, as well as the Japanese) and would arguably not happen in the United States. Nonetheless, the NRC, INPO, and the nuclear utilities have made a concerted effort to learn any possible lessons from what happened, and the root causes of what made it worse, to see what, if any, improvements need to be made to our present design, operating procedures, and emergency preparations in the US.

Speaking of design, we have nuclear plants that have been designed in the 40-year hiatus in building nuclear plants that are much more passively (rather than actively, i.e., requiring equipment and/or operator action in the case of an emergency) safe when an upset condition might occur. We are presently building two of these type of plants in Georgia and but the two that started construction in South Carolina have been halted indefinitely due to financial issues. There are plans for two plants in Texas, which have been delayed by contractual issues, and plans to resurrect two other plants in the Southeast.

I am hopeful that these efforts mark the beginning of the resurgence of nuclear power in this country. It is a vital constituent of a diverse and flexible energy portfolio and required for energy independence, which is necessary for our country's security and prosperity. With that diversity in mind, I need to mention one possibility, which I believe has significant benefits. That is, electrical energy and process heat generation from thorium. I am principally talking about the Liquid Fluoride Thorium Reactor (LFTR). In retirement, I joined the Energy from Thorium Foundation (EFTF), now known as eGeneration, which is focused on the use of thorium in the next generation of reactors. It would be used in something called a Liquid Core Molten Salt Reactor (LCMSR), which has many advantages over the present-day Light Water Reactors (LWRs).

As mentioned earlier, our country has needed a viable energy policy and plan for more than 45 years, ever since the first energy crisis back in 1974. Instead, since that time our surplus supply of electrical energy has gone down with no new broad-based electrical generation plants of any type built (due, in my opinion, to excessive over-regulation, as well as high interest rates and other financial considerations). Our dependency on foreign fossil energy supplies has increased, which puts our country in a precarious posture with respect to national security. In the meantime, our concern for the environment has increased significantly. While this is appropriate, many of the actions and limitations imposed on industry and business as well as utilities are, in my opinion, unreasonable, even unrealistic, and, in some cases, counterproductive to protecting the environment.

Industry is not very engaged in the development and eventual deployment of advanced reactor systems because the focus is on the next quarterly report bottom line. Since the denial of licenses to plants with considerable capital investment back in the 1970s and 1980s, the utilities will not pursue anything that might not come to fruition. The barriers to deployment of new designs are significant and will require government support to overcome both technical and institutional challenges. These challenges range from relatively modest licensing issues to decade-long fuel and materials research and development needs. For the range of advanced systems discussed here, the LWR-based SMR designs are likely to succeed in deployment first due to several factors, including:

1. Minimal technical issues needing resolution

2. The LWR reactor-centric mindset of the utilities, the NRC, and Congress

3. Proven safety and operational characteristics of water-cooled systems, resulting in few licensing issues to industry and the NRC

4. A rapidly growing customer base of utilities considering SMRs as affordable, incremental capacity or as carbon-free replacements for older, smaller fossil plants.

Even for these designs, however, government support and resources are needed to facilitate demonstration of the new engineering, regulatory, and business models for first-mover SMRs. An aggressive public/private partnership to deploy the new designs could result in the first commercial plants being ready to operate by 2020, but probably later. High-temperature and fast-spectrum reactors, while offering important new functionalities, will likely take longer to achieve commercialization and will require more extensive government support for research and demonstration. In addition to addressing a more extensive list of technical and regulatory challenges, introducing high-temperature reactors to the process heat market requires that the customer base become more familiar and comfortable with the technology. Similarly, fast-spectrum reactors face a comparable number of technical and regulatory challenges and an uncertain customer base. Deployment of these advanced systems may be possible by 2025-2030 with appropriate government support and demonstration.

The reactor design I favor is the LFTR, mentioned above, which is a version of the LCMSR. The Molten Salt Reactor is on the DOE's Generation IV list; but it is at the bottom, and it is the type that uses solid fuel versus the liquid fuel approach of the LFTR. The eGeneration is trying to encourage Congress to instruct the DOE (and, as required, the NRC) to move this reactor design up in priority. Meaningful collaborations with other countries that are also seeking to develop these same technologies will be very important to integrate knowledge and minimize development costs.

In summary, emerging nuclear technologies, such as high-temperature, fast-spectrum, and small modular reactors have the ability to offer clean, affordable, and abundant energy for the United States and should become key components of the future energy portfolio. The problem with nuclear is that it is unpopular, a victim of a 50-year-long concerted effort by fossil fuel, renewable energy, anti-nuclear weapons campaigners, and misanthropic environmentalists to ban the technology. In response, the nuclear industry constantly apologizes for its best attributes, from its waste to its safety. The nuclear industry has promoted the idea that, in order to deal with climate change, "we need a mix of clean energy sources," including solar, wind, and nuclear. It was something I used to believe, and say, in part because it's what people want to hear. The problem is that it's not true. France shows that moving from mostly nuclear electricity to a mix of nuclear and renewables results in more carbon emissions (due to using more natural gas) and higher prices (due to the unreliability of solar and wind). Oil and gas investors know this, which is why they made a political alliance with renewables companies, and why oil and gas companies have been spending millions of dollars on advertisements promoting solar, and funneling millions of dollars to said environmental groups to provide public relations cover. What is to be done? The most important thing is for scientists and conservationists to start telling the truth about renewables and nuclear, and the relationship between energy density and environmental impact.

Obviously, the above situation is a concern for my children's generation and my grandchildren's generation if left unaddressed. I believe it is one of the first questions that we must ask our elected political leaders to address (right after term limits, tax reform, tort reform, and requiring actual reading of legislation before voting on it). Safe, available, reliable, ecologically sound electrical energy is as important as preserving potable water supply for the future generations of Americans and, for that matter, the whole world. There are technologies available right now to solve those problems with the right national resolve, and nuclear power is one of the most important of those technologies.

Safe, available, reliable, ecologically sound electrical energy is as important as preserving potable water supply for the future generations of Americans and, for that matter, the whole world.

CINDY

My wife Cindy inspired the very best in me, including this book. She was by my side as I wrote and published the first edition, and in my heart each day as I have endeavored to build upon that first achievement in producing an even stronger second edition for new readers and future leaders. I hope that by reading about my life and career, you have felt you came to know *her* as well. She was the very best of me. I tried to express that very sentiment when delivering her eulogy, after her passing on August 11, 2018. In preparing this second edition of my book, I had considered adding a transcript of Cindy's eulogy to the Appendices section of the book, which follows. But Cindy was not an "appendix" — not a mere supplement or something extra. She was *everything*. So I leave you, as you finish this book, not with more words about project management, leadership lessons, or the nuclear industry, but with my most personal reflections on what matters most.

Cindy's Eulogy

Dave and Cindy, 2012

"Thank you all for coming to this memorial service to celebrate a most remarkable woman. There are friends here from communities in California, Washington state, Idaho, Arizona, Illinois, Tennessee, Kentucky, Florida, Georgia, South Carolina, North Carolina, Washington, D.C., New York, as well as Ohio and 'the state up north.' In most of those communities, I was known as 'Cindy Amerine's husband.' Most of the time, when we arrived in a new location, my work initially consumed me. By the time I could socialize in the community, Cindy had already won over everyone's hearts.

"When I met Cindy, she was a girl, a college sophomore. *But what a girl!!* She was simply breath-taking beautiful with very long dark hair reaching below her waist, a killer figure, and a dazzling smile set in a Mediterranean olive complexion. From across the proverbial crowded room, I thought, *"What a babe!"* I just had to get to meet her. When I got close, I found that all that beauty was on a barely five-foot frame. She made me feel tall. She laughed at my inane jokes, so she made me feel witty. I am neither tall nor witty. So, as she did for over 50 years, Cindy made me feel good. Fortunately for me, that beautiful exterior housed an even more exceedingly beautiful soul. And as the inscription on our headstone says, 'She made me want to be a better man.'

"As the dedication in the book I wrote about my career states, nothing I achieved would have been possible without Cindy's support. She loved an adventure and a challenge, and she saw living with me and making a life with me as both. We owned 17 homes over the course of our marriage and the moves that my career required. She considered each one a canvas on which to express her considerable decorating skills.

"The program for today's service lists Cindy's various activities and achievements. Through her work for the Red Cross, and through her song and videos for the ALS Association, Cindy has touched lives all over the world, many more than she could ever imagine. Maybe that is God's purpose for inflicting such a vibrant person with this horrible disease. However, perhaps the most important achievement is not mentioned and that would be mother to our two girls. Thanks to their mother, our daughters have grown into two beautiful, accomplished women. Like her, they are very good athletes, good students, fun-loving, and adventurous, successful women in their respective endeavors. And like their mother, they are loving wives and mothers. They are a living testimony to her. And, using Cindy's words, 'They have given us five grandchildren, one more exquisite than the next, if I may say so!'

"Cindy's father was Sicilian, and her mother was Irish. That combination meant our marriage was … colorful. Cindy could be argumentative one second and loving the next. Her sense of humor was always a compliment to any situation. She was passionate about many things, ranging from art to politics. Fortunately, I was on that list. I was always playing catch-up to her feisty and loving moods, but it was a merry chase. I will miss it with all my body, all my heart, and all my soul.

"As you sit there, imagine if you will, that you needed to scratch your eyelid. However, when you tell your arm to move your hand to your eye, nothing happens, no matter how hard you try. Imagine that you have a loved one sitting next to you who you would trust to do something so simple yet so delicate. But you can't get their attention and even if you did, you could not speak to tell them what you wanted. How utterly frustrating, debilitating, and even embarrassing for you, especially if you were always a vibrant, independent, can-do person. And yet Cindy faced that situation with courage, tenacity, dignity, and even humor. Through her studies, she came to know that the cure for ALS will unlock knowledge about how our bodies and minds work and are affected by our environment. That cure will be a major medical and scientific breakthrough. That is why the beautiful song she and our wonderful and talented friends, the O'Regans, created is dedicated to not only ALS victims, families, and caregivers, but also researchers.

"Now many of you, especially you children, but even the middle-aged present, think of folks in the retirement bracket as old and feeble. At age 63, when we retired, Cindy was anything but. She loved Aiken, South Carolina, and her friends there. While Cindy contributed to every community in which we lived, she thought Aiken was special. However, we did not have a Great Lake in our front yard. So, we decided instead to retire to Catawba Island, which Cindy had come to love. Cindy really considered herself to finally be at home. She made such good friends here and threw herself into community activities with a vitality that was contagious. Cindy's smile was infectious and always there for friends and strangers alike. I bought her a Jaguar XK convertible for a retirement present and, as she tooled around Port Clinton and Sandusky, even at age 63, she still turned heads. I am sure a guy or gal, seeing her at a stop light, thought, '*What a babe!'*

"And she was becoming a Buckeye. At the Sandusky High School Sensational Sixties football teams' reunion, when she heard Earl Bruce speak with that locker-room passion as only he could, she turned to me and exclaimed, 'I want to play football!' Later, that same Earl Bruce, when he learned of Cindy's disease, came across a room at a gathering in Naples, Florida, better known as Ohio South, grabbed her hands and said, 'I am rooting for you, Cindy.'

"Before ALS began to take its toll, Cindy was looking forward to traveling, to helping her community, and to taking on new challenges, including the daunting task of teaching me ballroom dancing. Although she was robbed of all those benefits of the retirement stage of life, she sensed God's purpose and could feel the love that she had given to so many being reflected back to her. Technology helped her adapt to the debilities of ALS, as did her precious nurses, Kathy Lambacher, Jami Lano, and Miranda Pasch, as did the ALS Association, most especially Lisa Bruening. Cindy's sense of humor was evident with her caregivers, as she labeled her angels Nurse Ratchet, Mother Teresa, and Florence Nightingale. She even tagged me as Doctor Strangelove.

"Because she was at peace with her Lord and Savior, Jesus Christ, even in the suffering with ALS, Cindy felt graced by God to experience how loved she was. Her way was to always think of others first and it is what motivated her to write her song of inspiration about ALS. To use her words, 'I am a child of God who tried to please Him. I was rewarded with a beautiful life. I thank God for this time on this earth. Even in the suffering with ALS, I was graced by God to experience how loved I was, and how loving and kind people are.'

"Cindy will now be decorating and rearranging things in heaven with her mother. The angels will be busy moving furniture. I have asked her to enlist her mother's help in pleading my case to those angels. It is my only chance. She is so looking forward to seeing her mother, she wants this day to be a celebration of her life as reflected in the song she chose to close out the ceremony.

"I am reminded of the end of the movie *Saving Private Ryan*, when Mr. Ryan, as an old man with his family, is visiting the Normandy

American Cemetery and Memorial, where some of the soldiers who sacrificed their lives to save his life were buried. He asked the question of his family, "Have I been a good man?" It is a worthy question of all of us. In Cindy's case, the answer is a resounding "YES!" She was a good woman.

"I am blessed to have been the one with whom she chose to live her life. What a beautiful presence in this world Cindy was! What a vibrant life she led! *What a babe, indeed!*

"Cindy, as you turn to go, know that I will be dying slowly until your next hello. We will be together again, you and me. For I love you now and will through eternity. In the meantime, I will be looking at the moon, but I will be seeing you.

"L'amore sei tu. Ti amero per sempre."

SECTION V

APPENDICES, BEHIND-THE-SCENES INSIGHTS, AND PARTING THOUGHTS

ACRONYM LIST

AB	Advisory Board
ACA	Apparent Cause Analysis
AEC	Atomic Energy Commission
AEW	All-Employees Meeting
ALS	Amyotrophic Lateral Sclerosis
APS	Arizona Public Power Supply
B&W	Babcock and Wilcox
BOQ	Bachelor Officers' Quarters
CAP	Corrective Action Program
CAPS	Cell Atmosphere Processing System
CARB	Corrective Action Review Board
CCA	Catawba Cliffs Association
CCB	Change Control Board
CE	Combustion Engineering
CEI	Cleveland Electric and Illuminating Company
CEO	Chief Executive Officer

CG&A   Calibration, Grooming, and Alignment

CNO   Chief Nuclear Officer

CONOPS   Conduct of Operations

D-B   Davis-Besse

DDI   Development Dimensions International

DOE   Department of Energy

DPO   Differing Professional Opinion

DWPF   Defense Waste Processing Facility

EBR   Experimental Breeder Reactor

E&C   Engineering and Construction

ECA   Effectiveness of Corrective Actions

ECP   Employee Concerns Program

EELV   Evolved Expendable Launch Vehicle

EFCOG   Energy Facility Contractors Group

EFTF   Energy from Thorium Foundation

EM   Environmental Management

EOC   Extent of Condition

EOOW   Engineering Officer of the Watch

EP   Emergency Planning

ERB	Executive Review Board
FBM	Fleet Ballistic Missile
FEMA	Federal Emergency Management Agency
FFTF	Fast Flux Test Facility
FLM	First-line Managers
HIRD	Harassment, Intimidation, Retaliation, Discrimination
HLW	High-level Waste
HPI	High Performance Initiatives
HuP	Human Performance
IAEA	International Atomic Energy Agency
INPO	Institute of Nuclear Power Operations
ISCA	Integrated Safety Culture Assessment
ISMS	Integrated Safety Management System
IVHM	In-Vessel Handling Machines
JTG	Joint Test Group
KPI	Key Performance Indicators
LCMSR	Liquid Core Molten Salt Reactor
LEIA	Lake Erie Improvement Association
LFTR	Liquid Fluoride Thorium Reactor

LHA	Little Harbor Associates
LOA	Letter of Authorization
LPSI	Low-pressure Safety Injection Pumps
NDA	Nuclear Decommissioning Agency
NFS	Nuclear Fuels Services
NEP	Nuclear Engineering Program
NR	Naval Reactors
NRC	Nuclear Regulatory Commission
NSRB	Nuclear Safety Review Board
NSSS	Nuclear Steam Supply System
OEP	Operating Experience Program
ORAU	Oak Ridge Association of Universities
OSU	The Ohio State University
OVH	Ohio Veterans Home
POD	Plan of the Day
POW	Plan of the Week
RADCON	Radiation Control
RAMP	Risk Assessment Management Program
RAPS	Radioactive Argon Processing System

RCA   Root Cause Analysis

RTF   Replacement Tritium Facility

SCIP   Safety Culture Improvement Plan

SCIR   Safety Culture Implications Review

SCUBA   Safety Culture Board of Advisors

SCWE   Safety Conscious Work Environment

SEW   Senior Engineering Watch

SINS   Ship's Inertial Navigation System

SMR   Small Modular Reactors

SMR   Small Nuclear Reactors

SOP   Standard Operating Procedure

SRE   Safety Related Equipment

SRS   Savannah River Site

SRTC   Savannah River Technology Center

SSRC   Safety and Safeguards Review Council

SWPF   Salt Waste Processing Facility

T&Q   Training and Qualification

TMI   Three Mile Island

TSG   Technical Support Group

WANO   World Association of Nuclear Operators

WBS   Work Breakdown Structure

WGD   Washington Government Division

WGI   Washington Group International

WIPP   Waste Isolation Pilot Project

WSRC   Westinghouse Savannah River Company

APPENDIX A

Decision Analysis

1. **State the desired outcome**
   As an example, "I want to decide between several alternatives. Which one will provide the best career path for me and the most stability for my family?"

2. **List resources**
   - Professional friends
   - Personal friends
   - Family
   - Consultants
   - Reference material
   - Internet

3. **List "musts" (non-negotiable)**
   If alternatives do not meet any items on this list, they are dropped from further consideration.

4. **List "wants"**
   Each of these items has a spectrum of satisfaction. You want the highest degree of satisfaction but will accept less (and not unhappily).

5. **Rank each "want" relative to the other "wants" (e.g., 1 to 12)**

6. **Weigh each want**, giving no. 1 the top weight. This can be any arbitrary number, but when the next lower want is weighted, it is

relative to the preceding item. This is a subjective activity, but you can seek help from any of your resources.

7. **Build a matrix** with each alternative across the top horizontal axis and the wants listed on the left-hand vertical axis.

8. **Put two columns under each alternative**, left to right labeled "Ability to Meet" or "ATM" and "Subtotal" or "ST."

9. **Determine the ATM of each want** for each alternative on an arbitrary scale of 1 to 10, with 10 being "meets perfectly."

10. **Multiply the weight of each want times the ATM of each alternative** for that want with the result listed in the ST column. This can be across the alternatives for each want (relative) or down one alternative at a time for all wants (absolute).

11. **Add the STs for each alternative** to obtain a value for that alternative.

12. **Compare the outcome of the alternatives to each other.** The alternative with the largest number should be the apparent choice. However, if two or three alternatives are relatively close, you should repeat the process after eliminating the alternatives that are not close.

13. **After settling on the alternative as numerically determined above, wait some period of time and do it all again.** One variation might be to alter the ATM approach from relative to absolute or vice versa. Use your resources to review and challenge your weightings and ATMs. You need to be able to defend those numbers even though they are subjective.

14. After you have decided on an alternative, then you need to **speculate on potential outcomes as a result of your choice**. For each speculation, you need to list the impact of the outcome (negative or positive), the magnitude of that impact (high, medium, or

low), and the probability of each speculation happening (high, medium, or low). If any potential outcome results in a high probability, high impact, and negative result, you need to re-examine your decision.

Having gone through this exercise, you are in a good position to defend your decision or rethink your position. You have compartmentalized your thought processes, and you and others can examine each constituent.

Example

Wants	Rank	Weight	Alternative #1		Alternative #2		Alternative #3	
			ATM	ST	ATM	ST	ATM	ST
ABC	4	40*	2	80	4	160	0	0
XYZ	5	30*	8	240	4	120	5	150
MNO	2	43	10	430	5	215	8	160
FGH	7	20	5	100	10	200	8	160
UVW	9	10	5	50	10	100	9	90
DEF	1	50	8	400	2	100	5	250
IJK	6	35*	10	350	5	175	7	245
QRS	8	15	0	0	6	90	7	105
LPO	8	40*	4	160	9	360	4	160
				1,810		**1,520**		**1,320**

* It is okay to weight items equally or discover the weighting proves the ranking wrong.

If I choose Alternative #1, then the following could happen:

Probability	Impact	Magnitude
WXYZ	NEG LOW	MED
ABCD	POS MED	MED
MNOP	NEG MED	HIGH
GHIJ	NEG HIGH	LOW

Because there is no NEG/HIGH/HIGH, Alternative #1 looks like a good choice.

APPENDIX B

Business Philosophy

The following several pages contain the elements of my overall Business Philosophy — from my life and workplace priorities, to how I have thought about everything from safety to leadership, management, communications, teamwork, and more throughout my career. Across my 45-year career, I was known to present variations of these very lists and diagrams, via PowerPoint, to my colleagues, employees, and clients.

Life Priorities

- God
- Family
- Health
- Work

Workplace Priorities

- Safety
- Quality
- Schedule
- Cost

Safety

- Set at the highest priority
- Make it every employee's first responsibility
- Be responsible for fellow workers safety
- Report unsafe conditions immediately
- Observe posted safety instructions
- Stop work for any safety reasons
- Practice good housekeeping
- All injuries are preventable

Safety Conscious Work Environment

- Any employee can bring up any issue without fear of retaliation
  - With confidence their concern will be addressed in a fair and timely manner
  - Knowing the issue will be dealt without ascribing motive, but on its own merit
- There will be zero tolerance for harassment, intimidation, retaliation, or discrimination

Safety Culture and SCWE

Safety Culture and Safety Conscious Work Environment (SCWE) are two distinct, but related concepts:

- Safety Culture refers to the necessary attention, personal dedication, and accountability of all individuals engaged in any activity that has a bearing on safety.

- SCWE refers to the willingness of employees to identify safety concerns and other issues without fear of reprisal or apathy.

SCWE is an *attribute* of Safety Culture.

Relationships

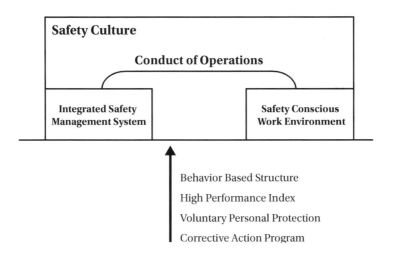

Conduct of Business

- **Personal Accountability**
  (Willing to sign your name at the end of the day)
- **Procedure Compliance**
  (Combine with training and experience = best chance of success)
- **Technical Inquisitiveness**
  (Never assume; wonderment)
- **Willingness to Stop** (If not sure)
  (Treat as act of honor and integrity)

Safety Conscious Work Environment (SCWE)

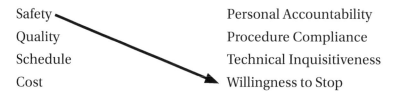

Safety   Personal Accountability
Quality   Procedure Compliance
Schedule   Technical Inquisitiveness
Cost   Willingness to Stop

SCWE = Allegiance to Safety will prevent proceeding in the face of uncertainty.

Workplace Leadership

- Set priorities for the workplace
- Be a servant leader
- Practice humility (before being humbled)
- Surround yourself with people smarter than you
- Be visible in the workplace with a purpose

Integrity: Willing compliance with the unenforceable.

Most Powerful Things a Leader Can Say

- Thank you
- I was wrong
- I am sorry

If you find yourself saying the last two too often, it may be time to self-assess.

Management Philosophy

- Leadership
    - Must first serve
    - Principles lead to paradigms; paradigms lead to vision
    - Promote teamwork, inclusion, diversity
- Participative Management
    - People are energized by a common focus
    - Individuals are accountable
    - Empower employees: they know the solutions
- First Line Managers are the most important members of the management chain
- A project can only have one schedule
    - Only do things in the schedule
    - Each item in the schedule must have an owner
    - People (not the schedule) make people do things
- Good housekeeping is vital
    - Fundamentally tied to safety
    - It is the first impression of visitors
    - It says volumes about the workforce
- Have an intolerance for equipment deficiencies
- Metrics are vital
- Celebrate successes
- Comply with regulations and other requirements or get them changed

Operations Philosophy

- Apply Conduct of Business to all activities
    - Personal accountability

- – Technical inquisitiveness
- – Willingness to stop
- – Procedure compliance
- Pre-job briefs are essential
- Continuous improvement requires feedback
  - – Post-job reviews are vital
  - – Worker involvement in job critiques is essential
  - – Self-assessments are important
  - – Have a "Lessons Learned" program
- Three-way communication is a must
- First question when an event occurs is "What was the First Line Manager's involvement?"
- Training is the responsibility of line management

Administrative Philosophy

- Meetings
  - – NO SIDE BARS: They are discourteous and distracting
  - – There must be an agenda
  - – Listening is essential
- Correspondence
  - – Have an executive summary
  - – Spell out acronyms on first use
- Training requires an exam; otherwise it is indoctrination
- Feedback is required for continuous improvement
- All engineering functions report to the Design Authority

Business Philosophy

- Treat the business as if you owned it

- Orientation
    - Be cost effective
    - Practice continuous improvement
    - Base tactical decisions on the strategic plan
- Plans
    - Strategic Plan > Business Plan > Business Development Plan
    - Have a Succession Plan, a Rotation Plan, and a Hiring Plan ... and use them
    - Have an Employee Development Plan

Team Philosophy

- Questions
    - Can I trust you?
    - Can you trust the team?
    - Are you committed to the team?
- Directives
    - Do the right thing
    - Do your best
    - Treat others as you would be treated
    - Trust but verify

Integrated Safety Management System

- Define the scope of the work
- Analyze the hazards of the work
- Develop and implement hazards controls
- Perform the work
- Provide feedback for continuous improvement

Participative Management

- Leader genuinely solicits input
- All input is sincerely considered
- Leader makes decision
- Success is shared all around
- Setback is the leader's responsibility
    - No finger pointing
    - Regroup around lessons learned

Requirements for Success

- Clear roles and responsibilities defined
- Clear expectations set
- Senior management visible in workspaces
- An effective feedback and improvement program
- Effective planning, work control, change control, and project control
- All the above clearly, effectively, and repeatedly communicated

Teammate Characteristics

- Are hard working
- Are aggressive
- Are thorough
- Have perspective (have a sense of humor)

Communication Philosophy

- Hardest part of any job
- Practice no surprises; raise issues early
- WHY: Explain or ask whenever you can; leads to support/compliance
- Seek first to understand
- Be courteous; listen
- Stories are a useful way to illustrate a point
- All the cards on the table, face up, all the time
- Listen to the client, customer, regulator
- Emails and texts are the poorest form of communication; face-to-face is the best
- Conceptualize with drawings, fragnets, and cartoons

And...

No Surprises

Bring problems and challenges to achieving commitments to the leadership team early, so that they can help find resources and solutions to avoid or mitigate impact.

Business Imperatives

- Safety first
- Discipline operations
- Continuous improvement
- Cost effectiveness
- Teamwork

Management-Employee Relationship Evolution
During the Last 50 Years

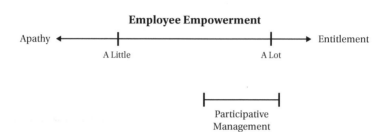

APPENDIX C

Various Talks and Presentations

Appendix C1
My Exit Talk to NFS

This All-Employee Meeting is a little different in venue and format from the first two. The agenda for this meeting is as follows:

- I have some opening remarks, which I am in the process of providing right now.
- That will be followed by a discussion about our Safety Culture Improvement Plan.
- After that, I have a few observations on activities in the workplace.
- Then there will be a personal announcement.
- That will be followed by food!

The food and this venue are meant to be a celebration. We have returned the plant to full service, with the exception of the processing of the UF6 cylinders, which is scheduled late in the first quarter of 2011. We have successfully transitioned to the new organization alignment, and the Work Control organization is becoming more effective every day. The revised Work Management procedure will be in effect very soon. The People Team and the ombudsmen programs are up and running and you are using them. The Nuclear Safety Review Board (NSRB) is about to have their second visit and we are acting on their useful observations from their first visit, as you will hear in a few moments. We have almost completed the Safety Conscious Work Environment (SCWE) refresher training and had our second quarterly First Line Manager (FLM) training. Both the new Metrics Program and the Strategic Plan are on schedule to be rolled out by the end of the year, as is the Streamlining Effort. You will hear more about these programs in the upcoming weeks, which will measure our performance like the rest of the nuclear industry, increase our administrative efficiency of things like Corrective Actions and plant changes, and lead us to a sustained future and continued employment. Of course, all of this depends on our performance.

But before proceeding further, I want to conduct the quiz I promised last time. Cheating is allowed. *[I then went out into the audience, and asked various individuals about the Workplace Priorities and the Conduct of Business Attributes.]*

I want to do one more thing. I know you think this is my "man bag." It is really my Franklin Planner, which I have used for many years to help me remember all the things I have to do, both professional and personal. Besides all my meeting schedules and action items, I also have items in it that I want to remember. One such item is a poem I would like to read to you now.

The Sculptor's Attitude
Author Unknown

I woke up early today, excited over all I get to do before the clock strikes midnight.

I have responsibilities to fulfill today. I am important.

My job is to choose what kind of day I am going to have. Today I can complain because the weather is rainy or ...

I can be thankful that the grass is getting watered for free. Today I can feel sad that I don't have more money or ...

I can be glad my finances encourage me to plan my purchases wisely.

Today I can grumble about my health or ... I can rejoice that I am alive.

Today I can lament over all that my parents didn't give me when I was growing up or ...

I can feel grateful that they allowed me to be born. Today I can cry because roses have thorns or ...

I can celebrate that thorns have roses. Today I can mourn my lack of friends or ... I can excitedly embark upon a quest to discover new relationships.

Today I can whine because I have to go to work or ... I can shout for joy because I have a job to do.

Today I can complain because I have to go to school or ... I can eagerly open my mind and fill it with rich new knowledge.

Today I can murmur dejectedly because I have housework to do or ...

I can feel honored that the Lord had provided shelter for my mind, body, and soul.

Today stretches out ahead of me, waiting to be shaped. And here I am, the sculptor who gets to do the shaping. What today will be like is up to me.

I get to choose what kind of day I will have!

Safety Culture Improvement Explanation

As a result of some issues back in 2006, management committed to some changes in the NFS culture and the NRC requested that the efficacy of those changes be assessed by an outside entity. This action resulted in a first report from a team called the Safety Culture Board of Advisors or SCUBA. For reasons you have heard before, a second assessment was commissioned and resulted in June of this year in another report referred to as the Independent Safety Culture Assessment II. We have committed to the NRC and, more importantly, to ourselves to address the Integrated Safety Culture Assessment (ISCA) II High Priority Recommendations from that report. Here are the actions underway to do so:

- The High Priority Findings and Recommendations of the 2009/2010 Independent Safety Culture Assessment Report (often referred to as the SCUBA II report) are being actively addressed by seven teams led by high-priority recommendation (HPR) champions (senior staff members) and supported by 12 "Safety Culture Trait" subject-matter experts (SMEs).

- These teams are in the process of binning all high-priority findings and recommendations into categories, such as "already completed," "currently underway," "not yet started," "don't intend to do," and "will get to later."

- For those actions already completed, objective evidence of completion is being obtained, reviewed, and archived in a process similar to that used during the recent restart. This step is very important because a lot of good things have been happening at NFS to address issues raised by the SCA. However, some of the actions taken have not been adequately documented with objective evidence of completion and thus might not be accepted as evidence for considering the item completed or closed.

- Those actions not yet started are being evaluated by their respective teams to determine the resources necessary to address the findings and to determine their relative priority for near-term accomplishment. The priorities developed by each individual team will be consolidated into a site-wide priority listing. As resources become available, actions necessary to address and resolve these high-priority findings and recommendations will be uploaded into the site's resource-loaded schedule and tracked and given status like all other site activities.

- All actions taken to address high-priority findings and recommendations will be evaluated to ensure they are providing the intended results and do not fall off the radar screen.

- A strong safety culture can take many years to implement. We are off to a good start and I'm confident that we have the ability see the process through and emerge as a safety culture model that others want to emulate.

I have contracted Ed Morgan, who I introduced to you at the last AEM and who is a very experienced individual in the area of safety culture, to lead this effort.

What does all this mean? Since the December 2009 shutdown, there have been a number of important initiatives to address the causes of that shutdown from a systemic basis (i.e., what were the underlying cultural issues that contributed to the events of last fall and how can they be corrected). I came here at the beginning of March of this year and, of course, I brought my own paradigm about how to change cultures and improve safety and CONOPS. These approaches and how to express key attributes were based on my experience at the successful recovery efforts of seven other nuclear facilities where I was a member of the leadership team brought in to restore those units to operation. While each one was different, just like NFS is unique in many respects, they also had many similarities, just as NFS does to them. After getting my feet on the ground here and getting the lay of the land, so to speak, I introduced many of the concepts and terminologies of those past experiences ... tailored to fit NFS. These concepts and directives ranged from the workplace priorities to organization realignment to administrative processes streamlining (which, as I said, you will hear more about in upcoming communications) to establishment of an Ombudsman Program.

One of the things I have initiated is the Nuclear Safety Review Board (NSRB), an outside collection of experts who will come in periodically, usually once per quarter, to assess how we are doing and make recommendations to me and the chairman of the Board of Directors on how we might improve. On their first visit in August, I asked them to look at the safety culture initiatives, including the response effort to the SCUBA Report II. Their review led them to conclude we had many good initiatives, perhaps too many, but there was no overarching theme that folks could easily identify as the Safety Culture Vision. The senior staff and I took that criticism to heart and met off-site to forge such an explanation of where we are and where we are headed. We were very fortunate to have that meeting facilitated by the world's leading expert in SCWE, Ms. Billie Garde.

What follows is a brief introduction to that conceptualization, presented as what I call the Safety Culture Improvement Plan. You will soon see the diagram posted at the entrance to this tent and on our new website here *[gesturing]*. A further breakdown of each block can also be found on the website. Today, I just want to introduce a brief overview of what you will see there, and the document called the Safety Culture Improvement Plan, which will soon be available.

The starting block is our NFS Vision, which is ... [*read from the diagram*]. That Vision leads to a definition of the Safety Culture we want here at NFS, which is ... [*read from the diagram*]. From there, you can go to two places — one of which is our Core Values, which remain unchanged. The other place you can go is to our Workplace Priorities. You know those, as indicated on the quiz we just participated in. In a few moments, I will say more about the balance we must achieve and are already achieving. From the Workplace Priorities, you can go to the Attributes of Conduct of Business, which we just discussed. You can also go to the supporting metrics or Key Performance Indicators (KPIs). In all cases, you can click to see the Priorities and Attributes and an explanation of each, or click to see the KPIs.

From there, you can go to the Employee Expectations, which have been codified in Policy and discussed in recent Newsletter articles.

I have asked the management chain to discuss these expectations with each of you before they were ever published. Again, you can click on that box to review those expectations.

Finally, there are several boxes along the bottom that provide the building blocks for what we do and how we go about doing it. Clicking on those boxes will lead to the bullets, which describe each one of those building blocks. This website illustrates how all these things hang together and depend on each other, just as we depend on each other to accomplish our mission and commitment to the Navy and the DOE.

Now let me continue with a Message of Hope to all of you.

As I was leaving the hotel on my recent travels to the NRC and B&W corporate, I met a lady who was cleaning the glass front door of the hotel entrance. She held the door open for me, and smiled and said, "Good morning, sir. Isn't it a beautiful day?"

I said, "Every day is a beautiful day," and commented that she was doing a good job on the door glass. She said, "I am just glad to have a job to feed my family. I owe the company that pays me to do my very best at whatever they give me to do." Hold on to that thought.

Every group or organization has a past, a history. There are good memories and notable achievements we all share. There is also some hurt and disappointment. Like any relationship, the key is to hang on to the good memories and let go of the hurt. It is also important to realize that NFS today is different from those past decades and must be so out of necessity. We need to think of ourselves as a team, driven to do so because we have a common goal, the safe and efficient delivery of our product to our client and in accordance with the requirements of our regulators.

I want us to be driven to meet this challenge because we are professionals and that is what professionals do. But let there be no mistake, we are on trial. These are different times, and our clients have changed in accordance with their new approach. They will not tolerate unreliability. Unreliability manifests itself in poor quality and higher costs. Our clients and, therefore, our parent corporation, cannot afford either. If we don't work together to meet these expectations, we could easily find ourselves (eventually) out of work and out of a job.

I have personally met many of you and talked to you and gotten to know you over the past year. I like you. I know that most of you are good people wanting to do the right thing and wanting to do your best. I also know some of you have been hurt by management decisions in the past. I can only promise you that that style of management and that approach to the workforce, hourly and salaried alike, is history at NFS. We are creating an environment of mutual respect and trust, up and down the management chain.

Before I go further, let me make sure you understand that my comments are directed to all NFS employees, not just those in the hourly category. With respect to being on trial with NR and DOE, you can choose to believe me or not. You may say we have always been here, we always will be. You may choose to hang on to the hurt and let it affect your attitude and your performance. But why take that chance?

Let me use an analogy to the very industry in which we are employed — probability and risk impact. On one hand, continued past performance and attitude may have little impact. Let's say the probability is high that it will only result in difficult relations with our clients and our regulators, reduced profit, less bonus and merit pay for those who qualify, but life will go on as it has and let's say the probability of that scenario is high. On the other hand, let's say that I am correct and poor productivity and low reliability leads to NR and DOE taking their business elsewhere, but the probability is low, say 15 percent. What is the consequence though? It is loss of work and unemployment for all of us. This would be a high unfavorable impact I am sure you would all agree. So, on one hand we have high probability and little negative impact and, on the other hand, we have low probability but disastrous impact. Is that a chance you want to take? We would not take that chance in nuclear safety space. We would take action to reduce even that low probability and/or the potential high impact.

What is the delta between these two situations? Quite simply, it is just doing the job you were hired to do. Acting as professionals, doing your best, treating each other with respect, giving eight hours of effort for eight hours of pay, is what you are supposed to do anyhow. To do less jeopardizes our very existence. The smart thing to do is not take that chance. Let's do the right thing and survive. Please reflect on what the lady at the hotel door had to say to me and count your blessings.

One other topic I must address is schedule pressure. Like any viable, vibrant business, we have schedule demands and time constraints. We must do our best to meet our third and fourth priorities — SCHEDULE and COST — if we are to be a viable business. However, we must never sacrifice our first two priorities — SAFETY AND QUALITY. Besides being the right thing to do, in the long run honoring them first always will serve to create the best business metrics. On the other hand, we cannot afford to wrap ourselves in the cloak of safety or quality just to avoid our business obligations. Instead, we need to look for innovative solutions and then make conservative decisions.

I was very encouraged by our actions during the recent Uranium Aluminum processing line startup. When we first discovered the configuration management issue, from operators to senior management, we took the right action. Operators, engineers, and FLMs determined the problem and its impact. Senior management deliberated long and hard on whether the extent of condition might move us to stop Navy Fuel and Uranium Oxide operation. In the end, we determined that we were into repetitive operation on both those endeavors, and that those operations had been successful and we were not going to be doing anything different, so we kept operating. However, we did extensive "extent of condition" reviews of the plant in Navy Fuel and Uranium Oxide, as well as Uranium Aluminum. Everyone pitched in and did a good job. We kept Uranium Aluminum shut down at great cost for two weeks because it was the right thing to do.

When we did start up the Uranium Aluminum processing line again, we ran into one issue after another. For example, an engineer determined through technical inquisitiveness that we had not properly tested an SRE (Safety Related Equipment). We stopped, did an extent of condition on that situation, and fixed both that SRE and the other SREs as well as the procedures that had led to that oversight. There were other issues that plagued us as we headed into the weekend. We thought about stopping and waiting until Monday when a full complement of the workforce would be available to help address these issues as well as any other that might come up. I encouraged the team to keep going. We needed to be able to respond to these kinds of situations if we were to be successful. We kept going. The team found more issues ... and more solutions. We gained time instead of losing it and we did it safely and appropriately. It indicated to me that we were maturing as a workforce in our ability to balance safety and conservative decision-making with the need to make progress.

And now I have a Personal Announcement to make ...

I have some medical issues I must address over the next several weeks. I can no longer put off doing so. Therefore, I will be gone from the site for a little while. In my absence, I have chosen Gary Darter to act for me. There are many reasons for this choice, not least of which is Gary's very capable ability to do so and his overview of NFS operations and strategy gained from managing Program Management. We will be bringing in an expert in project controls, with whom I have worked for many years in various parts of the nuclear industry, to assist Gary so that he can better shoulder both his responsibilities as well as mine. I know you will give Gary your full support.

While I am gone, preparations will be put in place for a Housekeeping Day in early November. This is an opportunity for us to pull together as a team to address housekeeping and facility material conditions. It is an opportunity to have some fun, change roles for a day, and celebrate our wonderful plant. We will have some really good food and other fun while we relax from our mission for one day. I have done this before on an annual basis at other facilities and everyone came away feeling good. We can do that here. You will hear more about the preparations soon.

While I am gone, you will not be far from my thoughts, my prayers, and my heart. I will be in touch with Gary by phone and by the dreaded email. I will return to fulfill my obligation to you. We have the structure, the checks and balances, and the momentum. I know you will support Gary as you have me in safely keeping the momentum. Finally ... be good to each other.

Let me close by returning to my "man bag" *[my Franklin planner]* and reading to you a prayer my wife gave me.

> *Let all things be healthy*
>
> *Let all things be peaceful*
>
> *Be sure to count your blessings at least once per day*
>
> *Forgive those who have hurt you*
>
> *And those who have offended you*
>
> *But forgive yourself for what you have done,*
>
> *And let go of what you have failed to do*
>
> *That which is done, there's no need to speak of*
>
> *That which is past, there is no need to blame*
>
> *Have self-control, self-knowledge, self-respect, and the courage to dare*
>
> *Be tranquil, the light of intelligence will shine*
>
> *Strive to make the spot where you stand beautiful*
>
> *Then beauty and harmony will follow you*
>
> *In all your ways and through all your days.*

Appendix C2
Closing Speech to NFS Management

First, thank you all for coming here tonight. It means more to me than you might imagine. I will keep my remarks as brief as possible.

I have spent the past several weeks talking to all of you and others who are not here tonight, in your workspaces, to appropriately let all of you know how I have grown to appreciate you and consider you friends as well as teammates. I do appreciate greatly all the calls, the emails, and the cards I have received from people across the workforce spectrum.

My wife has appropriately advised me that the strongest posture to take at this time is to move on. I know she is right but the hurt of knowing this is the end of my time in the nuclear arena makes doing so difficult. But she has been my companion for more than 40 years, and her advice and counsel and intuition are usually spot on. I know it is in this case as well.

I updated my résumé to include my time at NFS. The Ohio State University will need it to reflect this important part of my career. Billie Garde and I are putting together an abstract for a course I plan to teach there. At the very end of the résumé there was the statement of the time I have spent in this nuclear industry. I noted in my update that any accomplishments I have made during those 45 years would not have been possible without Cindy's support. What is the key to a successful relationship of that duration? As I have told all of you many times, the hardest part of our jobs and our relationships is WHAT? That's right, *communication*. Even Cindy and I have miscommunications at times. Here is an example. Near one of her birthdays, I overheard her say as she looked in the mirror, "I would love to be six again." So, when her birthday came, I treated her to a day of a six-year-old. We ate Cap'n Crunch cereal, went to an amusement park and actually rode the rides, had Happy Meals for dinner, and watched a Disney movie. When I asked her how she liked her day being six again, she looked into my eyes and said, "You idiot! I meant my dress size, not my age!"

Continue to work hard at communicating with each other. You will still have misunderstandings, but you can minimize the number with "repeat backs" and other techniques we have talked about this past year. And continue to support each other and work with each other as a team. What you do at NFS is so very important to our nation and to world security. I see a bright future for NFS if reasonable minds prevail at corporate and you give them no excuse to see you for other than what you really are — a tremendous resource, a reliable work-force, and a dedicated asset.

I will never forget all of you, those present and those not present. I will remember your support, your hard work, your humor, and your patience with me and what I tried to bring to the table. I hope these policies and programs endure because I think they are the right things to do. I hope my replacement goes about things in a measured way as he invariably puts his own fingerprint on NFS as he must do. If I know Joe Henry at all, I am sure he will not invoke change for change sake. Joe is a good man and I am glad he is following me.

But because I will not forget you, I want to give you something visible by which to remember *me* too. I hope you find a fitting place, at least for a little while, where all the workforce can see this poster and remember me and the things I have said about teamwork. *[Then handed them the poster entitled "TEAMWORK" showing five Buckeye football players piled on one poor Michigan son-of-a-bitch foot-ball player.]*

It has been an honor to be part of the NFS team. Thank you and God bless you.

Appendix C3
Expectations

Clear expectations about workplace conduct are, in my experience, the foundation for inspiring and maintaining that desired conduct. As such, I was known in my career to talk and write a great deal about expectations. Below is the essence of a document I prepared as guidance to all employees — so they understood my expectations about how they were to conduct themselves in the workplace:

Expectations of Management Team

1. Practice safety in all endeavors.

2. Treat employees with respect.

3. Support our workplace priorities, a SCWE, and good Conduct of Business.

4. As much as possible, explain why when you give direction.

5. Listen to feedback from employees to understand their concerns.

6. Clearly set your expectations for employees.

7. Manage union employees in accordance with company rules and the contract.

8. Document problems and short comings; keep senior management and HR informed.

9. Discipline employees who deserve it, in accordance with company guidelines

10. Upper management is to support lower supervision in the enforcement of work rules and contract provisions (enlist the support of labor relations if unsure of contract interpretation).

Expectations of Employees

1. Practice safety in all endeavors.

2. Treat management and each other with respect.

3. Support our workplace priorities, a SCWE, and good Conduct of Business.

4. Seek to understand management's direction.

5. Display a questioning attitude in a professional and courteous manner.

6. After providing input, do what management directs.

    a. Unless the direction is unsafe, illegal, or immoral.

    b. If you believe 6a is the case, elevate your concern to the next level.

    c. If you are a union employee and you feel the instruction is in violation of the contract, follow the grievance process.

4. Report to work areas at scheduled time in appropriate work dress; union employees are to adhere to the provisions of the contract in this regard.

ACKNOWLEDGMENTS

In the dedication of this book, I recognized the support and encouragement of my late wife, Cindy. Her influence on my life and my career is threaded throughout this book, as it was in my life for more than 50 years. She was an incredible person, talented, loving, funny, and beautiful. Although I miss her every day, she still influences my actions and thoughts daily.

The book makes it clear that my parents set an example and provided a grounding that made me the man I am. They were loving in actions, if not in words. They were supportive of me and my siblings without being over-indulgent or overbearing. After setting definite boundaries, they let us do our thing and picked us up when we stumbled.

And then there are my daughters. They were our pride and joy as girls. They amaze me as the strong, grounded, successful women they have become. I credit my wife for the example she set and the nurture she provided. I thank Erin and Alyssa for the joy they gave me and Cindy, the insights they gave me regarding women, and the beautiful grandchildren and wonderful husbands they have brought into our lives.

I think the first part of the book indicate that I was exceedingly fortunate to grow up at a time and place that I did. It seems to me that it was a more tranquil and grounding time in our country's history. The Sandusky, Ohio, school system and just the town itself provided for me a solid basis from which to enter adulthood and the working world. I would be remiss if I didn't thank Malcolm Gladwell for his book, *Outliers: The Story of Success*, which encouraged me to keep the background of my growing up as part of this book.

Throughout my book, I have introduced many of the mentors I have been fortunate to have throughout my career. I have also been influenced by colleagues, people who worked for me, and friends. Some of them have been kind enough to endorse this book. I am incredibly honored that Mike Morris took the time to contribute the foreword.

I also need to thank the Silver Tree Publishing team for making this second edition possible. Kate Colbert's editing, Stephanie Feger's social media direction, Courtney Hudson's design and typesetting talents, and Penny Tate's behind-the-scenes project management have taken the book and the awareness of it to another, higher level I could not even imagine. Thanks, team.

KEEP IN TOUCH

As mentioned in the prologue, I welcome any questions, comments, or suggestions regarding the content of this second edition of *Push It to Move It*. I commit to respond, if a response is requested. The easiest and best way to contact me is to send an email:

✉ **DAmerineD@Gmail.com**

I will take phone calls as well at 419-635-6319. That is my cell phone; Catawba Island, where I live, is in the Eastern time zone, USA.

If you want to mail something, the address is:

🏠 **4221 East Cliff Road**
Port Clinton, Ohio 43452

Find, follow, and share on social media:

f **Facebook.com/David.Amerine.5**

in **LinkedIn.com/in/DaveAmerine**

BEYOND THE BOOK

I still consult on project management and other challenges faced by large complex endeavors ... or even smaller ones. I have two companies through which I consult, depending on the assignment. I have the following criteria for accepting an assignment:

- The assignment or task needs to be interesting
- I need to feel I can add value to the endeavor
- In general, I do not want to be away from home more than two weeks at a time.

I know that these criteria limit the types of assignments or tasks that I can take on, but that is the intent. I welcome your initial calls to discuss how I might help your organization. If we mutually feel there is a fit, then I will have one of the consulting companies with whom I collaborate contact the appropriate person in your organization to set up a contract.

I do enjoy speaking to various groups, ranging from schools and civic organizations to businesses and professional associations. Depending on the engagement and assuming travel expenses are covered, I may consider waiving my speaking fee. I look forward to the opportunity of working with you.

ABOUT THE AUTHOR

David Amerine is a United States Naval Academy graduate who began his career in the U.S. Navy before transitioning to the commercial nuclear industry, where he held several positions including executive roles  leading multi-billion-dollar companies. Often brought in to recover troubled facilities and projects, David ultimately served as the President of Nuclear Fuel Services, which is vital to national security as the sole producer of fuel for our nuclear Navy, brought in to lead its recovery from an NRC mandated suspension of operations.

Today, David continues to advise top nuclear agencies and organizations, and is a sought-after consultant, coach, and speaker.

Connect with David via email at DAmerineD@Gmail.com and on LinkedIn at LinkedIn.com/in/DaveAmerine.

Made in the
USA
Monee, IL